WHO OWNS INFORMATION?

Who Owns Information?

FROM PRIVACY TO
PUBLIC ACCESS

Anne Wells Branscomb

BASIC
B
BOOKS

A Member of the Perseus Books Group

Designed by Ellen Levine

Library of Congress Cataloging-in-Publication Data
Branscomb, Anne W.
Who owns information? : from privacy to public access / Anne
Wells Branscomb.
       p.   cm.
Includes bibliographical references and index.
ISBN 0–465–09175–X (cloth)
ISBN 0–465–09144–X (paper)
1. Intellectual property—United States. 2. Privacy, Right of—
United States. 3. Freedom of information—United States. 4.
Data protection—Law and legislation—United States. I. Title.
KF2979.B67   1994
342.73'0853—dc20   93–44348
[347.302853]   CIP

99 00 01 02 ❖/RRD 9 8

CONTENTS

FOREWORD

Anyone who thinks that the ownership of information is an arcane pre-occupation for lawyers and economists will think again after reading this book. Using some of the most practical and painful examples possible, Anne Wells Branscomb demonstrates the urgency and importance of the collision of intellectual property rights and privacy for all citizens, whether they are high-level executives or entry-level or blue-collar workers. She pointedly asks questions that all too often have been ignored by others who have observed, praised, or lamented the march of technology and the massive growth of information and data sources. She raises questions that go to the heart of individual identity and personal privacy, such as who owns your name, telephone number, medical history, image, or record of videos you might have rented. In the process, the author, a distinguished attorney and communications scholar and longtime observer of new media technologies and their impact, demonstrates the inadequacy of present laws and regulations in this fragile and unsettled environment.

All this has been brought on by the fast-paced communications revolution of recent years, ratcheted up even more recently by corporate machinations that are building a giant information superhighway. What was once the stuff of graduate seminars on information theory or communications policy is now truly in the public arena, where it is beginning to dawn on people that the information revolution may affect them in helpful or harmful ways. In part, the message here is that what you don't know or don't protect can make your life quite perilous.

What seems to be a simple question about who owns information really is not. Most often, the answer from the players in this field is that they simply don't know, while the courts, scrambling to fashion solutions to daily problems, typically answer that "it depends." The reason is that existing laws at the state and federal levels in the United States are light-years behind new technologies, which raise heretofore unheard-of questions. And while the law of intellectual property is not often helpful in solving pertinent problems or answering critical questions, neither is the law of privacy very clear.

With stakeholders in the communications revolution competing vigorously for control of the conduits through which all kinds of messages will travel, all eyes are on corporate mergers and hostile takeovers, while the ordinary consumer is left far, far behind. Few are representing the economic rights of the citizen/consumer in this process, nor are many worrying about public access for ordinary people. As yet, these topics are not on the national radar screen or of much concern to people as the courts grapple with inadequate precedent and outdated laws. Clearly, as Anne Wells Branscomb urges, economic principles must be established, new policy guidelines drawn, and new laws written. At the same time, she acknowledges, in a global society where information travels across national boundaries, the control of information is even more complex.

While recognizing that most of the conflicts over information ownership and personal privacy will occur in the private sector and likely involve the countinghouse, the author nonetheless worries about public access to information for those who might be dispossessed. Again, there is a need to consider the balance between voluntary action and formal regulation. In many areas, as the book points out, there is little useful experience that comfortably maps the way for policy makers, entrepreneurs, or citizens.

Anne Branscomb makes sense of a world of new machines with new capabilities. A passionate advocate of the liberating potential of new technologies, she is at the same time a vigilant sleuth who is equally concerned about their potentially negative consequences. In the midst of fierce fragmentation, she makes a reasoned plea for coherent principles that will protect both the creators and the users of information at all levels. Unlike many commentators who watch only the interplay between giant corporations and marvel at the potential for human communication, the author sees all this through the prism of rights, whether those of individuals or institutions.

Having had the pleasure of watching the evolution of Anne Wells Branscomb's work on this critical question for nearly a decade, and before that appreciating her humanistic sense-making in a field that is often laced either with engineering terms or futurist musings, I am enthusiastic about the unique path blazed by this important book. Some of this work began when Ms. Branscomb was an inaugural fellow at what was then the Gannett Center for Media Studies at Columbia University,

where she tried out her ideas on colleagues in lively conversations and
seminars. Now, thanks to the publication of this book, many others can
join in that conversation and benefit from her deep knowledge of a new
and emerging field as well as her good judgment and wisdom.

Everette E. Dennis
Executive Director
The Freedom Forum Media Studies Center
Columbia University
New York City

ACKNOWLEDGMENTS

First, I owe a debt of gratitude to Robert White, President of the National Academy of Engineering, for drafting me to become involved in some of the efforts of the academy to sort out the problems involved in protecting intellectual property rights in scientific research. Next, to Everette E. Dennis, Director of the Freedom Forum Media Studies Center, who offered me the opportunity to pursue this new interest in information assets as an Inaugural Fellow of the center, then known as the Gannett Center for Media Studies. It was there that I wrote an introductory essay entitled "Who Owns Information?" that became the forerunner of this longer and more exhaustive study.

In my efforts to address the varied kinds of information and related proprietary interests, it was impossible to address each subject in the detail that it deserved and in the depth achieved by scholars who have been immersed in that special field for their entire professional lives. However, I have been most fortunate in having professional colleagues with such expertise agree to contribute their views and/or to review chapters in which they have a special interest. No doubt I have failed to live up to the expectations of many of them, and the responsibility is mine. I hope, in the process, to have made their fields more accessible to a wider range of readers and to entice these readers to examine further the topics of special interest to them.

I am indebted to these colleagues for their assistance in my efforts to include as many different kinds of information as possible and to integrate the varied topics into some kind of rational orientation. I am especially grateful to Audrey Bashkin and Bob Gellman for their contributions to the chapter on names and addresses and to Professor Mary Culnan for sharing with me her research on the Lotus Marketplace controversy; to Willis Mog for keeping me up to date on his legal efforts and to Professor Eli Noam for checking the chapter on telephone numbers; to Joan Jacobson for her contributions to the chapter on medical records; to Janine Ann Petit, Joanne Johnson, Brian Kahin, Marc Palumbo, David Shefrin, and Paul Doering for their views on the image chapter; to Ron Katznelson and Larry E. Rissler for their help on the antipiracy efforts of the cable television industry; to Professor Frank Moore Cross and Dr. William Moffett for tireless efforts to help me untangle the mysteries of the Dead Sea Scrolls (indeed, Professor Cross is responsible for whatever prompted me to step into this hornet's nest) and to Professors Wacholder and Abegg for sharing with me their efforts to deploy the computer in deciphering some of the manuscripts; to Mitch Kapor, Pamela Samuelson, Bob Bigelow, and Ellin Sarot for their efforts to set me straight on the complexities of computer software protection; to Kent A. Smith and Dr. Harold D. Schoolman of the National Library of Medicine for sorting out the entanglements of the litigation concerning Medlars; to David Johnson for reviewing the chapter on electronic mail and to Brian Kahin for monitoring entries on the Internet concerning the White House efforts to manage the E-mail; and to Professor Alan Westin for reading the entire manuscript for legal errors.

To my colleagues at the Program on Information Resources Policy at Harvard University, I owe a debt of gratitude not only for offering me physical space in which to work and access to many information resources, both print and electronic, but for their support and encouragement during the months of gestation. I am especially indebted to John LeGates and Tony Oettinger, who read most of the chapters, offering sage advice and often caustic criticism. Lastly, to my husband, Lewis Branscomb, not only for serving as a technical adviser when I failed to understand the capabilities of some of the information technology but also for his considerable expertise as an editor and for his moral support when the task I had set for myself seemed endless.

With these many inputs and editors, it would seem unnecessary to undergo more editing. However, Basic Books was not without its experts as well. The very able Susan Rabiner, as acquisitions editor, guided my steps at every turn and kept me on the straight and narrow path. I hope these many efforts will enable readers to comprehend the vast terrain of legal activity in which information assets are being privatized, publicized, commercialized, and shared. More important, I hope that they will take an interest in designing a legal infostructure that will serve us wisely and well.

Anne Wells Branscomb
Cambridge, Massachusetts
December 1993

WHO OWNS INFORMATION?

INTRODUCTION

Control of the Legal Infostructure

Pick up any newspaper reporting on new government efforts to keep the nation competitive; open any book attempting a thoughtful analysis of what we as individuals and as a society must do to prepare for the twenty-first century; sit in on any discussion about the impact of new technologies on our industries, our educational systems, our ability to wage war and to keep peace, and invariably there will be one point of consensus: as we embark upon a plan for the future, we must first come to terms with what it means to be in an information age.

It is only in the past two decades that we have come to realize that information has taken on a new character, that it has passed from being an instrument through which we acquire and manage other assets to being a primary asset itself. Until very recently, for instance, commentators referred to our society as a post-industrial, service-based economy, descriptions that accept the idea that information industries were becoming more and more important but that still failed to recognize the emergence of information as a commodity, now calling out for protection and definition of ownership rights. A natural consequence has been that our courts and our legislatures are now being asked to address information issues never before the subject of contention. What has changed between then and now to make information ownership and use the hot new legal issue?

One can assume that the very moment our earliest ancestors realized that speech is capable of communicating ideas—rather than just emotions—they began trading facts, judgments, condemnations, and insights. They did so in the planting fields and in the marketplace, in the privacy of their own homes and in public arenas, in small and in large groups—wherever two or more people came together.

Not surprisingly, in virtually all societies, control of and access to information became instruments of power, so much so that information came to be bought, sold, and bartered by those who recognized its value. Infor-

mation experts—from those who could glean from the heavens information useful to the farmer planting his fields, to those who could fathom the
medical value of different plants, to those community gurus who acted as
repositories of tribal history—were guaranteed status if not wealth in
every society in which they existed. Advisers to kings, elders of local societies, information vendors whose judgments were sought on a variety of
issues, were all at the right hand of power. But they were not considered
the society's property owners. Their cache of information, however valuable, was not of a class with a few ounces of gold.

Information acquired even greater value with the development of written language, and then the printing press. Both these developments
greatly expanded the reach of this exchange, so that like-minded people
could now communicate across miles and even across generations. In
time, those who organized and analyzed information sought protection for
their interpretations, and it soon became apparent that some sort of legal
redress for unauthorized use was necessary.

The arrival of radio and then television made inter-community, international, and even intercontinental communication almost immediate, alter-
ing in important ways our sense of what constitutes a community, as well
as introducing a new and much-expanded commercial value to the information being communicated. Yet despite the high value humankind has
always placed on information, and the stresses placed on the law by
changes in the commercial value of many kinds of information, until very
recently the law governing information exchange—for the most part,
intellectual property law—has been evolving with the creep of a receding
glacier. When the law lags behind changing conditions, conflicts arise that
present new questions, ones that are not easily answered by reference to
established precedents. In the early 1970s such new questions began to
arise with greater and greater frequency.

In some of these cases, there was a traditional aspect to the ownership
conflict, the what-I-own-you-can't-have notion, newly applied to information. Both sides intended to commercialize the contested block of information, that is, to make it available for sale to anyone who could afford to
pay for it. Not surprisingly, such cases often involved older businesses in
conflict with newer information-age businesses, and conflicts such as
those were most likely to reach the courts. One such issue is the argument
over who can control the use of telephone numbers. Telephone numbers
have been treated as facts, residing in the public domain, available for the
taking, without accounting for the change in circumstances that has led
communications companies to fight over what has become a valuable corporate asset—and also a personal identifier over which we want personal
control.

Such cases may have tested the limits of copyright, in that they tried to include the information itself as an asset worthy of protection, rather than just its expression or organization. While historically society has always recognized that some kinds of information lay outside the economic sphere, no matter who had collected it and at what cost, the victor fully intended to come out of the dispute with the right to commercialize the disputed information.

But at the same time two other groups of conflicts began to emerge, and these would present more difficult questions. In the first of these, one of the two parties might allege that no one owned the information in question—indeed, that it was inherently public property, too important to the welfare of the society for any one commercial enterprise to have the power to restrict its use or availability. In the second, a very different argument was made: that commercialization of the information is in conflict with established notions about the right of individuals to privacy about certain personal information. The question here was not *who* had the right to traffic in this information, but whether *anybody* did.

What explains this sudden explosion of questions about the legal status of information? At one level the answer is obvious: information that formerly resided in encoded scribblings on sheets of paper in dispersed locations, difficult to find, laborious to collect, and virtually impossible to correlate, can now be collected easily, read by electronic laser beams, recorded in magnetic patterns invisible to the human eye, and quickly aggregated and correlated. Collections of data that had once been dispersed to cubbyholes and file drawers now wend their way as patterns of electronic impulses into vast databases where, by virtue of their comprehensive nature and instant cross-accessibility, they become commodities more valuable than the sum of their independent parts. Information whose value could once be protected by guarding against those who would try to copy from the paper on which it was recorded could now be compromised in ways invisible to the human eye and at speeds almost unintelligible to the human mind.

But the technological revolutions of the past decades have brought about changes more troubling than those revolving around the question of who owns what piece of information. The new speed and accuracy of collection and correlation methods have given value to previously worthless information (in terms of its value in the marketplace), creating new ownership interests and conflicts and a tension between the need to foster new technology-based information businesses and to determine what will be responsible social behavior in an information society. A great deal of information we consider to be highly personal, and of interest only to ourselves and the town gossip—our names, telephone numbers, marital status, educational accomplishments, job and credit histories, even medical, dental, and psychiatric records—is now being sold on the open market to anyone who believes he or she might be able to use such information to turn a profit. These transactions usually take place without our knowledge or consent.

In their most benign use, these transactions generate telemarketing calls that intrude upon our private hours or bring a deluge of mail into our homes, tempting us to purchase items we did not know we needed and forcing us to dispose of mountains of paper we did not request, eventually clogging up our communities' disposal and recycling efforts. Put to more dangerous use, this marketing of our personal information determines whether or not we will be offered professional opportunities or promotions, be subjected to surveillance by government agencies, or be accepted for medical, property, or life insurance.

Most of us are bewildered by the amazing new array of instruments for acquiring, organizing, and accessing information. Even the law has found itself in disarray in trying to apply the old rules to a new game. Some factors that have changed the world of information collection and retrieval include:

- An explosion of replication techniques that facilitate the wide distribution of information clones, often almost indistinguishable from the originals in terms of legibility and utility: computer disks, CD-ROMs, videocassette recorders, digital audio, audiotapes, and facsimile transmissions;
- The deployment of satellites in a geostationary earth orbit where information can be collected from and dispensed to all corners of the earth at almost the speed of light;
- The advent of powerful mainframe computers that can search vast quantities of data, identifying similarities and differences beyond the capability of human time and patience;
- The arrival of the bar code and electronic "smart cards," which record so many of our personal transactions: purchases, trips to the bank, the doctor, the drug store, the auto repair shop, the movies, schools, even the supermarket;
- The democratization of access to information has made many of us accessories after the fact. The proliferation of the personal computer and certain of its common accoutrements—such as the modem and the fax card—has rendered every one of us a potential user, publisher, or distributor of information products.

If annoyance to the general public were the only by-product of the new information society, enacting legislation to rectify abuses might be an easy task. But the information society has produced a rich marketplace of new information products, and the ease of entry into the new marketplace attracts a large number of small entrepreneurs who depend for their livelihood upon access to these new information resources. As a consequence, the information industries are among the fastest-growing sectors of our economy and a growing foundation for economic success in the global market. Past legislation told us little about how these new industries should be allowed to operate—in their dealings with each other or with the general public.

What was a more or less orderly information marketplace, based upon oral communication, the handwritten note, and the printed word, and enhanced by radio and telephone, has evolved into a multimedia melting pot of new information businesses that find this treasure trove of archived information a valuable resource for many utilitarian as well as charitable purposes. What the future portends, we are told, is an information distribution system that can transmit five hundred or more channels of information services (voice, video, text, or a combination of all three) to our homes and places of businesses with the additional capability of interacting in innovative ways.

The law will lumber along like an unwieldy dinosaur wending its way to extinction if it cannot keep up with the pace of change in this new interactive, information-intense environment. But the law is by nature conservative, attempting to bring order out of chaos only as fast as consensus can be reached among social groups willing to conform to norms they believe are fair and workable. Human beings are by nature social animals, desirous of interacting through whatever means are readily available. However, in order to interact without stepping on each other's toes or offending each other's sensibilities, we develop social conventions and norms and ethical behavior. As time goes by these behavioral norms are written into statutes and constitutions that then govern future human behavior. The law is—or should be—a sociopolitical process through which free citizens agree on the norms and rules of behavior. It is too important to be left to the lawyers. Everyone must contribute to the vision of how an information society should function.

The difficulty with today's information societies is that we have not had enough experience to agree upon acceptable behavior. We are like children trying out all the toys to see how they work. Until something goes awry and the injustice of it becomes immediately apparent, we sit back and wait to see what will happen next. However, once a concerned citizenry becomes irate, our legislative representatives respond with remarkable alacrity. When Judge Robert Bork was nominated for appointment to the Supreme Court and an enterprising journalist got hold of his rental records from a videocassette store, hoping to find some salacious titles to disclose to his readers, the public rose up in indignation at this invasion of the judge's privacy, even though nothing detrimental was disclosed and no harm done. Congress lost no time in enacting the Video Privacy Act to prohibit video stores from disclosing the nature of their customers' tastes in videotaped material.

Users of personal computers with modems connected to public electronic mail and conferencing services are finding that they too can generate a considerable ruckus over issues that pique their concern. An effort of Lotus Development Corporation to market a new product containing the names and purchasing habits of some 120 million Americans prompted an electronic maelstrom of protests, convincing Lotus to withdraw the product from the market.

Such widespread use of computer conferencing to enhance electronic democracy has challenged the White House and Congress to reorganize their telecommunications capability both to send and to receive electronic messages from their constituents. At the same time it has generated concern that only those citizens with access to computers and modems may be able to participate in self-government, increasing rather than ameliorating the gulf between the information-rich and the information-poor. Yet the information technology itself has the great virtue of not recognizing race, color, or inhibiting physical characteristics. The electronic encounter has been called a true meeting of the minds. Furthermore, the transmission can be directed in any and all directions without favoring urban over rural areas and without requiring individuals to travel great distances to acquire the information they need.

In this new electronic environment that has come to be known as cyberspace, computer-literate inhabitants are carving out their own information domains in much the same way that pioneers homesteaded the Western frontiers. Common practice is "first come, first served" and "what is yours is mine" because it is so easy to copy whatever strikes one's fancy.

There is as yet no law of cyberspace. But it is clear that a genuine revolution is brewing in which the revolutionaries are unwilling to recognize and unlikely to observe laws imposed upon them by outside jurisdictions. They are coming to realize that cyberspace is a place or a universe of many places where users are making their own jurisdictional boundaries and developing their own standards of fair play and acceptable-use policies. It is not necessarily a lawless place, but lawless places do exist in cyberspace as well as in the real world. The real clash will come between the geopolitical boundaries (which the technologies of information ignore) and the electronic boundaries (which have no geopolitical counterpart). Whose rules and regulations will apply? And what sanctions are appropriate?

Cultures clash with cultures, and often in the place where minds are meeting there is no consensus, only ferment, argument, and disagreement. Often the technical boundaries between what can be maintained under personal or professional control and what may freely circulate for others to capture and manipulate is not clear.

The legal system is struggling to draw these lines with greater clarity. Constitutional principles embodied in the First Amendment proscribe government restrictions upon freedom of speech and favor an uninhibited information marketplace. But two bodies of law have come down to us over the centuries that have imposed limits on the exchange of information in the marketplace. One, *intellectual property,* offers legal controls over the creative productivity of the human brain, and the other, *privacy law* (a much more recent legal innovation), maintains boundaries through which curious eyes may not penetrate to invade those areas over which we may maintain exclusive personal control.

However, facts, which computers can record, compare, and manipulate most competently, do not come within the reach of either body of law. Neither does the labor involved in collecting, recording, and distributing such information carry intrinsic value for which compensation can be assured through appeal to court precedents without a specific contract signed and agreed upon between the two parties. A recent Supreme Court decision has buried the efforts of lower courts to carve out a "sweat of the brow" theory of compensation to protect the efforts of what have become the most rapidly growing sectors of the economy: the gathering, storage, manipulation, and distribution of information.

Today the most developed economies have become information-dependent, whether or not they lay claim to being information economies. They cannot afford to give away their information assets. Yet the legal infrastructure established to govern the fruits of the industrial age—intellectual property laws (patents, copyrights, and trade secrets)—are stretched, some of them to their limits, by new forms of creative endeavor such as computer software interfaces, which do not appear to fit comfortably into any one of the existing legal categories.

As a consequence, many of us are becoming apprehensive that we may not derive income from the intellectual labors that produce the valuable information assets of the information age. We are also concerned about the unauthorized commercial use of facts over which we seemingly have no control and for which there seems to be no viable legal protection.

The purpose of this book is: (1) to explore several instances where individuals and groups are challenging the existing legal structure as inappropriate or inadequate to protect information assets they consider valuable and proprietary, or alternatively, a critical component of a public domain; (2) to derive some basic principles that are evolving through their efforts to carve out a law governing the use of information assets in an information-intensive society: and (3) to urge individuals who gripe about invasions of privacy by information entrepreneurs to stop complaining and bring their concerns to their elected representatives so that a more humane and comprehensive law governing information assets can be devised.

No information society will reach its potential without addressing the legal foundation upon which information is exchanged. That foundation is as necessary a component of the information infrastructure or "infostructure" as the electronic global highways that we are rapidly constructing.

The boundaries between what is considered to be public information and what is considered to be private have been moving targets for several generations now. Unless we are able to reach a consensus on the fair uses and prohibited abuses of information, we will never achieve the promise of living in an information society.

1

Who Owns Your Name and Address?

Carl Oppedahl, a practicing patent lawyer in Manhattan, spent several years trying to protect his mother from the assault of direct mail solicitations delivered to her home. These would vary from a postcard offering a fabulous vacation at a pittance to a letter advertising some hugely expensive item at a bargain-basement price. You probably receive two or three such solicitations a week and immediately throw most of them into the wastepaper basket. Carl's mother, however, responded to many of the 800 numbers and provided her MasterCard information for verification or to cover the modest cost of shipping her bargain. When the credit card statement came the charges were often higher than what she believed she had committed herself to pay. Carl tried to persuade his mother to stop responding to these outlandish offers, most of which were scams.

Recognizing that his mother's current name and address were irretrievably stored in the computers of many highly skilled but irresponsible marketers, he determined to move his mother to a new address, hoping to free her from the endless onslaught of come-ons in the mail. In an extraordinary precaution most of us would never think necessary, Carl did not disclose his mother's new residence on the change-of-address form he filled out at the post office. Instead, he had her mail forwarded to his office, knowing that the new address would promptly be entered into a national computer database.[1]

Every night the U.S. Postal Service, through its 200 regional data processing centers, consolidates all the change-of-address postcards filled out that day by unsuspecting postal customers. The cards are then sent to a computer in Memphis, Tennessee. Here they are conformed to a national address system at the National Change of Address (NCOA) database and to a Delivery Sequence File (DSF) that contains almost all the deliverable postal addresses in the country. The NCOA list is then made available to some twenty-odd licensed address list managers who service the mass mailers who in turn fill up our mailboxes with direct mail solicitations, providing revenue for a whole range of people from the post offices to the many direct mail companies that access the list.

The change-of-address postcard does warn that the address *may* be given to others. The truth is that it *will* be. Not many of the 40 million Americans who file change-of-address cards each year are aware that this information is available to anyone willing to pay three dollars for it.[2] Moreover, the Postal Service offers its customers no alternative. If you want your mail forwarded, you must accept that within days, if not hours, your new address will be in the hands of the major direct mail marketers around the country.

According to the USPS, providing individual customers with a way out of this arrangement would be too expensive and time-consuming. Besides, the USPS claims its role is not "to monitor the preferences of individuals or to tell mailers to whom they can or should address the mail. We believe that the difficulties and the cost of such an undertaking far exceed the inconvenience to an individual customer of disposing of unwanted mail."[3]

Indeed, the USPS claims that using the computerized and standardized addresses saves it some $30 million a year for every 1 percent of the more than 160 billion pieces of mail automatically processed by computers; it also claims that dissemination of computer-coded mailing addresses greatly enhances its ability to deliver the mail promptly, besides holding down the enormous costs associated with forwarding mail to customers who have relocated.[4] The USPS claims to give the changed addresses only to mailers whose computers already have those customers and only to companies acting as its agents.

The master NCOA file, the only USPS file containing actual names, records some 90 million moves.[5] Mail managers who have an address that can be "matched" in the NCOA will receive the new address promptly, but those that do not will not be able to use change-of-address forms to build up their lists unless they already have at least 90 percent of the addresses within a given ZIP code.[6]

Moreover, although the name of the new occupant may be unknown, the old address is still known to the computer, which explains the large amount of mail addressed to "occupant." If one out of every five U.S. households changes domicile every year,[7] then it is reasonable to assume that any efficient mailer would, over a period of half a decade, manage to have in its database the great majority of correct addresses.

Because of presorting and computer coding of envelopes, selling address changes to direct mailers is a profitable business for the USPS, despite the discount the mailer gets off regular first-class rates. The direct mail or mail-order business, which generates what many call "junk mail,"[8] generates $53.4 billion a year from more than half of us.[9] In 1990, more than 63.7 billion pieces of third-class mail wended their way across the national landscape, producing purchases and contributions by 92 million Americans who responded to the solicitations of charities, political campaigns, environmental entreaties, sweepstakes, magazine subscription offers, investment opportunities, food, fashions, gardening supplies, even dieting secrets. Bulk mail constitutes about 40 percent of USPS volume, and the average American will spend the better part of a year of his or her life sorting through it.[10]

The average consumer is on approximately a hundred mailing lists and in at least fifty databases.[11] Many of these lists are made up of public information in the public domain, required for public purposes and from which our names cannot be removed. For those who are overburdened by excessive mail addressed to them, attempting to get out of the clutches of the database managers is almost a full-time job. I can vouch for this, because I have spent the last five years trying to withstand the assault of direct mail marketers on the post office box I rented to relieve the overstuffed mailbox at my home address. When I asked the post office employees to stop stuffing the post office box with unsolicited mail addressed to "occupant," duplications of the same occupant mail overstuffing my mailbox at home, I was informed that they could not legally comply with my request. It is this kind of effrontery that leads the Carl Oppedahls of the world to take extreme precautions.

Here we have a classic conflict, between the interests of those who wish to maintain a modicum of control over the mail they receive and the economic interests of the USPS in partnership with the direct mail marketing industry. Current practice comes down on the side of the USPS, which does have a legitimate interest in streamlining its operation and continuing to provide employment for its three-quarters of a million workers.[12] The real winners are the direct mail marketers, who have their mailing lists automatically updated though the efforts of unwitting USPS customers and employees.

The ultimate losers may be the planet's forests, devastated to produce the mountains of paper that go into unwanted mail pieces. Judging from response rates—only 1 to 2 percent of us respond to direct mail solicitations, although surveys indicate that a larger number do have an interest—a great deal of it goes into the trash unopened, or at least unread. According to the Stop Junk Mail Association, an area as large as Los Angeles County is consumed by the estimated 41 pounds of direct mail sent to each adult annually. There is also the cost of disposing of these unwanted arrivals,[13] leading inevitably to higher taxes. Recycling costs escalate, much of the increase going for the recycling of paper that has not yet had a useful first life. Indeed, many conservationists propose the abolition of "junk mail" as an important step in rescuing the planet.[14]

All of which comes back to the simple question, Who has the right to control access to your name and address? The simple view is that your name and address are a peculiarly personal asset and should be under your strict control. The more realistic view is that your name and address are public knowledge, in most cases available to anyone who wants to take the trouble to collect them.

What the Law Protects

Certainly the fact that each of us exists is not considered private information—birth and birthplace are duly recorded in public records. But full access to such information is not an absolute right, as standing practice has long permitted the use of aliases as well as the changing of one's name.

Most of the legal cases seeking to establish or strengthen a personal right to protect names and addresses from unauthorized dissemination have come to the courts under the settled law that federal agencies can deny access to public records under Exception Six of the Freedom of Information Act (FOIA),[15] in instances where the courts might find a privacy interest in names and addresses sought by an FOIA petitioner. Most of the courts, however, while recognizing a proprietary right of federal employees in their names and addresses, have found this right to be minimal. Seldom has it been found important enough to bar access when confronted with a compelling public interest favoring disclosure.[16] The issue is not entirely settled. Some courts have justified the protection of names and addresses if it is felt that individuals might be harassed.[17] Other courts have found the protection of names and addresses more compelling when combined with the protection of financial information.[18] Still others have concluded that they could prohibit disclosure of names and addresses only of those employees who had requested that their employers keep the information confidential.[19]

On the state level, courts are becoming more protective as citizens whose privacy has been invaded are beginning to seek legal redress. A suit was filed in 1989 in New York protesting the release of names and addresses to the Federation of New York State Rifle and Pistol Clubs of people who had been issued shotgun and rifle permits by the New York Police Department. The court determined that this was an unwarranted invasion of privacy. Because the sale and release of the names and addresses would be used for commercial fund-raising purposes, no governmental purpose would be served by public disclosure of such information about private citizens.[20]

As far as the mail is concerned, the Supreme Court has acknowledged the somewhat fanciful notion that a person's home is his or her castle, and that the occupant should have sole control over what passes over the threshold.[21] However, this quaint idea is contained in a decision that provides only a modicum of control over what mail will be delivered to the castle. You may bar "erotically arousing or sexually provocative" mail from your household if you submit a signed request to the post office.[22]

The Privacy Act of 1974 could be seen as proscribing release of names and addresses of postal customers. Nonetheless, the managers of the USPS's NCOA and DSF databases claim that their disclosure of addresses, contrary to the provisions of the Privacy Act, is permissible under an exception permitting disclosure for "routine use," "for a purpose which is compatible with the purpose for which it is collected."[23]

Since the purpose of collecting address information is to assure efficient delivery of the mail, and to avoid the costs and delays attributable to the one-third of the mail that is misaddressed, the USPS considers the disclosure of addresses to commercial mail managers consistent with the purpose for which the addresses are collected.

Who Owns Your Mailbox?

There is a statute forbidding the postal box or mailbox attached to your premises from being used for any purpose other than as a receptacle for USPS mail, strongly suggesting that it is, for all practical purposes, USPS property, not yours.[24] This legal view has been found necessary to uphold the USPS monopoly over first-class mail by denying non-USPS carriers the convenience of a mailbox at every stop.[25] It also explains the separate depositories some newspaper circulation departments provide their customers. They are prepared to go to this expense despite the fact that subsidized rates for postal delivery of printed matter were long ago established specifically to facilitate the delivery of the news. Many bulk delivery services for local advertisements bother with neither names and addresses nor receptacles; they merely toss their messages willy-nilly at every residence in the area.

An additional piece of information required to sort out the views of the USPS is that it is more and more under duress to have mail delivery pay its own way. For most of its two centuries of existence the mail has been delivered as a public service, on the assumption that an infrastructure assuring low-cost exchange of information is crucial to the binding of the nation. In recent years the USPS has been required to operate within a more balanced budget.[26] In former years first-class mail supported third-class mail, for which special rates were applied. But now the rate structure has been changed to better reflect the actual costs of delivery of the different classes of mail. Presorted, computer-accurate and computer-addressable mail, which now constitutes almost half of the total, is cheaper and more efficient to dispatch, and the USPS relies upon these major mailers to sustain its service. Thus it is in partnership with the industry that helps it struggle out of the red.

The legal position of Title 39, section 412, of the U.S. Code is that the USPS may not on its own provide names and addresses to any member of the general public. It skirts the spirit of the law by declaring managers of mail lists not separate and independent entities but "agents and licensees" assisting the USPS in getting the mail to you in a timely and cost-effective manner.

One concerned citizen, Albert G. Ertel of Rockville, Maryland, took this provision of the statutes seriously and set out to find out why the USPS was ignoring the law. When he approached his local post office in June 1990, he received the practical, not the legal, answer. The USPS did indeed sell mailing lists; there was no possibility of having one's address removed from this list; the sale of such lists was earning income for the USPS.[27]

Feeling strongly that a federal agency should not be in the business of selling address lists, Ertel wrote to his Congresswoman, Constance A. Morella, for assistance in sorting out the legalities. The double-talk he received in response informed him that the USPS did not deem itself to be in contravention of the law because the law "does not prohibit the USPS from providing any 'address'; the prohibition applies only to 'lists' of addresses. . . . We do not consider that addresses which are provided to mailers through address sequencing services constitute 'lists' of addresses for the purposes of section 412."[28]

The plain truth is that the USPS will provide 100 percent of the mailing addresses in any ZIP code if the entity seeking the 100 percent already has 90 percent of the addresses contained therein. There is no possibility—absolutely none—of having your address deleted from such distribution, even though your name might not be included. How can you *not* conclude that ownership of your address and mailbox resides not with you, but with the USPS?

Opting In or Opting Out

Only a few years ago Americans seemed to accept the impossibility of having one's name removed from lists distributed by direct mail merchandisers. Now there is growing resistance to the use of names and addresses without permission. In May 1990, New York Telephone provided the opportunity for its 6.3 million residential customers to "opt out" of a list that it intended to rent to direct mailers. A record-breaking 800,000 people took advantage of the offer.[29] As more and more people find these mailings a burden, the most responsible of the direct mail merchandisers allow their customers to prohibit redistribution of their names and addresses to other direct mailers.

The Direct Marketing Association has since 1971 maintained a list of persons who do not wish to receive any direct mail solicitations. Although customers, according to the DMA, appreciate the opportunity to opt out, fewer than 2.5 million postal customers have done so in the two decades during which the DMA has offered its Mail Preference Service.[30] Members must purchase the list in order to purge their mailings of these names, and many direct mail merchandisers either do not belong to the association or do not purchase the lists. Moreover, the DMA is smart enough to require customers to request that their names and addresses be removed from *all* lists. They know that most of us like some of the catalogs we receive.

A Postal Service survey found that 60.3 percent of the respondents did not mind receiving solicitations of no interest to them, and one of every six Americans has made at least six purchases by mail (whereas only one in seven has bought an item through home shopping clubs on television or from telephone solicitations).[31] Direct mail is clearly a lucrative vehicle for advertisers. In 1992 more than 10,000 mail-order companies sent out 13.5 billion catalogs, and more than half of the adult population purchased $51.5 billion in merchandise by mail.[32]

Equifax,[33] the leading provider of information for consumer financial transactions, has attempted to set up a system whereby recipients can specify which types of materials they are happy to receive and which they are not, but it apparently abandoned the effort.[34] Such selective marketing becomes burdensome, but it is actually what many customers want—information directed toward their special needs and requirements. Given a choice, they would like the right to determine to whom their name and address are distributed and for what purpose.

This right is provided to customers of the cable television industry. The Cable Communications Policy Act of 1984 provides that the cable operator must disclose to cable customers what information about their use of the cable system is to be collected and cannot disclose such information "without the prior written or electronic consent of the subscriber concerned."[35] This system is called "opting in" and is afforded to all postal customers by the Deutsche Bundespost in Germany.[36] Mary J. Culnan, a professor of business administration at Georgetown University who studies privacy issues, recommends that direct mailers offer a voluntary opt-out service to save money by not mailing solicitations to non-receptive consumers.[37]

Big Brother in the Information Marketplace

Far more pernicious than being submerged beneath a sea of catalogs, solicitations, and notices that you may have already won a million dollars is the compilation of data gathered from many sources, then correlated by computerized analysis to formulate profiles of our tastes, interests, and activities. This capability recalls the horror of George Orwell's novel *1984* in which Big Brother knows all about everyone and uses this exhaustive and reliable knowledge to manipulate their lives. Indeed, this kind of world still exists in most Communist-dominated regimes and is sharply etched in this description from a newspaper article:

> Behind a locked door on the second floor of the Beijing Engineering Design Institute is a small room stacked with files from floor to ceiling.
> There is a file here on each of the institute's 600 employees, and although they are never allowed to peek inside, they live all their lives with their files looming over them.
> As a part of China's complex system of social control and surveillance, the authorities keep a dangan, or file, on virtually everyone except peasants.
> Indeed, most Chinese have two dangan: one at their workplace and another in their local police station. . . . A file is opened on each urban citizen as he or she enters elementary school, and it shadows the person through school to college and employment.
> Particularly for officials, students, professors and Communist Party members, the dangan contain political evaluations that affect career prospects and permission to leave the country.[38]

The specter of growing government-collected and government-controlled information about its citizens, inaccessible to them, is what prompted Congress to enact the Freedom of Information Act,[39] which permits an individual to see files held by government entities, and the Privacy Act of 1974,[40] which places restrictions on government entities collecting information about individuals. What the Privacy Act prohibits is a government agency's use of data collected for one purpose being used for another. It does not govern commercial information gatherers in the private sector.

Today it is becoming more and more apparent that it is not merely government entities that threaten the confidentiality of information. Commercial vendors of name and address lists, marketing what many individuals feel is private information, are being recognized as a threat to personal privacy. According to a Harris survey panel of 2,254 adults in June 1990, three out of four people think consumers have lost control over how information about them is circulated and used. These respondents were more worried about information collected by private business than by the police, Federal Bureau of Investigation, or Internal Revenue Service.[41]

In January 1991, Larry Seiler, a Massachusetts computer consultant, discovered that the Lotus Development Corporation[42] was joining forces with Equifax to produce and sell a CD-ROM (a laser disk with the capacity to hold 104,000 pages of information). Called Lotus Market-Place: Households, it would contain information on the buying patterns and estimated incomes of 120 million Americans. Astonished at this prospect, he took prompt action, dispatching a letter to Lotus in protest of this new product, "an incredible intrusion [that] ought to be illegal."[43]

At the same time, Seiler distributed the letter on an electronic mail system. Within hours, computer networks as far away as Saudi Arabia burned with angry discussion of Seiler's news, and some 30,000 letters of protest were soon sent to Lotus and Equifax. As a consequence, the two companies decided to cancel this product and a similar one, Lotus MarketPlace: Business, which contained information on 7 million U.S. businesses and had already been on the market for a few months.

Jim Manzi, president of Lotus, explained that Lotus MarketPlace: Households found itself "at the apex of an emotional firestorm of public concern about consumer privacy. While we believe that the actual data content and controls built into the product preserved consumer privacy, we couldn't ignore the high level of consumer concern."[44] Manzi went on to argue that technology is radically changing the way we use information, and that "balancing the advantages of easier access to information with the individual's right to privacy is only the first of many new issues our industry will grapple with in the coming years." But in the end he conceded that "the product is not part of our core business, and Lotus would be ill-served by a prolonged battle over consumer privacy."[45] Jack Rogers, Jr., president and CEO of Equifax, echoed Manzi's disappointment: "Despite our significant consumer education efforts, consumer misperceptions about this new product offered through this distribution channel persist."[46]

In developing Lotus MarketPlace: Households, Lotus and Equifax had made what they thought to be an honest effort to address privacy concerns. These practices included:

- Limiting the data. Specifically excluded from the product were telephone numbers and individual personal data such as actual income, credit data, and purchase history;
- Offering the data only to legitimate businesses, through a controlled purchase process;
- Educating and advising users about the proper legal and ethical responsibilities for list usage; and
- Providing several Lotus- and Equifax-funded options for consumers to have their names removed from the database.

Lotus MarketPlace, which was to have been offered in 7,000 computer stores around the country, was a set of ten compact discs containing the names, addresses, and detailed marketing information on 120 million consumers, 80 million households, and 7.5 million businesses. Directed toward the market of small and medium-size businesses, the system was priced at $695, which included a set of only 5,000 names according to the purchaser's locale or business interest. Additional names could have been purchased at eight cents apiece. Names could also have been matched with other databases acquired from different vendors.[47] What the new products offered, in fact, was equitable access for small businesses to the kind of sophisticated data that had been supplied by Equifax and its competitors to large businesses for several decades.

Apparently these facts were not known to the protesters, and the efforts of the vendors to protect the privacy of members of the general public were not sufficient to satisfy privacy advocates. These consumer misconceptions may have killed off a goose about to lay a golden egg, providing equitable access for small businesses to an expanding information marketplace.

The incident provides a good example of the power of an aroused public to take advantage of the new electronic networks to influence public opinion. It also highlights the hazards faced by budding information entrepreneurs if they fail to address the legitimate concerns of their consumers for personal autonomy over their own information assets.

Ironically, what the Lotus MarketPlace products were intended to provide in the way of information represents merely the tip of an iceberg of information already being accumulated and stored in the computers of countless businesses around the world. The market for such transaction-generated income is thriving.

The Threat to Privacy of Targeted Marketing

Recent advances in computers have made possible "point-of-sale" data collection systems similar to one used at Dahl's Foods Inc., in a prosperous Des Moines, Iowa, suburb. Each checkout counter holds a color computer screen and an electronic gadget to read the "frequent-shopper" cards the customers carry. Buried inside each plastic card is a computer chip that records every item purchased, along with the buyer's name, address, age, social security number, employer, income, debts, children, pets, and other personal information. Those frequent-shopper cards are tools in a technological revolution changing the marketplace in a way that should stir fears that personal privacy is being invaded on a scale more massive than ever before. Shoppers use the cards voluntarily, receiving in exchange special offers directed to their personal preferences, but are unaware of the additional use to which the store puts their cards.

Frequent-shopper programs are only one of a number of new techniques that business and industry are developing to collect information about their customers. Most systems are sponsored by marketing giants like Citicorp, Dun & Bradstreet, Procter & Gamble, IBM, and National Cash Register. Citicorp, for example, is building a National Household Purchase Data Base covering 40 million households—nearly half the homes in the United States—with information to be gathered from 12,000 retail stores, and is eager to sell what its databases contain. Gerald Saltzgaber, chief executive of Citicorp's Point-of-Sale Information Services, disclosed with pride: "Imagine how Coke would like to know the households that drink Pepsi by name and address and then be able to track them. This is targeted marketing based on absolute knowledge of what the household actually purchases."[48]

During the summer hay fever season, television viewers were offered an 800 number to call for information about the pollen count in their ZIP code area. Half a million people responded. What resulted was a barrage of sales pitches for Benadryl, an allergy medicine produced by Warner Lambert, the big pharmaceutical company, which had sponsored the pollen count program. The automated number identification system recorded the telephone number of the caller, which was then used to ascertain the address and name of the caller and correlate it to information gleaned from other sources.[49]

The baby goods industry has been most successful in reaching prospective mothers by direct mail. Between 3 million and 4 million women give birth annually in the United States, and a great deal of information about these births becomes part of the public record. But many marketers of baby goods obtain lists of prospective mothers long before they come to term. As they purchase maternity clothes and baby furniture or enroll in parenting classes, pregnant women leave behind a well-documented record, requiring only systematic collection and organization. Names can even be obtained from obstetricians and gynecologists.[50]

American Baby magazine also collects and sells names of its new subscribers.[51] Thus one specialized area of names and addresses is well serviced, assuming that the prospective mothers feel neutral or pleased about the stream of solicitations they soon start receiving. But imagine the distress this barrage brings to the woman who experiences a miscarriage after her name has appeared in the expectant mother pool. The flood of smiling babies in the arms of smiling mothers will continue to fill her mailbox right through the date her baby would have been born and into what would have been the first months of the infant's life.

For another field, the marketing of Porsche cars in the United States depended upon identifying the 300,000 most likely purchasers of this prestigious sports car. Porsche managed to target potential customers in a legal manner. A labor-intensive effort was initiated to identify the 2 million most affluent from a list of 80 million car owners, then to target only those households with an annual income of over $100,000. The appeal was tailored to the specifics of each targeted customer's interests. According to the London *Economist,* a typical direct mail letter mentioned the recipient's career, current car, and corresponding pursuit of excellence in all things, suggesting that this was a quality shared "with Dr. Ferry Porsche, the creator of the original Porsche automobile."[52]

Mountains of detailed data are piling up in computers, just waiting to be mined for their commercial value. Such transaction-generated information (TGI) is produced every time a credit card is used to make a purchase, an 800 or a 900 telephone number is called, a hospitalization becomes necessary, a mortgage is needed, or a loan is sought. Each of us is providing information to someone with almost every action we take: when we sign our name to a check, when we purchase a new car, when we visit the doctor, when we move to a new condo, take a trip, or buy the "Uh-huh" cola instead of its competitor. All these transactions generate data that, when accumulated and matched with our demographics, give a pretty reasonable portrait of our behavioral patterns. Only when we rent an X-rated videotape or watch cable television does the law provide protection against disclosure.[53]

The Federal Fair Credit Reporting Act permits credit information to be shared only with employers, insurance companies, government officials, and for a vaguely defined "business transaction involving the consumer."[54] However, violations are common. For example, a reporter for *Business Week* had no difficulty gaining information contained in Vice President Dan Quayle's credit record.[55]

Furthermore, not only is it possible to know everything about you, it is also difficult to hide from those who seek to find you. Lawyers in the Washington, D.C., area, received the following solicitation from Equifax: "If you ever have difficulty locating a missing witness, an heir to an estate, debtor, shareholder, or any other person, we have great news for you. . . . [Equifax could] provide you with the current addresses of almost anyone you may need to locate."[56]

Such a locator service is one of many new products offered by the big three credit bureaus, Equifax, TRW, and TransUnion. The Equifax claim is based on information in its files on over 160 million Americans. The files are updated daily from reports submitted by thousands of merchants covering every purchase made on a credit card. These credit reports are available to more than 50,000 businesses. To manage the prompt distribution of these reports, tens of thousands of Equifax employees must be given access to credit files.[57]

Professor Culnan summarizes the data collection process in this way: "It feels like someone is filming you in the shower. . . . Little by little, the stores track who you are and what you buy. When they put all this data together, they know an awful lot about you. . . . The only way to keep your privacy is to drop out of the [credit] economy—pay cash."[58]

Why We Should Worry

Should we worry over what is recorded in the memory of a computer? If the information seekers are our alma maters looking for money, we may be inclined to forgive the intrusion and give generously. If the file is vulnerable to crooks looking for likely targets, then we worry. If a direct mail solicitation comes from an antiques dealer who has just located the most fabulous bargain in a pre-Colombian pot, which we happen to collect, then we are delighted that the dealer was able to target us so efficiently.

Viewed in this light, it is not difficult to understand why 80 percent of those polled report that they are concerned about privacy but why so few of us are willing to ask the DMA to remove our names from all solicitation lists. What most of us want is to receive the kind of information in which we have a special interest, and to receive it at a time and place of our own choosing. What we get is a daily deluge of undifferentiated advertisements out of which we are often unable to find that one piece of information that might interest us. It is lost in a pile of unwanted papers.

As a consequence, those of us who do take an interest tend to blame the culprits who are littering our houses, threatening the environment by cutting down our forests, overburdening waste-disposal plants, interrupting the dinner hour, and generally causing havoc to our peace and quiet—about as good a definition as you can find of the violation of personal privacy.

Millions of businesses are collecting data about the purchasing habits of specific people, along with their lifestyles, political preferences, shopping habits, credit history, and payment practices. Evan Hendricks, editor of the newsletter *Privacy Times*, summarized the situation as follows: "There has been an explosion of activity in this area in the last couple years. . . . People suddenly realized this data has commercial value; they are packaging it and selling it."[59]

One of the most efficient miners of such information is the American Express Company. By sifting through the files detailing the purchasing patterns of its credit card holders, American Express has divided its lists into six categories: Rodeo Drive Chic, Fifth Avenue Sophisticated, Fashion Conscious, Savvy and Established, All Around Traditional, and Value Seeker. By further sorting its cardholders by categories such as frequent air travel, car rental, use of hotels, and gift or apparel purchases, it can create lists that become of great value to companies seeking to dominate the purchasing power of these cardholders. Airlines, hotels, and travel agencies are eager to contact consumers who have both the desire and the ability to purchase their services and products.

Accommodating the Concerns of the Consumer

In a settlement that could become a model for privacy protection across the country, Robert Abrams, attorney general of New York and former candidate for the U.S. Senate, effected an unprecedented agreement in May 1992 with American Express. The credit card company agreed to inform its 26 million cardholders that it records their buying habits in order to compile marketing lists that it then sells to other merchants.[60]

According to American Express spokespersons, the agreement merely confirms what have been established practices in the past. Cardholders have long been advised, the company contends, that their names may be released to merchants who may wish to offer them quality products, and permitted to opt out of such service if they so choose.[61] The agreement with the attorney general makes explicit a right of the cardholder to be informed of the many uses to which the name might be put, with a complete description of the procedures for opting out.

Companies named as recipients of the information included Saks Fifth Avenue, AMR Corporation's American Airlines, Marriott Corporation's Marriott Hotels, and Ford Motor Company's Hertz Rent-a-Car unit, to which American Express offered joint marketing ventures. Such merchants generate substantial annual sales through the use of American Express cards. In turn, American Express shares in the revenues generated by their targeted advertising campaigns.[62]

A spokesman for Abrams said the investigation arose from an earlier probe into practices at TRW, in which the credit-rating firm was found to be breaking down credit information and selling lists of consumer types to direct mailers. The probe resulted in a lawsuit by nineteen states, including California, that was settled when TRW agreed to change certain practices and entered into a consent decree with the Federal Trade Commission.[63]

American Express agreed to tell customers once a year that it develops mailing lists based on "information derived from how you use the card, which may indicate shopping preferences and lifestyle." Prior to the agreement, customers were informed that their names were distributed to others but they were not told that their shopping patterns were disclosed.[64] According to American Express, many customers were delighted to receive special offers from quality firms and had no objection to the disclosure of their names and addresses.

The prestigious Platinum Card appeals to credit card holders who seek expensive restaurants, lavish hideaways, and luxurious travel accommodations. Indeed, not everyone treasures privacy. Many take a certain pleasure in (maybe even gloat over) the fact that they have been placed on special lists restricted to wealthy, privileged, or discriminating buyers. Being on such lists allows them the luxury of poring over catalogs full of quality items at their leisure, sparing them the ordeal of shopping with people of random taste and resources.

The settlement underscores how computers allow lenders and merchants to collect information about their customers, and how they are able to use it for purposes other than simply tracking a transaction for billing purposes. Custodians of the legal system are just beginning to understand the extent to which the computer can store and manipulate information about individuals and their behavior patterns. To date, direct mail marketers have assumed that all the people responding to a solicitation with a purchase or donation have knowingly and willingly released their names and addresses to them for whatever purpose they deem desirable. It is doubtful that many people doing business with a mail-order firm have any idea of the legal presumptions they have generated, and it is only beginning to become apparent that many are incensed over it.

Robert Ellis Smith, publisher of the *Privacy Journal,* chided American Express for what he described as a "breach of trust with its consumers." Smith warned that a large number of people would want their names deleted from the company's lists if they knew how they were being used. With full disclosure, Smith predicted, the marketplace would resolve the controversies without further legislation.[65]

The New York attorney general, in announcing the landmark agreement with American Express, stated: "A consumer who pays with credit is entitled to as much privacy as one who pays by cash or check. . . . Credit cardholders should not unknowingly have their spending patterns and lifestyles analyzed and categorized for the use of merchants fishing for good prospects."[66] Abrams announced that he would propose legislation in New York requiring all credit card companies to get permission from cardholders before providing "portraits" to merchants.[67]

Richard Kessel, Consumer Protection Commissioner for New York State, announced a public hearing on privacy issues, which he characterized as "the consumer issue of the 90's," and commented:

> We're very concerned about new technology, from telecommunications to cable television to the whole credit area. Consumers seem to be vulnerable to serious infringements on their privacy and we need to take a look at how to protect them. We're going to look at the freeness with which people seem to distribute lists of consumers without their permission. . . .
>
> We have to take a look at whether or not consumers getting a credit card or a driver's license automatically give away rights to their own name, and information that might accompany the name.[68]

Alan F. Westin, a privacy law expert and professor of public law and government at Columbia University, predicted that the American Express agreement carved out the direction in which regulation was headed: "One of the principles that is beginning to emerge is that when information is collected from a consumer directly, there is an obligation to disclose any additional uses of that information beyond the immediate transaction."[69]

Federal Initiatives to Address Consumer Concerns

In the summer of 1994, Congress took action to protect citizens from the excesses of public access to state motor-vehicle registration and driver's license records. The new statute was prompted by concerns about the murder in 1989 of Rebecca Schaefer, whose home address was obtained by the killer from motor-vehicle records, and by concern for doctors performing abortions, whose addresses were being obtained by anti-abortion activists for the purpose of harassing them.[70] Entitled "Driver's Protection Act of 1994," the new statute provides that states must enact, within three years, legislation to prohibit the disclosure of personal information about individuals obtained by them in connection with registrations.[71] However, the act is riddled with so many exceptions that David Flaherty of the Privacy Commission for British Columbia charged that anybody who really wanted access to the records could get them. Nonetheless, it marks one small step toward the exercise of more choice and control over personal information.

Yet another congressional committee was examining the practices of the USPS. Congressman Robert Wise, Jr., of West Virginia introduced into the House of Representatives in mid-1992 a bill that would permit the USPS to disclose names and addresses of postal customers only if permission to disclose has not been denied, and only if the change of address was obtained through a form notifying postal customers how and to whom their names and addresses would be disclosed, and to provide them with a mechanism to deny permission.[72]

Jonah Gitlitz, president of the Direct Marketing Association, recognizes these threats to his industry and has warned his membership:

> For a business that is totally dependent on the use of information for marketing purposes, unwise and heavy-handed . . . restrictions in this area can completely alter the way we do business.
>
> Perhaps the most draconian legislative threat that could severely impact the direct marketing business, as we know it now, is the increased threat of positive consent—that consumers should not receive solicitations unless they specifically request them. Such legislation is growing in popularity at both the federal and state level.[73]

Direct Mail Marketing and the First Amendment

The DMA has established a Freedom to Market initiative to protect
direct marketers' claimed First Amendment rights to communicate
information to consumers, and the consumer's alleged First Amendment
right to receive marketing information. Such a lobbying effort could cost
as much as much $2.5 million, to be funded by DMA members. But the
original intent of the First Amendment was to protect political discussion in a democratic form of government. Only recently has the
Supreme Court conceded that First Amendment rights apply to advertisements.[74] It is not apparent that an asserted right of direct marketers
to peddle their wares would override the First Amendment right to privacy that has been evolving over the past several decades.

When the Supreme Court considered the First Amendment challenge to the congressionally sanctioned right of postal customers to prevent "sexually provocative" advertisements from being delivered to the
home,[75] the decision suggested that there would be no constitutional
impediment to a far more reaching congressional action requiring mailers to remove unwilling postal customers from their distribution lists:

> In today's complex society we are inescapably captive audiences for
> many purposes, but a sufficient measure of individual autonomy must
> survive to permit every householder to exercise control over unwanted
> mail. To make the householder the exclusive and final judge of what
> will cross his threshold undoubtedly has the effect of impeding the
> flow of ideas, information, and arguments that, ideally, he should
> receive and consider. Today's merchandising methods, the plethora of
> mass mailings subsidized by low postal rates, and the growth of the
> sale of large mailing lists as an industry in itself have changed the mail-
> man from a carrier of primarily private communications, as he was in a
> more leisurely day, and have made him an adjunct of the mass mailer
> who sends unsolicited and often unwanted mail into every home; it
> places no strain on the doctrine of judicial notice to observe that
> whether measured by pieces or pounds, Everyman's mail today is
> made up overwhelmingly of material he did not seek from persons he
> does not know. And all too often it is matter he finds offensive. . . .
>
> The Court has traditionally respected the right of a householder to
> bar, by order or notice, solicitors, hawkers, and peddlers from his
> property. . . .In this case the mailer's right to communicate is circum-
> scribed only by an affirmative act of the addressee giving notice that
> he wishes no further mailings from that mailer.
>
> To hold less would tend to license a form of trespass and would
> make hardly more sense than to say that a radio or television viewer
> may not twist the dial to cut off an offensive or boring communica-

tions and thus bar its entering his home. Nothing in the Constitution compels us to listen to or view any unwanted communication, whatever its merit; we see no basis for according the printed word or pictures a different or more preferred status because they are sent by mail. The ancient concept that "a man's home is his castle" into which "not even the king may enter" has lost none of its vitality, and none of the recognized exceptions includes any right to communicate offensively with another.[76]

Direct mailers may be more successful in their efforts to educate us about our rights by also assuming greater responsibility with respect to the names and addresses entrusted to them. Gitlitz acknowledged the need to address consumer concerns and recommended a strategy for forestalling the initiatives of privacy advocates by "developing a proactive educational program to encourage companies to develop in-house suppression programs for customers who request that their names not be rented to others. Giving the consumers [a] choice as to whether or not they want to participate in the marketing process not only makes good business sense, but also meets the concerns of consumers head-on."[77]

Conclusions

Direct mail marketers will be more successful as they deploy information technology to help their customers find the particular products they want. Computers are very good at finding the needle in the haystack. If potential customers know exactly what they want, there are information services that can help winnow down the choices to those products with just the right features.

For example, in the summer of 1991, I decided to purchase a four-wheel-drive vehicle for driving on the high mountain trails of Colorado. On CompuServe, provider of on-line access to electronic databases offering a variety of information services, there is an automobile shopping service that allows the potential purchaser of a new or an old vehicle to gather all the comparative information on currently available models. One can seek a particular model or a comparison of several makes and models, all of the models of a particular manufacturer, or all of the manufacturers of a particular type of vehicle. Such are the ingredients of free choice. My only worry was that I would be deluged with direct mail solicitations for camping equipment from hopeful companies anticipating that my four-wheeler would lead to camping expeditions.

The problem today is that the mailing list managers have unlimited access to our names and addresses without much opportunity for unwilling recipients to curb the excesses of their zeal. There is a real danger that the benefits of computerization may be lost in a backlash against the proliferation of all those unwanted information products that computerized name and address lists make possible.

As a consequence we have become more concerned about what the computer is doing to us than what it might do for us. The current thrust of legal protection contains some real threats to the information industry and some genuine inhibitions to the healthy expansion of the information marketplace.

Commercial information procurers and providers of information are riding a surfboard on a wave of public indignation, which may turn into a tidal wave if they do not act rationally and promptly to calm the waters. Many subscribers and consumers feel that they are drowning in too much information, while remaining without easy access to the information they really want and need.

In which direction does the law appear to be moving? We are becoming more and more concerned about the manipulation of personal data. We seek a more equitable relationship between ourselves and direct marketers. The effort is not merely to provide greater protection for Carl Oppedahl's mother but to offer more personal autonomy over all of our names and addresses. As *Privacy Journal* publisher Smith has concluded: "[T]he right to privacy includes a sense of autonomy, a right to develop a unique personality and living space, and a right to distinguish one's own persona from everyone else's."[78]

The release of names, addresses, and personal data should become a transaction in which the two parties negotiate the nature of the transfer of information between them. At the least we should be offered some quid pro quo for the release and use of our names, addresses, and purchasing profiles.

The information industry must not become a Peeping Tom whom we must catch in the act of violating our privacy. It must seek to become a responsible partner, helping us find the information that will allow us to make reasonable purchases of things we need or want at prices we can afford. American consumers are avid shoppers, more likely to opt into than out of the information marketplace.

Direct mail marketers should treat consumers as equal partners, avoiding the pitfalls and taking advantage of the opportunities of the information age. If they deploy their computers to offer information products tailored to the needs and desires of differentiated groups of consumers at times and places convenient to the users, entrepreneurs will be assured a healthy income and their efforts will greatly enhance the information marketplace.

Our names and addresses and personal transactions are valuable information assets worthy of recognition that we have property rights in them. Unless we assert these rights we will lose them. If such information has economic value, we should receive something of value in return for its use by others.

2

Who Owns Your Telephone Number?

Willis Mog, an attorney in Lebanon, Illinois, was fed up with having his dinner hour interrupted by telemarketing calls: "My phone used to ring off the hook from about 5 in the evening until 10 o'clock at night. . . . If you're having dinner, you can't get through it because you get 15 calls during the dinner hour. I'd go outside or not answer or disconnect the phone or go away to eat, and that's not right."

Mog decided to take legal action. First he joined an organization called Private Citizen, Inc., founded in 1985 by a fellow sufferer, Robert Bulmash of Warrenville, Illinois, the sole purpose of which is to fight what Bulmash dubbed "telenoyers." For a $20 annual membership fee, Bulmash will include your name on a notice he distributes to some thousand telemarketing companies and other businesses known to generate unsolicited calls. His notice warns: "I am unwilling to allow your free use of my time and telephone for such calls. . . . I will accept junk calls, placed by or on your behalf for a $100 fee, due within 30 days of such use. . . . Your junk call will constitute your agreement to the reasonableness of my fee."[1]

Soon thereafter, Mog's telephone solicitations dropped precipitously, as did those of other members of Private Citizen. However, the retailer J. C. Penney either didn't get the warning or persisted in ignoring it. In response to a call from that company, Mog sent a bill for $100. When Penney refused to pay it, he filed a complaint in the St. Clair Circuit Court for damages in the amount of $2,500 "for use of Plaintiff's telephone equipment and Plaintiff's services in answering Defendant's telephone solicitation on January 26, 1989 . . . and [for] mental anguish."[2]

Mog named as defendants both J. C. Penney and Advanced Telemarketing Corporation, the company J. C. Penney employed to make its calls. Although the case languished for more than three years and the defendants hired expensive Chicago attorneys to fight the charge, Mog was confident of a favorable outcome. But he was prepared to stick with it as long as it would take:[3]

> If I win, it's a precedent. The file is about a foot thick at this time, and it's not easy. It takes a lot more time and money than I'll ever receive, but I believe in the principle—the right of privacy. I don't want to be bothered in my free time. You couldn't hire a lawyer to do this for you because it takes so much time and research and running to the court-house. A person with no legal training would lose the first round. I am litigating my right to privacy, and if I have to go to the Supreme Court, that's what I'll do.[4]

Unfortunately for the annals of legal history, Mog's complaint did not make it to the Supreme Court. J. C. Penney capitulated to a lower court but in a closed decision, which means the details of the settlement cannot be revealed.[5] Not one to give up, Mog has filed a similar complaint against another company.[6]

Mog, Bulmash, and the 900 or so other members of Private Citizen are by no means voices in the wilderness. In a national survey, 70 percent of those questioned considered unsolicited telemarketing calls "an invasion of privacy"; 61 percent of those called reported terminating the call within seconds; and only 6 percent reported committing themselves to a sale, a donation, or an appointment. This may seem a small return on investment, but 6 percent is markedly higher than the 1 to 2 percent return typical of direct mail advertising.[7] Residential consumers account for $115 billion of the telemarketing business's $435 billion in annual sales.[8] This industry is certainly not about to go away the first time someone suggests that it intrudes on the right to privacy.

Thus, it was not surprising that when Bulmash wrote his first letter in 1985 to Illinois Bell claiming a legal right to prevent access to telephone numbers, Robert L. Sherman, general counsel of the Direct Marketing Association, countered by describing telemarketing calls as just "one of life's little annoyances"—all you have to do to rid yourself of them is to hang up the phone.[9]

More than a decade earlier, Walter S. Baer, a telecommunications analyst at the Rand Corporation, had tried to deal with the problem by filing a complaint with the Federal Communications Commission. Although Baer was concerned about all "junk telephone calls," he restricted his petition to automated unsolicited calls to increase his chances of success.[10] The FCC opened a docket to examine the issue of use of automated dialer and recorded message players, or ADRMPs.[11] Such automated and unsolicited telephone calls constitute a potentially serious nuisance, even, perhaps, an invasion of privacy, Baer pointed out:

The widespread use of ADRMP devices by advertisers could bring a barrage of unsolicited phone calls to random homes at any hour of the day or night, with no means of controlling or stopping them. It could prevent other calls—even emergency calls—from being received while a pre-recorded sales pitch for facial cream or detergent is being delivered. An unlisted telephone number would provide no protection since the ADRMP can call numbers at random or in some numerical sequence. Rather, widespread use of ADRMPs may drive many subscribers to install answering recorders or just stop answering the phone.

Overall, the widespread use of ADRMP devices may significantly degrade telephone service for all subscribers. There are at present no FCC or state regulations regarding the use of ADRMP or similar devices. Regulatory action is needed now—before these devices are widespread—to prevent their possible abuse.[12]

Unsolicited telephone calls, Baer claimed, are far more intrusive than direct mail or television advertising. Direct mail arrives once a day with the regular mail and can simply be thrown away unopened;[13] television programs can be changed or turned off entirely. But telephone calls come at all times of the day and evening. They cannot be distinguished from personal calls by the sound of the ring. They cannot be ignored easily even by someone willing to miss a personal call, because the sound of a ringing telephone is so demanding of one's attention. Just think about how expected and common it would be for someone you may have flown across the country to visit to pick up the telephone in your presence and take a local call.

To his credit, Baer, a scientist, did point out that there could be technological solutions to the problem. Classes of calls—commercial, personal, long distance, emergency—could be represented by different audio tones programmed into the system. Automated display of the calling number is another alternative, one that many customers already use. But it has created, as Baer predicted, inherent conflicts of interests between the privacy of the caller and the privacy of the called.[14] Other alternatives include: (1) temporary blocking of all calls during periods when subscribers do not want to be interrupted; (2) recording of calls at a central location with subsequent selective access by the user (a choice simplified by voice messaging and automatic answering machines); (3) selective call blocking of commercial advertising lines with appropriate equipment to permit subscribers to prevent access to their telephone service from these intruders.[15] Obviously, annoyed subscribers could also successfully block the intrusion of unwanted calls by disconnecting the phone or taking it off the hook.[16] If you have ever tried the latter, however, you know that you will soon hear a persistent and loud sound on the line. You are also giving up all incoming calls during that time.

The only prior effort to legislate some restrictions on unsolicited telephone calls was an ordinance adopted by the City Council of Tampa, Florida, in 1964. It was vehemently opposed by local merchants and the telephone company (which stood to lose no small amount of money if such calls could not be made) and was repealed almost before it could be enforced.[17] That same year a law student at Stanford proposed to Pacific Telephone and the California Public Utilities Commission that users desiring to avoid unsolicited calls should be identified in the telephone directory with an asterisk warning telemarketers not to call those numbers. Pacific Telephone declined to adopt the system and the California PUC refused to require it, holding that the legislature was the appropriate forum for such action.[18]

Although the FCC also decided not to take action restricting telemarketing,[19] Baer's petition identified a sensitive issue that has not gone away. By the mid-1980s, junk telephone calls were on the minds of more than a couple of malcontents. In a 1985 survey in the state of Washington, 75 percent of respondents favored some form of regulatory action. Washington then led the way to new legislation designed to curb the practice of unsolicited telemarketing calls.[20] By 1986 only five states did not have statutes prohibiting harassment by telephone with the intent to annoy, but only fifteen states had enacted legislation regulating calls originated by ADRMPs.[21] In October 1991, the Consumer Federation of America, a consortium of organizations representing consumer interests, called a meeting for the sole purpose of assembling a group to recount their junk-call grievances. Those assembled complained of phone calls to unlisted numbers, calls to the elderly who had to struggle to reach the phone, and calls that tied up phones needed for emergency or other purposes.[22]

Congress responded by enacting legislation to regulate such calls. Statutes in more than half the states had already addressed some of the issues, but state legislation could not affect interstate calls.[23] Many telemarketing calls are made over the 800 WATS lines. On December 20, 1991, President Bush signed the Telephone Consumer Protection Act,[24] prohibiting "any telephone call to any residential telephone line using an artificial or prerecorded voice to deliver a message without the prior express consent of the called party, unless the call is initiated for emergency purposes or is exempted by rule of the Commission."[25]

The legislation also bans the use of automated dialing equipment or artificial or prerecorded messages to an emergency phone line, a patient's room in a hospital, an elder care home, or a cellular telephone service where the recipient pays for the call.[26] What the statute does is shift the burden to the callers to ensure that they do not disturb unconsenting or disabled parties. The purpose of the legislation is to curtail the most egregious abuses of the telemarketing industry but not to foreclose the use of the telephone for business solicitations altogether.

The FCC was given nine months to work out the details of setting up a nationwide directory of names of individuals unwilling to receive telemarketing calls. The legislation permits telenoyed individuals to sue offenders for as much as $1,500 per call.[27] Citizen advocates commended Congress for taking care of part of the problem but admonished them for permitting two loopholes in the legislation, one for charitable solicitations and the other for political purposes.[28]

As an example of how these loopholes could lead to trouble, consumer advocates told the story of an AIDS patient who complained to the medical board of California when his physician gave his telephone number to a political candidate whose staff called to solicit support from HIV-positive voters:[29] "I felt like that was an invasion of privacy and was a disclosure of medical information to a person who had no right to the access of that information. Here I was called by somebody who has no connection with the medical office."[30] Of course, this type of call offends for reasons other than its unsolicited nature. According to Janie Cordray, speaking for the medical board, it would be considered unprofessional conduct to disclose any information about a patient other than for medical purposes.[31]

The Telephone Consumer Protection Act also mandates the FCC to explore alternatives for identifying those who do not wish to be solicited, and to consider the establishment of a single national electronic database to identify these telephone numbers as well as private- or public-sector agencies to set up and manage this information.[32] It also explicitly provides that state laws requiring more restrictive intrastate behavior will not be preempted by the federal rules.[33]

The legislation had hardly come to life before it was challenged in court. Kathryn Moser, who operates a chimney-sweeping business with her husband in Keizer, Oregon, and not incidentally holds the presidency of the National Association of Telecomputer Operators, took the FCC to court. Her complaint was that the legislation treated small telemarketers like herself differently from the larger ones, which could afford to use more sophisticated and discriminating telephone dialing equipment. The federal district court in Oregon agreed with Moser.[34] Its rationale was that an unreasonable burden would be placed upon her, unjustifiable under First Amendment challenge. While threatening the livelihood of her business, the restriction would reduce the worrisome calls by only 3 percent and leave uncontrolled many other types of calls that also threaten the privacy of telephone consumers. What the court said, in effect, was that the FCC might reasonably forbid all telemarketing calls but could not discriminate among different types.

Despite efforts to derail some of the provisions of the 1991 act, telephone subscribers are not satisfied with the status quo. Representative Edward Markey, Democrat of Massachusetts and chairman of the House Committee on Communications, planned to introduce into Congress a privacy bill of rights for telephone subscribers. The legislation would require telephone companies to empower consumers to block transmission of their telephone numbers, to stop incoming calls from the "blockers" if they did not wish to receive unidentified callers, and also to prohibit reuse or sale of information supplied by calls to 800 and 900 numbers without the knowledge and consent of the callers.[35] While this legislation, if enacted, will address some of the concerns about the use of the telephone to invade privacy, it does not address the fundamental right of who owns the telephone number.

Do Property Rights Exist in the Telephone Number?

Telephone numbers were first used in Lowell, Massachusetts, in 1879 when a local doctor contemplated the confusion that might ensue if all four of the local operators were to become ill or unavailable. Prior to that, operators relied on their memories to guide them to the appropriate receptacles on their switchboards for every call. The decision was made to assign each subscriber an individual telephone number.

Historically, telephone companies have viewed the telephone number as belonging to them. They assign the numbers and change them when the customer moves out of the residential area assigned to that number. They list them in a telephone directory, charging a premium to those customers who do not want their numbers listed.[36] They produce and distribute the listing, known to all as the white pages, free to all customers. They also publish a separate list of business telephone numbers for those customers who wish to be listed and also sell advertising space supported by their own campaign touting the benefits to consumers who use the yellow pages—a substantial source of income for telephone companies.

The emergence of new information technologies has facilitated access to this listing of numbers and affiliated services. In France, for example, a simple and easy-to-use computer terminal called a Minitel has been substituted for the telephone book in millions of homes. New telephone numbers are updated often, so that customers need not wait for new telephone directories to be published and distributed and operators do not have to spend time looking up new numbers. In addition, telephone customers may use the Minitel to send electronic messages to their friends, to order goods and theater tickets, and to make travel reservations. Newspapers have even offered services over the system.

In the United States, however, newspaper executives viewed this kind of electronic directory as a threat to their classified advertising pages, a major source of their income. When the Bell system sought permission from the Public Utilities Commission in Texas to computerize its yellow pages, the Harte Hanks newspapers, representing the interests of all the newspaper publishers in the country, succeeded in stopping it.[37]

When the Department of Justice successfully brought to fruition its effort to break up the Bell system monopoly of telephone services, Judge Harold Greene was also persuaded, by lawyers representing the newspapers, to prohibit both AT&T and the regional operating companies from providing electronic yellow pages or any other information services. AT&T was subjected only to a seven-year ban, which expired in 1991.[38]

Judge Greene has remained reluctant to unleash the Baby Bells to provide information services.[39] However, public sentiment favors a competitive market in the distribution of telephone numbers electronically together with the information services that the public might benefit from using. Telephone companies were free to provide information services, except video services, which might compete with cable television systems,[40] although this statutory prohibition has been held unconstitutional by a federal district court in Virginia.[41]

It should be clear from this discussion that if telephone companies do own the telephone numbers they assign to their customers, they are not free to do with them as they like. Telephone numbers are a valuable asset, attractive to telemarketers and to their customers as well. If the courts have not looked favorably on telephone company claims of proprietary rights to the telephone numbers of their subscribers, it is also true that they have been no more supportive of such proprietary claims when made by the public, even when such claims revolve around the issue of privacy. The Supreme Court, in essence, has refused to recognize that a telephone customer has either a privacy or a property interest "in information he voluntarily turns over to third parties."[42]

In March 1976, subsequent to a robbery, Patricia McDonough of Baltimore, Maryland, started receiving threatening and obscene calls from a man who claimed to be the robber. In order to track down the culprit, the police requested that the telephone company install a "pen register" on McDonough's telephone, which would reveal the telephone numbers directed to her number.[43] Michael Lee Smith, thus identified, claimed a constitutional right of privacy to the telephone numbers he had dialed. (Today the numbers would be revealed automatically by the computerized recording of all calls for billing purposes.)

At the trial Smith moved, under the "search and seizure" clause of the Fourth Amendment, to suppress the pen record of the telephone numbers he had dialed, claiming that they constituted an unwarranted search. The issue was decided by the U.S. Supreme Court in 1979. The Court held that Smith could expect this evidence to be withheld only if he had a legitimate expectation of privacy in the telephone numbers he used and called. The Court found no such basis for preventing evidence of the telephone numbers:

> We doubt that people in general entertain any actual expectation of privacy in the numbers they dial. . . . Telephone users, in sum, typically know that they must convey numerical information to the phone company; that the phone company has facilities for recording this information; and that the phone company does in fact record this information for a variety of legitimate business purposes. Although subjective expectations cannot be scientifically gauged, it is too much to believe that telephone subscribers, under these circumstances, harbor any general expectation that the numbers they dial will remain secret.[44]

Justices William Brennan and Thurgood Marshall wrote a strong dissent, stating that there could be no assumption of risk where there was no practical choice:

> [U]nless a person is prepared to forgo use of what for many has become a personal or professional necessity, he cannot help but accept the risk of surveillance. . . . It is idle to speak of "assuming" risks in contexts where, as a practical matter individuals have no realistic alternative. . . . Privacy of placing calls is of value not only to those engaged in criminal activity. The prospect of unregulated governmental monitoring will undoubtedly prove disturbing even to those with nothing illicit to hide. . . . Just as one who enters a public telephone booth is "entitled to assume that the words he utters into the mouthpiece will not be broadcast to the world" . . . so too, he should be entitled to assume that the numbers he dials in the privacy of his home will be recorded, if at all, solely for the phone company's business purposes.[45]

It may have been the case in 1979, when the Supreme Court handed down this decision, that users understood that their telephone numbers were public knowledge. But today, when asked, we are becoming more and more apprehensive about the disclosure of our own telephone numbers and those we dial. Indeed, the case that the Court cited in support of its finding,[46] a case that failed to protect bank records from being disclosed to the government, precipitated congressional response in the enactment of the Right to Financial Privacy Act of 1978.[47] Nonetheless, the claim of a property interest in telephone numbers is far from settled.

Can the Telephone Number Be Copyrighted?

A more recent Supreme Court decision, *Feist Publications v. Rural Telephone Service*,[48] confirms that claims of a proprietary interest in telephone numbers are not likely to be taken seriously by the courts in the absence of legislation conferring such rights. In this case a rural telephone company in Kansas refused to license the use of its telephone directory to Feist Publications, which packaged wider area directories. Feist went ahead and extracted the numbers it needed, claiming that they were facts and thus not susceptible to copyright protection. (Had Feist not openly admitted this, Rural Telephone would have shown that Feist included some fictitious telephone numbers that Rural Telephone had inserted for the sole purpose of entrapping would-be copiers.)

On the issue of whether telephone numbers were protected under the copyright laws, the Supreme Court ruled with Feist, saying they are not. With this decision it put to rest the labored efforts of a long line of lower court rulings attempting to craft a "sweat of the brow" theory to cover the substantial investment made by database providers who must gather, process, package, and market their information products. As Justice Sandra Day O'Connor wrote: "copyright protects originality not effort."[49]

Moreover, she noted, the requirement of originality was constitutionally mandated.[50] This means that Congress as well as the courts would be foreclosed from extending the copyright law to cover facts contained in otherwise copyrightable "expression." Compilations of facts are now included under the copyright statute, but only for the original organization of the facts, not the factual material itself. If "sweat of the brow" is to be protected, other means than the copyright statute need to be sought.

Although the Supreme Court decision was argued on the copyright issues alone, the justices were no doubt influenced by the fact that a lower court had found Rural guilty of antitrust violations by refusing to license use of its white pages to Feist in order to maintain its monopoly over this information.[51] The Court also noted that Rural was required by state law to publish the telephone numbers.[52]

The decision leaves one much to think about. It underlines the inadequacies of the judicial system as a vehicle for crafting new legal tools to cover changing economic circumstances brought about by new information technologies. Clearly, in the information age, telephone numbers do carry economic value. The law is deficient in not recognizing this, and it is likely that this decision will lead to legislative initiatives. It is also likely to lead to further litigation in which the courts more finely sort out what proprietary rights can be asserted to control the allocation and use of data such as telephone numbers.

Curiously enough, Rural conceded the factual nature of the telephone numbers together with the names and addresses included in the telephone directory without claiming any proprietary interest in the numbers. Justice O'Connor concluded: "there is nothing original in Rural's white pages. The raw data are uncopyrightable facts, and the way in which Rural selected, coordinated, and arranged these facts is not original in any way. Rural's selection of listings—subscribers' names, towns, and telephone numbers—could not be more obvious and lacks the modicum of creativity necessary to transform mere selection into copyrightable expression."[53]

In fact, the organization of telephone numbers is quite complex. Numbers in different countries differ in length. They do not necessarily have seven digits for local numbering, as in the United States. Exchanges have to be designated; area codes have to be assigned. Special services such as 700, 800, and 900 numbers, as well as emergency numbers such as 911, require special technical expertise, understanding, and, indeed, originality. This observation is corroborated by the extensive proceedings before the FCC to regulate the way telephone numbers are being handled among the various competing carriers in order to achieve an interoperable system. A telephone number is not like a mathematical algorithm or law of nature that lies waiting to be discovered and thus becomes the property of all, allocated forever to the public domain. Again, it seems strange that the lawyers for Rural did not make a good-faith effort to establish originality in the telephone numbers themselves. Perhaps Rural's lawyers recognized that the company itself did not construct the numbering system. What they use is the North American Numbering Plan, developed by the Bell Telephone Laboratories and now prepared by Bell Communications Research (Bellcore) on behalf of all of the operating companies.

Perhaps the case was ineptly argued or decided. On the other hand, it may be just another example, like computer software, where the utilitarian nature of the product is unsuitable for coverage under statutes designed for literary and artistic endeavor. Indeed, not merely telephone numbers but facts, organized into complex databases, have substantial economic value that may, in a market economy, require legal protection.[54] What is valuable is not just the fact but the ability to find it easily and quickly by complex and costly software. The proliferation of electronic databases of all kinds may eventually attract the attention of lawmakers as a commodity for which compensation is necessary when offered on the information marketplace. Depriving their content of legal protection is detrimental to the healthy development of an information marketplace.

Telephone Numbers as Corporate Property: WATS Lines and 800 Numbers

The 800 prefix for telephone numbers was an innovation introduced by AT&T in 1967 and designed to serve the business community, which desired to contract for wide-area telephone service (WATS) and to enable customers to reach their offices without incurring long-distance charges. From a customer base of only 653 users in 1967 making 7 million calls, in 1988 the 800 service had grown to half a million subscribers generating 6.3 billion calls annually.[55] By 1993 there were 700,000 businesses with 800 numbers receiving some 13 billion calls a year and generating $7.2 billion in charges.[56]

The use of the 800 number has been so effective in attracting new customers that advertising on broadcast and cable has become keyed to the number of 800 calls generated in response to it.[57] Moreover, several cable television channels are devoted exclusively to the marketing of consumer items ordered through 800 numbers.[58]

Some corporate customers have a considerable interest in acquiring as property the 800 numbers their customers use. Many have claimed numbers that spell out their corporate name to make it easier for the customer to remember them and also to attract interest in their product. Indeed, Clairol, Procter & Gamble, and other companies print their 800 numbers on their products, such as kitchen appliances, laundry machines, and computers, so that customers can seek advice and further information.

The 800 number was also used successfully in the 1992 presidential campaign by both H. Ross Perot and Jerry Brown. Brown's campaign claimed that $3.5 million in pledged contributions were received, resulting in $2 million to support the campaign. Perot reported 500,000 telephone calls to his 800 number within a twenty-four-hour period following his appearance on "Donahue."[59]

Ownership and control of the 800 number was not a serious problem so long as AT&T was the only carrier providing the WATS lines. When MCI entered the market in 1987, however, customers were reluctant to switch long-distance telephone companies. Even where the terms were more competitive, to change 800 numbers would mean releasing numbers they had spent their own advertising dollars to publicize. Consequently, customers wanted to "own" their numbers and be able to carry them along to their new telecommunications carrier. Carriers, on the other hand, had a vested interest in maintaining their number inventory and retaining the customer. An agreement with U.S. Sprint made clear in its contract for service that the customer did not acquire "any ownership interest or proprietary right in that number" and upon termination of the account "any US Sprint 800 service telephone number which had been assigned to said customer will no longer be made available for the customer's use."[60]

Commercial interests have urged the FCC to curtail the telephone companies' proprietary interest in the 800 numbers they assign to the customer. In response to a petition filed by Bell Atlantic in 1986,[61] the FCC has determined that subscribers may acquire what is called "number portability," at least of 800 numbers.[62] According to this decision, number portability will increase competition, provide customers with more flexibility, and permit more options in designing commercial systems.[63] Potential competitors to AT&T anticipated the May 1, 1993, date on which portability was to be instituted by an advertising blitz designed to attract away the 75 percent of 800 number customers still served by AT&T.[64]

The 900 numbered sequence may be even more valuable. This pay-per-call information service has grown like topsy from 233 information providers in 1988 to more than 14,000 today. Some analysts predict that this new industry will continue to mushroom from a billion calls worth about a billion dollars in 1990 and almost two billion in 1992.[65]

Special numbers to match special letters are an important information asset—for example, the use of 1-900-WILLARD for a weather service featuring Willard Scott, the weather forecaster for NBC's "Today" show. The *New York Times* has found a profitable service in its special number, 1-900-884-CLUE, which permits readers stumped by its crossword puzzle to seek answers. Other uses include sports scores, dial-a-joke, dial-a-prayer, even dial-a-bird to discover where rare birds have been sighted.

These examples represent information services that are respected and desirable, and they attract a large customer base. However, the 900 service also attracts rogues and shysters as well as the purveyors of obscene and pornographic materials. In August 1992, the FCC fined Tele-

Compute Corporation, a provider of adult entertainment telephone messages, $400,000 (eight violations at $50,000 each) for what it considered to
be "highly vulgar and degrading and appear to us to be patently offensive"
and prohibited by statute.[66]

A particularly troublesome application appeared that same year at
Christmastime in Seattle. An imaginative information provider advertised on television a service providing children an opportunity to place
calls to Santa Claus: they were to hold the telephone up to the television
set, which then played the tones for the 900 number.[67]

Confusion over the nature of the calls and the rights and responsibilities of customers, carriers, and providers prompted the FCC to make
rules for the use of 900 numbers[68] and Congress to enact the Telephone
Disclosure and Dispute Resolution Act in October 1992, affirming the
interim rules. Concerns about 900 pay-per-call services were by far the
most frequent subject of informal complaints.[69] Moreover, 20 percent of
the caller-paid bills were contested, compared with the normal rate of 1
percent for other types of calls.[70] The rules require a preamble with full
disclosure, understandably and audibly, of the name of the information
provider, the price, and a brief description of the product, service, or
information being offered. The customer must be given an opportunity
to hang up before being charged for the call. Calls of interest to children
under the age of eighteen must carry a special warning, and arrangements must be provided for customers to block all 900 services if
desired. The rules also require the carriers to make available the names,
addresses, and telephone numbers of all information providers to whom
they provide transmission service.[71]

Some 800 and 700 numbers, and as many as twenty different local
office codes, have also been used for pay-per-call information services,
creating some confusion. Consequently, the FCC has circulated proposals that would require all pay-per-call services to be restricted to the 900
series, with 976 exchanges available for intrastate pay-per-call services
and the 700 numbered sequence to be assigned to a new personal telephone number.[72] It also suggests that different office codes in the
intrastate calls be reserved for each distinctive category of pay-per-call service, for example, adult-oriented, entertainment, chat lines, and polling.[73]

None of these rules, designed to protect the customer, addresses the
question of property rights or portability. The 900 numbers, unlike 800
numbers, are often used for a single event, such as the one that initiated
the service in 1980, the opportunity for listeners to call in their choice of
whether President Carter or Ronald Reagan won the pre-election
debates. AT&T offered a "broadcast service" such as NASA coverage of
space activities in 1982, but no interactive 900 service was offered by

AT&T until 1989. Telesphere became the first competitor to offer 900 service in 1987, when 900 numbers were first assigned to competitive carriers.

The assignment of both 800 and 900 numbers remains the responsibility of Bellcore. As of September 30, 1992, of the 800 codes 523 were assigned to 143 long-distance carriers. At the end of 1992, there were 297 active 900 codes assigned with only 52 used by AT&T.[74]

Telephone Numbers as a Privacy Issue: Caller ID and Automatic Number Identification

Many members of the public are becoming more and more possessive about their telephone numbers and concerned about their disclosure without their consent. Almost a third (28.2 percent) of subscribers nationwide request an unlisted telephone number, a substantial increase from 21.8 percent in 1984. In some high-usage areas such as Los Angeles and Las Vegas, 59.9 percent and 58.3 percent, respectively, asked for unlisted numbers in 1991.[75] When Pacific Bell announced its intention to make lists of new telephone service orders available to telemarketers, more than 75,000 letters of protests were dispatched, persuading the company to cancel its plans.[76]

The question of who controls your telephone number has become most controversial with the advent of automated number identification, in which the calling number is displayed.[77] Caller ID also permits the holders of 800 numbers, primarily businesses, to greet repeat customers by their first names and to correlate their names and addresses with their purchasing habits. By overlaying demographic data from the census data with information generated from the use of credit cards, these businesses can get an accurate profile of your purchasing preferences.

The advent of Caller ID services has brought forth as many opponents as proponents. People are often delighted to be able to ascertain who is calling, in order to pick and choose which calls to answer. But the callers are often annoyed at being automatically identified on the video screen, especially if they are calling from an unlisted number. Some feel absolutely threatened. For example, Eileen Hahm is concerned that Caller ID may physically endanger her life. She counsels psychologically disturbed patients and would be inhibited from calling them on her home phone lest a disturbed patient track her down and inflict harm.[78]

On the opposite extreme, without the use of caller ID with 911, a person who is the victim of a heart attack, arson, or burglary has to enunciate clearly his telephone number and street address while under duress.

Help may never come if he or the operator has a weak command of English or a heavy accent. A young woman in Lexington, Massachusetts, died, perhaps needlessly, from a stab wound because the recording of her plea for help was difficult to understand, and the local office she called did not have the automatic E911 system, which would have flashed both her calling number and her address on the screen for prompt dispatch of help.[79]

For large retail merchandisers, Caller ID has been a boon, since it permits telephone operators to identify and pull up the files of callers even before they pick up the receiver. For a time, American Express greeted callers by name, but this disturbed a number of their customers and they ceased the practice. Privacy advocates have become indignant on behalf of their supporters in lobbying state and federal administrative and legislative bodies to stop the worst offenders.[80]

However, not everybody is as concerned as the privacy lobbyists about the identification of their telephone numbers. It can be a very efficient process. I once called L. L. Bean to order a jogging suit for a relative. Before I could give the name and address, I was asked for the ZIP code of the person to whom I was sending the gift. The operator read out a street address she had on file in that ZIP code and asked whether I was sending this order to the same address. The preservation of this information saved me and the agent from having to restate and record the information. I was not the least bit annoyed that this information had been saved in my file.

However, privacy advocates who appeared with me on a panel discussion where I reported this incident were appalled at my equanimity. I have since shared this incident with others who confirm that they also have found it useful in placing orders. It is only the unauthorized use of information by people with whom the callers have no previous experience and with whom they do not enjoy a consensual relationship that disturbs most consumers.

In a Louis Harris opinion poll for Equifax, over half of the respondents thought that telephone companies should be able to sell Caller ID systems. By category, men were pro–Caller ID more often than women, but not by a large margin; holders of unlisted numbers were for it by a smaller number than the average; and those with a higher level of education tended to favor it more often than those with less than a high school education.[81] Only 13 percent, however, felt that Caller ID should be completely unregulated, while 25 percent wanted it banned completely, and a persuasive 55 percent agreed that it should be subjected to regulation.[82]

The privacy scholar Alan Westin defines *privacy* as the ability for people to determine "when, how, and to what extent information about them is communicated to others."[83] Turning the release of the telephone number over to the discretion of the telephone company, without regulatory restrictions, is a practice many callers will continue to deplore as an infringement of privacy.[84] What is essentially in conflict in the Caller ID controversy is the right of anonymity of the caller balanced against the right of the called not to be harassed by unwanted intrusions.

A right of anonymity is a troubling legal concept, especially when it comes to information that may cause damage, and the person or institution originating the message may need to be held responsible. The law is not entirely consistent on when and in what circumstances a person enjoys such a right. Authoritarian states have been known to harass, torture, imprison, or even murder those who speak out against them. Even in democratic nations, politicians in power have a temptation to harass, embarrass, or otherwise discredit those who oppose them. Thus the common law in the United States has protected a First Amendment right to remain anonymous when speaking out and publishing material that enters the "marketplace of ideas."[85] On the other hand, the Supreme Court has upheld the constitutionality of requiring those who contribute money to political candidates to identify themselves and their occupations so that voters may know the various candidates' sources of money.[86]

The Supreme Court has also found a valuable government interest in personal and especially residential privacy. Justice O'Connor, writing the opinion for the majority in a case involving residential picketing, said:

> The State's interest in protecting the well-being, tranquility, and privacy of the home is certainly of the highest order in a free and civilized society. . . . Our prior decisions have often remarked on the unique nature of the home, "the last citadel of the tired, the weary, and the sick," and have recognized that [p]reserving the sanctity of the home, the one retreat to which men and women can repair to escape from the tribulations of their daily pursuits, is surely an important value. . . . One important aspect of residential privacy is protection of the unwilling listener. . . . [A] special benefit of the privacy all citizens enjoy within their walls, which the State may legislate to protect, is an ability to avoid intrusions. . . . There simply is no right to force speech into the home of an unwilling listener.[87]

The Harvard law school professor Arthur Miller, while recognizing that Caller ID brings into direct confrontation the privacy rights of the caller and the privacy rights of the called, also favors the latter:

> I believe that anonymity—not privacy—is what is being sought by a telephone caller who objects to having the telephone number revealed

by Caller ID. The question then is whether a person has a right to hide behind a veil of anonymity in making a telephone call over the public telephone network. . . . Society, for example, requires that automobiles have license plates to travel on a public road. This modest deprivation of anonymity is designed to promote accountability. Those who insist on anonymity in placing telephone calls are, in essence, saying that they do not want to be accountable on the communications network, which is quite analogous to driving without a license plate.[88]

The ultimate policy question, which has created a furor in public utility commissions all over the country, is: Does a public utility—the phone company—have the right to release phone numbers, particularly unlisted ones, to individuals and institutions willing to pay a fee for the information? Many holders of 800 and 900 numbers have been purchasing the telephone numbers of their callers from long-distance companies for some time already.

The issue has not been treated as a right to control the commercial value of the telephone number, but rather as a privacy issue. Some states offering Caller ID service, such as New Jersey, have reported that the number of harassing calls has diminished substantially. Other states have required the companies to offer a mechanism through which a caller may block access to the calling number in order to protect those with a legitimate interest in keeping their numbers secret. Some states require only that certain categories of personnel, including law enforcement officers and psychiatrists, be permitted to block their numbers. Others require that each call be blocked rather than putting a block on all outgoing calls, and one state, Pennsylvania, has held the entire service unconstitutional and a breach of the state's wiretap law.[89]

The deliberations in New York State are illuminating. The Public Service Commission declined to follow Pennsylvania's lead, stating that there were no call-blocking options provided by the offering in that state. While recognizing that many competing interests were in conflict, the New York commission authorized Caller ID services to be offered in New York State with certain provisos.[90] The capability to block transmission of the telephone number—either for all calls or on a per-call basis—was to be provided the customers at their option and without additional cost. The default configuration, if no choice were made, would be per-call blocking. New York Telephone was also ordered to conduct an outreach and educational program to familiarize customers with the options provided.

More sophisticated technological "fixes" were proposed, including an audible signal that would indicate to the callers whether their calling numbers were blocked or, alternatively, an 800 number that could be called to test whether the calling number was blocked. New York City urged that the company also be required to provide an option for the called parties to refuse all blocked (anonymous) calls.[91] However, these were rejected as unnecessarily expensive and cumbersome or not yet technically feasible, given how little experience was available to determine customer preferences and concerns.[92] The proposed requirements were found to be in compliance with the Commission's previously promulgated privacy principles that impose an affirmative duty upon carriers to recognize privacy as a guiding principle, to educate their consumers concerning the privacy implications of the communications services they offer, to permit a choice of various levels of privacy protection, and to forgo charging customers for assuring pre-existing levels of privacy while permitting charges to be imposed upon customers seeking a higher level of privacy protection.[93]

Taking these principles one step further into the federal arena, Representative Edward J. Markey, Democrat of Massachusetts, introduced legislation in November of 1993 (H.R. 3432) that would impose a right of privacy as a guiding principle for all carriers in the introduction of new telecommunications technologies and services. Addressing both the Caller ID issue (display of the number on the called party's telephone) and Automated Number Identification (an access signaling protocol used by carriers to provide billing and other information), the bill imposed upon the Federal Communications Commission a mandate to prescribe nationwide regulations governing the use of such services but prohibiting the imposition of charges on callers who request that their telephone numbers be withheld. Thus the bill recognizes the right of telephone callers to maintain their anonymity.[94]

The agitation over the use of telephone numbers grows more complex with each passing year, as technological advances make automatic solicitations easier as well as technological blocking devices more practical. The questions boils down to one of cost and who pays the bill. Technological solutions can be deployed that will provide almost limitless user options. The caller can achieve anonymity, but the called may choose to block all anonymous calls. Which one should be required to pay for the privilege?

Transaction-Generated Information

More disturbing than disclosure of the telephone number alone and its minor inconveniences is the disclosure of information that is generated by use of the telephone number. Concerns of telephone subscribers include: listings in the white pages, which usually print the address as well as the telephone number; records of calls made by an originating number; records of calls received by automated number identification in institutions such as police stations, emergency services, and fire departments; and information concerning the length of calls, repeat calls to the same number, concentrations of geographic contact, the amount spent for telephone calls, or the number of calls placed to 800 or 900 numbers. The value of such information, called Transaction-Generated Information (TGI), is high and accelerating.[95] Justice William Douglas once warned that a person could be defined by the checks he wrote, as they would disclose "a fairly accurate account of his religion, ideology, opinions, and interests."[96] The use of the telephone number may be even more defining.

For years, privacy advocates fought the use of the social security number as a universal identifier on the theory that much mischief could be wrought by permitting government agencies free access across database boundaries to correlate and compare information entered about the social security number holder. Much of this battle was successful in preventing such universal use, despite the continued and successful efforts of some states to use the social security number as the driver's license number, as well as its standardized use as an identifier on tax returns and bank records.

It seems to have gone unnoticed that the telephone number is becoming a more universal identifier, at least for commercial purposes, than the social security number. Whenever direct mail marketers take your orders through an 800 number, they request your telephone number, "just in case we need to call you about your order." In fact, it is used to gain access to your file when you call again. With the new automated number identification devices, such merchants can use the ten-digit number to access your files and your records of purchase without even asking for the number. Most of them seek, in addition, your ZIP Code, since this can be correlated to give very accurate data about lifestyles, real estate values in the neighborhood, and purchasing practices. All of these can be used to pigeonhole your family into a category of purchasing habits that indicates how attractive a target you are for direct marketing of a given product.

Representative Markey's proposed legislation also addresses the issue of carrier custody of personal information transactions and prohibits custodians from reusing or selling the telephone number or billing information without notifying the original telephone subscriber and providing an option to prohibit such reuse or sale, *unless* the telephone subscriber has "an established customer relationship" that is "directly related to the products or services previously acquired by that customer from such person."[97]

Regulation of TGI is a legal nightmare waiting to happen. The more computer networks that come on line, the more likely is the public to become aware of how their personal data is being gathered and used for business interests. With this awareness will come a greater demand for more personal autonomy over such information.

Telephone Numbers as a Scarcity Issue: Personal Communications Systems

The most ubiquitous and tantalizing technology to appear on the horizon in some time is the personal communications service (PCS).[98] Proponents of PCS predict global access to individuals wherever they may be through miniature telephones that can also accommodate computer terminals with interactive video, electronic mail service, and many other features. Many hope to merge the two technologies into a mass consumer service with these computer/phones costing users a mere $100 or so:

> Imagine having one, permanent telephone number and a small, wireless telephone that you could carry and use everywhere—at home, at the office, or in the car. Imagine having a laptop computer that had built-in radio functions and was connected to a wireless local area network. Imagine having a sensor in your car that was part of an Intelligent Vehicle Highway System that kept you apprised of traffic conditions and ideal commuting routes. These are just a few of the scenarios that may become everyday reality with the development of advanced personal communications services (PCS).[99]

Consumers who have participated in early PCS experimental field tests are impressed with the clarity of the sound but apprehensive about the short range of the coverage. The phones cannot be used while traveling, since the technology cannot pass calls between transmitters. However, with the cooperation of the regulatory authorities in the various countries and the acceptance of the consuming public, it is anticipated that individual service can ultimately be provided nationwide, even worldwide. Such individual access could solve the shortage of telephone numbers, since we would acquire a single telephone number for life.

The National Telecommunications and Information Administration (NTIA) placed PCS at the top of its 1993 priority list as the most promising new technology[100] that could constitute the next generation of mobile communications.[101] PCS is an advanced version of current cellular telephone technology, featuring lower-cost, smaller digital cells and inexpensive consumer receivers. In June 1993 the FCC allocated spectrum and adopted rules authorizing operation of PCS including paging, data messaging, E-mail, and facsimile transmissions.[102] The FCC had previously issued dozens of experimental licenses—many to cable television systems—to test PCS in Washington, Pittsburgh, Tampa, and other cities.[103] For the first time in history, licenses for use of these frequencies will be auctioned off to the highest bidders—at least three to a market—a move expected to fill federal coffers with an estimated $10.2 billion.[104]

If PCS becomes as popular as predicted, we will each carry our own handset everywhere with us. Contact with colleagues and friends will be as simple as calling their personal identification numbers.[105] Hewlett-Packard, Apple Computer, AT&T, and several other companies have more ambitious visions of the future. They intend to offer palmtop and pen-based computers with built-in radio and modem functions that would permit data exchange. The Apple Newton Messagepad became available in 1993 at less than $1,000. In addition, Apple proposes to serve wireless local area networks for portable computers.[106]

Researchers at Xerox's Palo Alto Research Center are experimenting with "active badges"—identification tags that transmit an infrared signal allowing them to be located by a computer anywhere in the complex.[107] Other projected uses include an Intelligent Vehicle Highway System in which each vehicle would be equipped with a computerized digital sensor that would contain a road map and the capability to monitor traffic conditions and notify drivers of the optimum travel routes.[108]

However, not all participants in the communications revolution are enthusiastic about the advent of PCS. Representatives of law enforcement agencies as well as utilities, railway, and petroleum companies (all high users of microwave frequencies) have protested the allocation of even a small amount of spectrum to those interested in launching PCS businesses. They warn that existing public safety and business interests should not be forced to share spectrum with "unproven technology" that might interfere with established microwave signals. Nor, they argue, should they be forced to relinquish their spectrum without compensation and being offered other reliable frequencies instead. The consultant Charles Jackson counters that PCS will produce many new jobs and new domestic revenues from business and consumer markets.[109]

PCS could also provide a lucrative opportunity for American manufacturers and operators to export PCS technology. Arthur D. Little, Inc., a market research and technology consulting firm, estimates that approximately 15 percent of all U.S. households (approximately 14 million households) will subscribe to PCS within three to five years, and more than 60 million people will subscribe within ten years. This could produce annual revenues of $30 billion to $40 billion.[110] Other analysts predict that there will be 150 million users of wireless networking services worldwide by 2010 in what may exceed a $50 billion-per-year international marketplace.[111]

It is not clear that this rosy future will materialize or that PCS will develop. There is a long way between its inception and its acceptance by the public. Cellular systems see PCS as a natural extension of their current capability, and telecommunications carriers—both local exchange and long distance—see it as a natural extension of their wired services to those persons who are highly mobile or who choose to carry their instruments with them rather than use public telephones. Cable television companies see PCS as an easy entry into the voice-messaging and data services, whereas their tree-branched systems do not offer a competitive service to the telephone companies' switched network. And, of course, there will be entrepreneurs who see it as a potentially lucrative business opportunity they cannot pass up.

If the potential comes close to meeting the advance advertising, all of the above may be true and PCS will become a highly competitive service. Indeed, it is possible, though not probable (at least not in this century), that personal telephones will replace fixed ones for all practical purposes. What is more likely is that PCS will become an adjunct to the fixed services, which provide greater security, reliability, and accuracy than airborne signals, offering a smaller and more portable size with greater clarity than the current cellular alternative. Clearly the argument over who will control access to PCS will heat up as it becomes a reality.

Hot upon the heels of the announcement, Bellcore, acting in its capacity as administrator of the North American Numbering Plan, notified the FCC that beginning August 1, 1993, it would start assigning telephone numbers for the PCS in the 500 service access code. However, the FCC responded to objections of competitors fearing a potential conflict of interest if Bellcore assigned the numbers. The FCC asked Bellcore to postpone the assignment, while it sought comments concerning ways to achieve portability of the numbers assigned as well as assuring assignment in a "fair, open, and nondiscriminatory fashion."[112]

Conclusions

The telephone number, standing alone, may seem an unlikely legal entity. Still, the right to control who may assign, use, and/or transfer the right to use the number is a matter of growing concern. Within a very few years we are scheduled to exhaust the numbers available to assign users, given the present system of ten digits. We could move to a numbering system so complex that the sequences of digits would be hard to commit to memory, or personal telephone number assignments could soon come into play.

Also, phone numbers are being used for purposes of identification and are, indeed, becoming a hot commodity in the information marketplace. At present many direct mail and telephone merchandisers seek to obtain and use the number to identify customers' files. As it also becomes a way of locating individuals wherever they might roam, protection of that identity and location will become a matter of great concern to the individual subscriber as well.

If the telephone number becomes a universal identifier, even above the protests of privacy proponents, should the number be assigned at birth or when a child reaches the age of potential use, whatever age that might be? As computer-literate parents seem to be introducing computers to their children at a tender age, before they are able to read or write, that age may become lower and lower. Whatever the future holds, ownership and control of the telephone number will continue to plague policy makers as well as the public for many years to come.

The Supreme Court ruling that telephone numbers are facts that cannot be protected by the copyright statute has left a void. Without a record before it substantiating the complexity and creativity with which telephone numbers are created and assigned, the Supreme Court pushed aside the last remnant of protection to which the industry had been clinging. Clearly innovative legal strategies will be devised to establish proprietary rights in telephone numbers. It is in the interest of the carriers as well as the consumers to seek portability. It is in the interest of individuals—assuming that the number becomes a personal identifier—to assert control over the release of that number by the carriers to third parties, especially telemarketers, and by authorized telemarketers to others. This is a fight for control of your telephone number that cannot be won by sitting back in the audience watching the carriers fight it out among themselves.

How telephone numbers are issued, used, protected, and marketed will come increasingly to the forefront of public debate, as users become increasingly agitated about their deployment. Moreover, companies will confront the increased costs and inconveniences of providing technological "fixes" or offering greater consumer option for protection as well as disclosure of telephone numbers.

Recognition that the telephone number is a valuable commodity rather than an inconsequential fact is the first step. Determining the locus or loci of control is the second. Should the issuer or the user of the number, or the government (which government?), have ultimate authority over its deployment?

To what entities must it be disclosed and for what purposes? If left to one's own devices, the choice to maintain anonymity (blocking the ID of one's calls) may inadvertently mean death rather than the life-saving aid of emergency workers if the 911 call you make is unidentifiable because you are incapacitated to respond vocally. Clearly there are trade-offs that must be considered in making choices available.

Most important, who is to pay for the imposition of technological "fixes" for serving diverse needs: the user, the provider, or the public coffers?

These are not questions that can all be left to an unfettered marketplace to decide or even to thoughtful judges and juries in case-by-case litigation.

Who owns the telephone number is not an issue that can be laid to rest.

3

Who Owns Your Medical History?

On November 7, 1991, Earvin "Magic" Johnson, the all-star basketball player, stood before a national television audience and announced that because he had tested positive for HIV, he was retiring from the Los Angeles Lakers.[1] A sports announcer for NBC-TV pronounced it a turning point in the history of AIDS. Now the world would know that the dreaded virus could be contracted by anybody—not just male homosexuals and drug abusers.[2] Others pronounced it "the second shot heard round the world," which would start a revolution to conquer this disease infecting millions and millions of people worldwide.[3]

When Johnson announced that he would make a national effort to spread the word that the only protection was to practice safe sex, the upbeat attitude of this universally admired athlete breathed new life and hope into AIDS professionals, who had fought long and hard to get the public to accept the wide reach of the virus. Perhaps Johnson's candid disclosure so early in the course of his disease, long before his deteriorating condition forced disclosure, would encourage others to share the information that they too were HIV-positive.

The history of public personalities with AIDS had been far from candid. Even after it became public knowledge that Rock Hudson, the macho screen idol, was dying from the side effects of AIDS, most AIDS victims continued to struggle to keep their infection secret as long as possible. For instance, none of the health professionals attending Perry Ellis, the popular designer, would confirm rumors that he was suffering from AIDS-related illnesses, and fashion designers in general went to considerable lengths to hide the devastation inflicted upon their number by the disease. Roy Cohn, the notorious New York lawyer who had served as chief counsel for Joseph McCarthy in the 1950s, repeatedly denied that he was suffering from AIDS.[4] That he did indeed have AIDS was confirmed by Jack Anderson, who cited documents from the

National Institutes of Health revealing that Cohn was being treated with the then-experimental drug AZT, used only for the treatment of AIDS. In 1986, the *Washington Post's* managing editor, Leonard Downie, Jr., enunciated a policy of printing the truth only postmortem (unless the afflicted was an important public figure), because that was when an illness became newsworthy.

In earlier years, even death did not end the coverup. The fact that a noted personality had died of an AIDS-related disease was almost always kept from the general public.[5] Indeed, the *New York Times* published only five obituaries in 1986 revealing AIDS as the cause of death.[6] Because AIDS was popularly regarded as the gay plague,[7] a certain amount of public apathy developed, based on the idea that it was restricted to small segments of the population who perhaps "deserved what they got."[8] More recently, we have had to recognize the possibility of acquiring the infection through a visit to the dentist or an encounter with the surgeon's scalpels—although transmission through these means remains highly improbable—or, more easily, via the placenta of a pregnant woman to the fetus.

For years the nature of the threat of contact with AIDS victims was unknown or unsure. Many people were apprehensive about even the slightest contact. Known carriers of the virus were shunned as though they emitted a lethal poison even in casual encounters. Ryan White, the young hemophiliac who contracted the infection from a transfusion of tainted blood received before the blood-screening test was developed in 1985, felt the full force of the prejudice surrounding the disclosure of HIV-positive infection. The people of his small community of Kokomo, Indiana, acted with little charity to have him barred from attending school with his friends, even while he was still healthy enough to participate fully in school activities.

The cases of Ryan White and Magic Johnson represent two points on a long journey, from reactions of pure fright to a great interest in hard medical information about the risk of contagion to the community and how infected persons should be treated by the public.

Shunning the Diseased: Ryan White

In order to plan steps to contain epidemics, to treat victims, and particularly to participate intelligently in decisions to allocate research funds to the search for satisfactory cures or immunizations, professionals must have precise statistical data. Alongside this strong need for information, especially in situations where a disease threatens to become an epidemic, is a strong personal aversion to sharing our medical history with anyone other than a close circle of physicians, family, and friends.

This aversion has a practical as well as an emotional basis. A case of the sniffles or a winter cold can win a little sympathy from cohorts, but the knowledge that you have a serious communicable disease can make you a pariah. Further, any suggestion that you have a serious, long-term illness, communicable or not, can cause others to speculate about whether you may be compromised in your ability to perform optimally on the job. Even a smoking habit, if known, can make a person less employable.

The legal tensions between these two forces are being worked out case by case, by such intrepid folks as the parents of Ryan White, who, under the Education for All Handicapped Children Act,[9] the Rehabilitation Act,[10] and the Civil Rights Act,[11] charged the school board with violating Ryan's rights in keeping him from attending school. They sought a court injunction to require the school authorities to readmit their son to classes with his peers, filing suit in the federal district court in the Southern District of Indiana.

The court, following the general guidelines defining the federal nature of our judicial system outlined in other Supreme Court decisions, held that because the Whites had not yet exhausted all the administrative remedies available to them, the matter was not ripe for federal intervention, and shunted the case back to the local level for resolution.[12] Rather than undergo the expense of fighting a long legal battle with the determined Mrs. White, the local school board capitulated, citing the inadequacy of public funds available for legal fees.[13]

The board's decision to take this action may have also been predicated on the national attention the case received and the compelling arguments of the medical profession that there was no credible evidence to support the belief that Ryan's classmates risked contracting the HIV virus from casual exposure to him in the classroom or on the playground.[14] Nevertheless, on the day Ryan returned, a number of students boycotted the school, and parents threatened to lobby the state legislature to enact a law prohibiting HIV-infected children from being taught in a classroom setting.[15]

Other families of children with AIDS were not so persistent. Children in Redondo Beach and Carmel, California, and triplets in Miami, Florida, just stayed at home without protest.[16] In Orange County, California, an eleven-year-old boy was excluded from school for over a semester because of HIV infection.[17] Despite a vast amount of medical information to the contrary,[18] public opinion polls at the time revealed that more than half of those questioned believed that HIV could be transmitted through casual contact. A not inconsequential number thought that AIDS was as communicable as the common cold.[19] As the information spread that this affliction would increase in number and severity in the coming years, school boards all over the country were challenged to develop a policy.[20] A virtual epidemic of concern erupted all over the country, as students boycotted schools where fellow students were known to be infected.[21]

Eventually Congress enacted legislation extending health care services to the afflicted and providing for testing, education, counseling, and aid to highly affected areas. The statute, known as the Ryan White Comprehensive Resources Emergency Act of 1990, recognized the right of an HIV-infected person to privacy of medical information except in cases where public health or the health of third parties would be put at risk through unwitting exposure to the disease.[22] The statute did recognize that there was a problem with those who had unwittingly been exposed to the HIV virus before the danger of blood transfusions became apparent, and required that these at-risk people be notified.[23]

Lawyers pricked up their ears at this news. A spate of law journal articles appeared in the aftermath of the Ryan White controversy and similar incidents around the country, dealing mostly with the logistics of providing access to education for the afflicted.[24] Indeed, in 1990 articles on AIDS were listed under "communicable diseases" in the *Index to Legal Periodicals;* by 1991 there were so many articles that they became entitled to a category all their own.

A Personal Right to Disclosure: Kimberly Bergalis

When is society entitled to know who does or does not carry the AIDS virus? In December 1991 a young woman named Kimberly Bergalis, only twenty-two when she found she had AIDS, became the first person known to have died of the disease after contracting the virus from a health care professional. According to the best available information, Kimberly was sexually inactive and drug-free, saving herself, as she put it, for "Mr. Perfect." Her mother, a nurse, surmised that Kimberly must have gotten AIDS from her dentist, Dr. David J. Acer, to whom she went for a routine extraction of two wisdom teeth.[25]

Shortly before her death, Kimberly wrote to the Florida State Health Authorities, "you ruined my life and my family,"[26] and begged them to "enact legislation so no other patient will have to go through the hell that I have."[27] She had, according to earlier reports, become a "celebrity by disease."[28] A year-long investigation revealed that four other patients of Dr. Acer had become infected with the same strain of the AIDS virus.[29]

The state health authorities were mystified about how the virus could have been transmitted, since the dentist had worn the mandatory rubber gloves while treating his patients. There were many theories propounded, from contaminated instruments to a bleeding cut to a deliberate act of injecting samples of his blood in the local anesthesia used on the patients. Efforts to track down Dr. Acer's sex partners were to no avail. And only 900 of an alleged 2,000 patients responded to a letter urging them to get an AIDS test, many of those saying that they did not want to know.[30]

Unfortunately, Dr. Acer was not around to help with the investigation, having died the year prior to Kimberly's discovery that she had contracted the disease from him. However, the dentist did leave a posthumous letter to his patients advising them to be tested.[31] Discovery of a sixth patient prompted speculation that Dr. Acer may have intentionally infected his patients. A friend of Acer, Edward Parsons, of Miami Beach, reported that Acer had discussed with him in 1988 his concern that mainstream America would continue to ignore the AIDS epidemic until "it starts affecting grandmothers and younger people."[32]

Kimberly spent the remainder of her short life in lobbying efforts attempting to persuade the state of Florida and Congress to require health care professionals to make it known if they harbor a dangerous virus. The Senate acted hastily to impose prison terms and fines on AIDS-infected health care workers who performed questionable procedures without informing their patients about the potential for transmitting disease[33]—this despite the fact that only 5.1 percent of reported cases of AIDS in 1988 had been contracted from health care workers.[34]

Bergalis sued Dr. Acer's estate as well as his insurance company.[35] She received a $1 million settlement from Acer's malpractice insurer after the CDC confirmed through genetic tests that there was a 99.4 percent certainty that she had contracted the disease from him.[36] She later received another $1 million from Acer's estate.[37]

Some 372 similar cases were filed between June 1989 and January 1991. According to Lawrence O. Gostin, a professor at the Harvard School of Public Health and author of a report on AIDS litigation: "There never has been a disease in American history, or even world history, that has produced a flood of litigation like this. There is still a basic fear, often an irrational fear, in society that is being litigated in the courts."[38]

The largest number of court cases, 107, involved discriminatory treatment of AIDS victims. Another 56 cases involved criminal law, and a third group of 45 cases concerned contamination of the blood supply. Unique to this disease, many cases involved infected people being sent to jail for biting or spitting on others, or HIV-infected sex partners failing to disclose their condition. Insurance companies that deny coverage for medical treatment and health care workers who refuse to care for AIDS sufferers make up another group.[39]

State legislatures moved quickly to enact far-reaching and sometimes unreasonable statutes. For example, if a woman contracts the HIV virus, even if she does not know it, and becomes pregnant, she can be considered a felon under the laws of Illinois, Louisiana, Missouri, and Oklahoma for "engaging in intimate contact with another"[40]

Doctors' Rights

Doctors who suffer from the disease have a special point of view. Dr. William H. Behringer, an ear, nose, and throat specialist, sued the Princeton Medical Center, where he practiced, for requiring his patients to sign a consent form acknowledging that they had been informed that he had tested positive for the AIDS virus and that there was a potential risk of transmission.[41]

Behringer's complaint argued that this consent form in effect excluded him from surgical practice at the hospital. He argued further that the hospital had breached his right to confidentiality both as a patient and as a staff member. The information about his state of health spread like a brushfire throughout the hospital and the community in which his patients lived. Dr. Behringer's exclusion from practice is not an isolated case.

Besides Dr. Acer there are no other cases of a doctor contaminating his patients,[42] yet the information that he had infected his patients opened a floodgate of national debate over disclosure to patients of any health professional's HIV-positive status. The CDC has published recommendations that professionals engaged in "exposure-prone" procedures seek the test and refrain from such procedures if they test positive, unless given permission to proceed by a review panel of experts. But the Association of Physicians for Human Rights in San Francisco claimed that the guidelines "feed into misplaced fears." Nonetheless, the American Medical Association has called for voluntary testing of all health care workers, and a *Newsweek* poll found that 94 percent of Americans surveyed felt that doctors should tell their patients if they are HIV-infected.[43]

Dr. Behringer suspected that he had contracted the disease while performing an emergency procedure on an infected patient's throat while not properly masked, thus permitting saliva and/or blood from the patient to be mixed with his own.[44] He had been informed of the patient's condition and failed to exert due care, but what about a situation where the attending doctor is uninformed? Does the doctor have a right to know whether the patient has AIDS?

A young intern tells of his experience attending a surgeon replacing an outmoded knee replacement on a young athlete, with inadequate tools for the circumstances. The operation was an unusually bloody one, during which bodily fluids spurted about the operating room in all directions. While attending the patient in the recovery room, the intern detected the telltale enlarged glands that suggested the young man had AIDS, which he had neglected to disclose to his attending physicians.[45]

Given the appropriate information, the surgeons might not have undertaken the difficult surgery in a patient with such a limited life expectancy. Had they decided to proceed they would surely have taken measures to protect themselves. Without sufficient information, they had exposed themselves to a dangerous but avoidable medical hazard.

Physicians have begun to speak up about not being given pertinent information to help them make judicious decisions in such cases. Over the past eleven years and after over 200,000 diagnosed cases of AIDS across the nation,[46] there are only fifty known instances in which a person with AIDS transmitted the virus to a health care worker.[47] However, to health care workers at risk daily, that is fifty too many. The law seems to be of two minds on the subject. In Los Angeles Superior Court, Judge David Horowitz found "no duty of patient to be truthful concerning her medical condition with her medical care providers," yet upheld a jury award of $102,500 for fraud for failure to disclose to a health care professional contaminated during a surgical procedure that she had been diagnosed as HIV-positive.[48]

Protection of Public Servants

The concern about exposure to AIDS on the job has extended to police officers, firefighters, prison wardens, and teachers, all of whom may be called upon to treat HIV-positive individuals under emergency conditions. Many legislatures are considering laws requiring mandatory testing of prisoners, prostitutes, accident victims—indeed, almost anyone hospitalized or arrested. Whether limited public funds would be better spent on testing or on massive distribution to the public of information about AIDS is highly controversial.

The transmission of AIDS in prisons, both to other prisoners and to prison wardens and guards, has become a serious threat.[49] It is a fact that both consensual and coerced homosexual sex is commonplace in most correctional institutions, putting many prisoners at risk.[50] In New York as many as 25 percent of prisoners are said to have been exposed to circumstances in which transmission of the AIDS virus is likely.[51]

Moreover, it has become difficult to reconcile the fears of penal system employees with the rights of prisoners. In Nevada, corrections officer who threatened to strike were given a list of all prisoners who tested positive, despite a study by the state attorney general's office maintaining that such disclosure would violate the state's confidentiality laws.[52] The Department of Education in California assigned an HIV-infected teacher to an administrative position, but refused to grant the person permission to teach in the classroom. The determination was upheld by a judge who stated that he could not be completely sure that the disease would not be transmitted.[53]

This observation is not entirely inconsistent with the experiences of ordinary folk, who often question the authority with which the medical profession pronounces one or another view as indisputable medical fact and then in the light of subsequent data changes the pronouncement—as it did with secondhand cigarette smoke, for example.

In an exercise of extreme caution, at least ten states analyzed in a study carried out by the National Prison Project of the American Civil Liberties Union found prisoners with AIDS and ARC (an AIDS-related condition) in the latter stages of degeneration housed with those who had merely tested positive. The thinking among AIDS professionals is that those who test positive but do not exhibit manifest symptoms of AIDS should be regarded as having an impairment but not as being diseased.[54] The current trend is toward mainstreaming those merely infected.[55] A federal statute went into effect on January 26, 1992, protecting victims of the AIDS virus from discrimination in housing, education, and employment. The statute has no provisions concerning denial of access to medical or life insurance on account of AIDS, another contentious point.[56]

Medical Records of Presidents and Presidential Candidates

At the opposite end of the spectrum from personal privacy and confidentiality is public access to the private and confidential medical records of public figures. No law requires disclosure, no matter how high the office. Much effort was expended to show President Roosevelt (FDR) standing in public without assistance, to conceal the fact that his affliction with polio left him wheelchair-bound. During the 1944 presidential campaign, when he ran for a fourth term, the serious deterioration of his overall health was not disclosed, other than by the lugubrious dark circles under his eyes. In fact, his press secretary prevailed upon the FBI to investigate a physician on suspicion of leaking the truth about his high blood pressure and weak heart.[57]

Since Roosevelt's death, only three months into his fourth term, the White House doctors have gone out of their way to disclose medical threats, as well as to dramatize their successes in forestalling the grim reaper from taking his toll. The public became conversant with the details of Eisenhower's heart attack in 1955 and his later attack of ileitis, for example. It was inevitable that such scrutiny would soon extend to candidates as well. The fact that JFK took steroids for Addison's disease was hinted at during the 1960 campaign, although his brother Robert went to great lengths to keep it from being confirmed. Members of the public cringed when LBJ proudly displayed a scar from an incision in his belly. In 1972 the Democrats lost Senator Thomas Eagleton as a vice presidential candidate when he failed to reveal that he had been under psychiatric treatment. Medical press releases emanated regularly from the George Washington University Hospital where Ronald Reagan lay stricken by an assassin's bullet. Interested readers were allowed to peruse medical arguments over the dosage of synthroid George Bush would have to take for the rest of his life in order to control a thyroid malfunction.[58]

To reassure their supporters that they are medically competent to withstand the rigors of four years of leading the country, today's presidential candidates are required, not by law but by popular demand, to disclose their medical records to the public. To convey a picture of robust medical health, Paul Tsongas, who had left the Senate to undergo successful bone marrow treatment for cancer some years back, made a point of appearing in television ads in his swimming trunks during his 1992 bid for the presidency. Only after he withdrew from the race was it disclosed that at one point he had endured a setback in his medical progress, and that a cancerous lymphoma had to be removed. This news made the public question the integrity of the information about his health disseminated during his short-lived candidacy.

According to Tsongas, the information about removing a cancerous lymph node, and successful irradiation of the area, had been told to some journalists but, with time, was deemed of minimal significance by his doctors. His doctors had drafted a letter stating the facts as they knew them but, respecting the confidentiality rights of the candidate, sought his review of the letter before distributing it to the press. By failing to allow the letter to be released, Tsongas left himself open to a subsequent charge that he was being less than candid with the public at the very moment he sought its absolute confidence in him.[59] In recognizing his mistake, Tsongas declared: "If I should surface again politically . . . I will have to prove I don't have cancer, no matter how many years will have passed. And there will always be people who would never vote for me because of fears about a disease they dread."[60]

The columnist William Safire, in an extensive essay on the subject of candidate candor, agreed with something else Tsongas said: all Presidential candidates would now have to submit to the utmost scrutiny of their medical histories and current state of health. Recognizing that physicians and hospitals were in a quandary between the opposing goals of respecting patient privacy and public responsibility, Safire confirmed that, at the presidential level at least: "Good health is a qualification for office. We do have a right not to be misled about the life expectancy of the person we make the most powerful leader in the world."[61]

Press Invasion of Privacy: Arthur Ashe

Where should we draw the line between those who have a responsibility to divulge their medical histories and those who don't? Magic Johnson chose to discuss the nature of his illness with the public, but another popular athlete, Arthur Ashe, did not. He released the information only after an inquiry from USA Today suggested to him that his condition was likely to become front-page news despite his desire to keep it secret: "I just didn't want to go public now because I'm not sick. I wanted to protect the privacy of my family. As of this moment, my life is going to change. I will deal with it because I know how to adapt. But it's wearying to have to fight misconceptions and the ignorance that people have about this disease."[62]

Ashe contracted the disease, he surmised, through a blood transfusion administered during either a quadruple bypass surgery following a heart attack in 1979 or double bypass operation in 1983. The infection was discovered when brain surgery in 1988 revealed that what was thought to have been a tumor was instead toxoplasmosis, a malady brought on by AIDS. Because it was feared that the revelation of this connection might lead to hysteria over blood transfusions, the doctor who attended Ashe said that he could not confirm that the blood product was the source. However, at the time of the first operation the practice of screening blood was practically unknown, and at the time of the second, it was only beginning to get under way.[63]

The chances of contracting the AIDS virus from contaminated blood are far smaller today—1 in 45,000, according to one source,[64] but only 20 units of the 18 million units of blood transfused every year have the capacity to transmit the virus according to another.[65] Whatever the risk, some 4,770 Americans have developed AIDS from contaminated blood transfusions, and federal officials at the Centers for Disease Control contend that another 10,000 will one day develop symptoms from blood transfused in past years.[66]

Should it have been left up to Ashe to determine when and how to reveal the details about his illness? He was not seeking high public office or trying to advance himself to any position where his condition might have interfered with his ability to perform optimally. Or is Ashe such a public figure that his personal wishes could not have been respected? Although many in the tennis community knew of his condition, they respected his privacy and managed to keep his secret from the prying press.[67]

Gene Policinski of *USA Today,* who broke the news, justified his act on the basis that, once given the information by reliable sources, it would have been professionally irresponsible not to report it. According to this view, Ashe was a public figure and AIDS a matter of public discussion meriting due exposure in the columns of his newspaper.[68] Indeed, while the Gannett Company, publishers of *USA Today,* stood by their editors' decision to pursue the story, and most of the editors at a national convention confirmed that they would have done the same, the decision was widely challenged both inside and outside journalistic circles.[69]

The coverage has provoked much debate in the journalistic community, with some editors coming down in favor of protecting the privacy of patients and others considering it a burden of sound medical reporting to expose such cases. Some felt that it was Ashe's notoriety that provoked the disclosure, concluding that "even if Arthur Ashe had bone cancer, I think we would have covered it."[70] Floyd Abrams, a First Amendment legal expert, confirmed that there were no legal prohibitions to the press's exposure of Ashe's malady. However, he added, in a note of warning to the press: "It seems to me that the harm it inflicted or has the potential to inflict is so great and the information it provides to the public so insubstantial that the story should not have been pursued and should not have been published. It also is a case of press survival. The press should realize the harm this story does to them. It makes the public angry, and it makes the courts angry. . . . To pursue under these circumstances is unseemly and self-destructive."[71]

Many commentators, agreeing with Abrams, were appalled at the callousness of the press's treatment of Ashe and his family, some calling it unconscionable to expose their private lives in this manner.[72] About 95 percent of the 700 readers who contacted *USA Today* about the Ashe story protested its appearance.[73] Even among those who consider the public's right to know limited when it comes to matters of personal privacy, many would urge public figures to disclose as early as possible if they are carrying an affliction of vital interest to the public.

Access to Your Medical Records

For those of us who are not public figures, confidentiality of medical records has long been recognized by public health officials and incorporated in most laws governing public health.[74]

There is no uniformity; the laws vary from state to state. For example, California and New York laws are markedly different in their treatment of death certificates. In California they are made publicly available, whereas New York and many other states do not permit open access.[75] This lack of consistency among the laws in various states leaves the statute books in disarray and the minds of the public both confused and concerned. Legislators can respond by saying that even among patients and the medical profession there are differences concerning what level of privacy should be protected in dealing with these matters:

> The law regarding release of medical records by health care facilities is currently ambiguous, confusing, and greatly at odds with the typical patient's expectations of confidentiality. The law of medical privileges was enacted at a time when medical care had little resemblance to our current health care system. Instead of fulfilling the public policies of providers, maintaining patient privacy and protecting the ethics of the health care profession, the law has given an inconsistent patchwork of protection which is not capable of logical interpretation.[76]

There is no common-law privilege—a right derived from established customs—to protect patients from disclosure of information they may have confided to their doctors or nurses or laboratory aides about their medical condition, so a right to confidentiality must be established by legislation.[77] The first physician-patient privilege statute was enacted in 1828 in New York.[78] Although federal courts are free to adopt a practice of respecting the privilege established as an ethical mandate by health care professionals, they have declined to do so.[79]

Under a rigid interpretation of most of the state statutes,[80] only the admitting doctors and dentists are covered by a legal requirement of confidentiality. However, all health care professionals are pledged to honor an ethical mandate to keep secret the communications of patients under their care,[81] and such ethical standards have been codified in many states.[82]

There exists a tort action available for redress of grievances if a health care professional breaches this care of duty.[83] A lawsuit may not be a suitable path to pursue, however, since the confidential information that is the subject of the lawsuit may then be disclosed publicly.[84] Most recent federal legislation has left to the state "the complex decision as to whether to require identifying information based on the State's assessment of whether gathering such information will discourage individuals from volunteering for counseling, testing and early intervention services."[85]

However, a recent study by the Office of Technology Assessment of the U.S. Congress has reviewed the current legal status of medical confidentiality and determined that

> [t]his patchwork of State and Federal laws addressing the question of privacy in personal data is inadequate to guide the health care industry with respect to obligations to protect the privacy of medical information in a computerized environment. It fails to confront the reality that, in a computerized system, information will regularly cross State lines, and will therefore be subject to inconsistent legal standards with respect to privacy. The law allows development of private sector businesses dealing in computer databases and data exchanges of patient information without regulation, statutory guidance, or recourse for persons who believe they have been wronged by abuse of data.[86]

Clearly the only recourse to the present stalemate is federal legislation. The 103rd Congress constructed a bill that would prescribe the duties of health information trustees, provide both criminal and civil sanctions for improper possession, brokering or disclosure, establish rules for patient education about access, correction, and deletion of information, establish requirements for informed consent to disclosure, require tracking of uses and abuses of the information, and introduce protocols for access as well as both rights and responsibilities of users.[87]

But do you as a patient have the right to your own medical history contained in the doctor's office, the hospital database, or the records of a large research institute? According to one way of thinking, the doctor's diagnosis of your medical complications may be proprietary to him and buried within his own undecipherable notes, which he would prefer to keep under lock and key, or at least beyond the reach of the patient or the patient's lawyer. The argument, of course, is that these are personal observations written in the hand of the attending physician, who alone can make sense of the entries. This may have made sense in the days when most such notes were handwritten, but loses some of its persuasive power when the information is entered into a centralized database of a large hospital or research institute.

While the information is arguably yours because you are its subject, the file containing this information goes into the care, custody, and control of the health care provider. Who then has access to it depends upon the state or jurisdiction within which you live.[88] In federally funded facilities, federal statute gives the subject access to the records.[89] Under state laws, rights of access vary. In California, for example, a defense attorney could prevent your lawyer from obtaining access to your own medical file, even though (and usually because) what it contains may help your case. In Georgia, on the other hand, any hospital employee may inspect your records if there is an indication that you may harbor the AIDS virus. This is an area of the law much in need of clarification.

The Public Citizen Health Research Group, a public advocacy organization operating from Washington, D.C., urges that all patients should have access to all their medical records and should review them on a regular basis to ensure their accuracy.[90] This group has conducted a poll suggesting that at least 75 percent of medical practitioners have no objection to having their patients see their own records. It should be an easy task to find a doctor willing to share your records with you.

Access to records contained in non-federally funded centralized databases is not so easy to obtain. Much personal medical data is contained in the records of insurance companies, who pay the largest portion of medical bills today. The Medical Information Bureau, of Weston, Massachusetts, a nonprofit centralized collection agency for medical data organized in 1902, provides access to the medical records of 15 million Americans to the 750 participating insurance companies.[91] Medical records denied to the patient because they are contained in the records of insurance companies, which are unregulated, may be available to third parties with no role in the medical care of the patient. Few of us realize that when we sign an insurance release form, we are relinquishing control over our medical history.

"Most people would have a heart attack if they knew how little medical privacy they had," according to Craig Cornish, a Colorado Springs lawyer.[92] According to the Office of Technology Assessment, a great deal of aggregated medical information is gathered and sold without the patient's knowledge or consent and the practice is entirely legal at the present time.[93]

The Role of the Government

The responsibility of the U.S. government in the centralized collection of medical data, its interpretation, and distribution to the public seems unquestioned. The national budget, after all, supports the medical research of the National Institutes of Health, and the National Library of Medicine, one of the earliest on-line databases, dispenses medical research information to research centers all over the world.

At a global level the World Health Organization collects medical data and makes it available to health care organizations. For example, it is only through the diligent collaborative efforts of collection facilities worldwide that we are able to evaluate the extent of the threat that HIV presents to the world community. It is predicted that it will affect some 40 million people worldwide by the year 2000, according to figures provided by the World Health Organization, but up to 110 million according to newer estimates made by a consortium of independent health care professionals led by Dr. Jonathan Mann of the Harvard School of Public Health.[94] The discrepancy between the two figures has been explained by the fact that the WHO medical information is supplied by governments, many of which are reluctant to disclose the true extent of the AIDS infection within their populations. Within any society, of course, the closer the estimates can come to reality, the better informed will be the public policy responses. But in the end the accuracy of such figures depends very much upon the legal requirements imposed upon disclosure and confidentiality of medical information.

Aside from the access to the aggregated information to which most citizens would claim a right, there is the daunting question of how reliable these statistics are. The unwillingness of many patients to have the nature of their illnesses revealed and the reluctance of their physicians to breach the covenant of confidentiality with their patients very much determine the value of the information collected and studied. This puts policy makers on the horns of an almost insoluble dilemma. Unless patients can be sure that confidentiality will be respected, and that they will never again be associated with the information provided about their own illnesses, the aggregated data is unlikely to be accurate. A statute requiring the reporting of certain named medical conditions to a governmental authority might make the collected data more reliable, but at what price? The Department of Health and Human Services is required to set up a data bank of research data, to provide a clearinghouse of information about HIV, and to provide a toll-free telephone number for inquiries from the public.[95] Without such centralized health information services, there would be no hope of containing the spread of AIDS.

Conclusions

Much of the medical information that is collected makes its way into computerized databases at the National Centers for Communicable Diseases in Atlanta, as well as into myriad other databases throughout medical institutions. These national databases are gold mines of information, but the question arises: Should we inhibit their use for fear of privacy invasion?

A very frustrated director of the Colorado Department of Public Health has complained: "Only if we identify and track cases by name . . . could health authorities accurately follow the epidemiology of an infection. With names they could track down individuals who do not return to clinics after testing positive. They could trace the infected person's partners . . . it is antithetical to the practice of public health not to use names. . . . [T]hat is what public health disease control is all about."[96]

The value of such tracking by name, including of those third parties who might have been infected, has been demonstrated many times. The successful demise of smallpox as a worldwide threat is attributable to the sleuthing project the global medical profession carried out to identify victims suffering from the disease and to track their movements and the threat they posed to others. Indeed, the last known case of smallpox was pursued by a team of medical trackers who hastened to inoculate the citizens of that person's village before he exposed them to it.[97] The benefits to be derived from such tracking are in evidence in many health problems, such as the link between cigarette smoking and lung cancer and the link between estrogen use and uterine cancer.[98]

Aside from the benefits of epidemiological sleuthing, there are other advantages to making personal medical information appropriately available through a computerized network. Given the migratory habits of today's global citizens, an individual may be taken ill or be involved in a blood-letting accident in some remote part of the world. Indeed, it is not unimaginable to find oneself hospitalized halfway across the globe from one's home, family support, and family doctor.

We are already at a technological level where providing access to medical records via telecommunications lines could almost instantly provide the critical information needed for survival anywhere and anytime. A study by the Environmental Science and Policy Institute outlines the many health care services that could be provided by Health Oriented Telecommunication Services to reduce the financial burden of health care in the United States as well as to improve the overall health of its citizens: an interactive personal health information system providing an overview of the state of one's health twenty-four hours a day; a lifetime health record available at a moment's notice anywhere anytime; improved access to the latest in medical care for underserved rural areas; public interest communications systems and electronic libraries providing a two-way flow of information from patient to doctor and patient to researcher; and greatly reduced administrative costs associated with more efficient computerized tracking of medical services.[99] The American Health Information Management Association, composed of 34,000 health information specialists, is actively engaged in monitoring the integrity and accuracy of medical records as well as ensuring that these records are accessible to individual patients. They also offer proposals for reforming the law to regulate access to medical records.

Aside from the financial cost of deploying such on-line services, the legal morass is challenging, because information on an individual may be contained in the records of various medical specialists, hospitals, clinics, and medical institutions from prior addresses dating back to childhood. Each custodian may require signed releases before making records accessible. What a miracle of medical prowess might prevail if we could centralize all of this information, providing an accurate portrait of our medical state of health at any given moment. But are we willing to have so much medical information about ourselves contained in so little electronic space, with possible access not only to us and the doctors treating us, but as well to our insurance companies, our employers, and the FBI, not to mention that bizarre world of computer voyeurs?

The technological marvels of microchips and minute memories can offer portability of medical records in a "smart card" that can be carried in your wallet and provide up-to-the-minute medical information concerning your care and treatment. Would this ensure complete confidentiality? Not if the institution downloading the data kept a copy of the records, which it would most likely be inclined to do. To have such a smart card handy would surely facilitate expeditious and beneficial care in all circumstances except when you forgot to carry the card or, through some mishap, the card was separated from you. A readily available centralized medical database, accessible via high-speed telecommunications lines, might save your life under these circumstances.

Such a centralized depository of medical information has been proposed by President Clinton in his health care package. The centralization of medical records is considered a high priority to cut the costs of administering health care, since it will save the excessive costs of duplication by many different institutions and health care providers. Centralization will also assure health care professionals timely access to patients' records. A smart card is not proposed at the present time, but a Health Security Card is. Every citizen and legal resident will be assigned this card, similar to those that activate bank-teller machines, with a magnetic strip containing basic information including your health care plan, insurance coverage, and an identification code that will assure that health coverage continues regardless of changing jobs or moving to another state.[100]

The assurance of privacy in the use of the health care records is considered essential, as 85 percent of the people polled considered privacy either "absolutely essential" or "very important" to the reform.[101] Although a majority of those polled (87 percent) feel that their own doctors are diligent in protecting access to their records, the same respondents overwhelmingly fear that the computer is creating mistakes in bills (75 percent) and patient records (60 percent) and causing medical information to be distributed willy-nilly to third parties without their consent (64 percent).[102] Indeed, although three of every four Americans believe that computers have improved the quality of life, almost a third of the adults polled (representing approximately 56 million Americans) express distrust of business and government to control the excesses of technological capabilities, and only 40 percent feel that their privacy is adequately protected by today's legal system.[103] These fears are not entirely unfounded, and there is evidence that clever computer manipulators have generated phony claims. For example, in the 1980s a man and his son collected $16 million in fraudulent Medicaid claims for nearly 400,000 phantom visits.[104] Another misuse of computers is "code gaming," or selecting a medical code for a more extensive surgical procedure or office visit than that which actually occurred.[105]

No doubt the precise language of the federal legislation to be enacted cannot be predicted. Several bills have been proposed in addition to that submitted by the administration. Senator Christopher S. Bond, Republican of Missouri, offered one of the first (S. 1494) in early September 1993. The Bond bill proposed establishment of an integrated electronic health care data interchange system requiring uniform processes and standard data entry and mandatory submission of data by all involved in the health care system. Moreover, stringent privacy principles are to prevail: (1) use of the information only to the extent necessary to carry out the purpose for which the information is collected; (2) use for a different purpose to be authorized explicitly by the individual unless the data is unidentifiable; (3) destruction of the information when no longer necessary for the function for which it was collected; (4) satisfactory procedures to assure the verifiability, timeliness, accuracy, reliability, utility, completeness, relevance, and comparability; (5) notification in advance of collection of the information whether the disclosure is mandatory or voluntary and the uses to be made of the information provided; (6) an opportunity to reject such uses at the time the information is collected; and (7) the right to inspect and correct any personally identifiable information.[106]

Today our health care records are in a state of too much diversity, too much duplication, and too little personal control over their ultimate use. Centralization, standardization, accessibility, reliability, and accuracy may all be necessary components of a national medical information system to contain costs and improve the quality of health care. To centralize the medical records would also provide a wealth of data for analysis by medical researchers on the correlation between health and geography, health and dietary habits, health and inoculations. What a treasure trove for medical detectives as well as health care workers who seek to optimize our chances of living longer, healthier lives.

Yet this dream of a medical millennium is clouded by fear about misuse of the information, including discrimination in access to insurance, employment, even medical treatment. How can we weigh the advantages of electronic disclosure against the threat of flagrant abuse? This dilemma will continue to plague us until consensus is reached concerning the proprietary rights to be assigned to which claimant for which purposes. Until we can become confident of the integrity as well as the security of our medical database, the fruits of information technology applied to our medical needs will remain beyond our grasp. So long as we remain apprehensive about providing the missing pieces of the puzzle that only we as individuals can provide, information gaps will persist. Personally identifiable medical information is badly needed to complete the medical mosaic researchers need to better serve our health needs. Yet such personally identifiable accurate records are far beyond our current reach, so long as we cannot rest assured that such information will be used solely for the advancement of medical knowledge and not to our personal disadvantage.

4

Who Owns Your Image?

A few days before Election Day 1990, John Silber, the Democratic candidate for governor in Massachusetts, was incensed to discover his distorted face featured in a television advertisement advocating the election of his Republican opponent, William Weld. Natalie Jacobson, a popular broadcast journalist in New England, had interviewed the two contenders in the gubernatorial race on her Channel 5 evening news program, and now a short clip from her long interview with Silber was being used against him.

Both men have large and prosperous families, and the interviews had taken place in the candidates' homes, within the warm circle of their family members. Jacobson's apparent intent had been to let viewers see the candidates' human side. When she approached the subject of professional and volunteer activities of family members with Silber, however, he became offended. He slipped into an outburst, berating the modern world for requiring women to leave the home for paid employment, an attitude that denigrated the inclinations of those who, like one of his daughters as well as his wife, chose to dedicate their lives to the care of husband, house, and children. While defending the lifestyle of his family members, he lashed out at women who, despite being married to lawyers making $75,000 a year, found it necessary to leave their children to third-rate nursery care rather than the first-class care of a stay-at-home mother. The implication seemed to be that mothers who worked were subjecting their offspring to a form of child abuse.

Silber's eruption could reasonably be predicted to ruffle the feathers of working women—many of whom were heads of household trying to make ends meet for their families—and Weld's campaign strategists decided to incorporate it out of context into their ad, which emphasized Weld's support for working mothers. Not only was proper authorization not requested from Channel 5 but the spot broke new ground in the manipulation of images. In the process of incorporating the program footage into the advertising tape, a decision was made to enlarge and tilt the angle of Silber's face to make it appear more menacing.

It created quite a stir. The Silber team cried foul and sought to have the ad quashed. This had the predictable result of provoking news editors to pick it up and rebroadcast it as news, thus adding to its impact. There is no question that the repeated showing of this film clip, including Silber's rancorous statements and menacing visage, had a substantial effect upon the electorate. By the time television editors were satisfied that they had used up the story's news value, all my acquaintances in Massachusetts with whom I discussed the matter had seen at least some portion of the Jacobson interview and, in this admittedly unscientific sampling, virtually all reported that it had influenced their vote.

Important legal questions arose from the various charges made by different factions interested in the outcome of the election, as well as by the management of the station. Did John Silber have a case against William Weld for defamation or slander? If so, what was the appropriate remedy? Should Silber have been entitled to a temporary restraining order to prevent television stations from showing snippets of the offending ad as part of their coverage of the dispute? Was there any way to prevent a political ad charged with being unfair from being replayed, and gaining impact, as part of news coverage?

Silber wasn't the only injured party. When the Weld organization, and then Channel 5's news competitors, carried the excerpt from the copyrighted news program, did Channel 5 have a right of action for copyright infringement? And if so, against whom? Did Natalie Jacobson have a right of action against the Weld organization for lifting the segment from her interview out of context or for distorting the image? Could she have moved against her TV competitors for showing a distortion of her original product? If so, would it be a vindication of the right of the artist/originator to protect the integrity of the artistic work, known as "moral rights" in European countries? Could the rebroadcast of her work product be defended as "fair use," a concept that allows quoting from a work as part of the review process? If so, just how much could have been rebroadcast without infringing upon her copyright or that of the station? Last, why should we care who does what with material that has already been made available to anyone who has a television set?

The short answer is that John Silber, by running for governor of Massachusetts, made himself a public figure, if his many earlier public statements had not already done so (as president of Boston University, he was already well known to the public and press as an outspoken advocate of certain conservative positions). Thus, according to the law, he had waived his privacy rights with respect to intrusion. In fact, he had invited Natalie Jacobson into his home because he sought television coverage of his campaign. As to any allegation that he had been defamed by an untruth, unless such defamation could be shown to have been made with malice— defined for the purpose of libel law as either having knowledge that the defaming material is untrue or displaying a callous disregard for whether or not it is true—Silber the public figure had no recourse. To further undermine Silber's position, the offending material was made up of his own words, which he would have to attack as untrue to make a case.

Although this was a state election and the statute governing broadcast licensees mandates access only for candidates for federal office,[1] Channel 5, according to its legal counsel, felt compelled to carry a political advertisement offered by a candidate for gubernatorial office. Having contracted to carry political advertisements from both candidates, it was prohibited by law from refusing to broadcast based upon the content of either's message.[2] It would also not seek to restrain other stations from retransmitting the political advertisement that included portions of its newscast, because the rebroadcast of such political speech, with its "high level of Constitutional protection," might be deemed to be fair use of a portion of their video presentation.[3] Ditto as to any action the station might have contemplated against the Weld campaign itself.

Taping the sound bite from the Jacobson interview could be construed as violating copyright laws if done for commercial purposes rather than for personal viewing at a later time. However, here it was used for political purposes, neither personal nor commercial, falling between the cracks of established law but probably making it off-limits for litigation.

The way the political ad was put together could have been considered an unfair and prejudicial campaign tactic, and might well have been the subject of proposed legislation, except that any resulting restriction might be deemed an unconstitutional restraint of free speech. An alternative way of handling such potential improprieties would be for an ombudsman or a public watchdog to review campaign practices and offer standards of acceptable advertising by which voters might pass judgment on their candidates.

In the end, it was left to the marketplace of political action to sort out the consequences. Once Silber called the electorate's attention to the Weld campaign's manipulation of the original tape, the incident might well have backfired against Weld, hurting his own chances for election rather than his opponent's.

The Power of the Image

Step into the Future of Television Graphics.

Connect to an on-line graphics library with thousands of high-resolution images, all formatted for television. AP Graphics Bank.

Step in any time, day or night. Find hard to find images fast. Maps
and flags; corporate and sports logos; head shots of heads of state,
national leaders, newsmakers, entertainers and sports figures. Complete graphics, and graphic elements. Plus images of late-breaking
news from around the world.[4]

This is an advertisement for an electronic archive offering instantaneous access to old news coverage from all over the globe. The satellite
delivery system of such archives can make photographic images available, if not quite with the speed of light, in a remarkably short time.

Make no mistake about the power of these images to move people.
The public disaffection with U.S. involvement in the Vietnam War has
been attributed, at least in part, to the fact that the blood and gore of an
ongoing war was forced on U.S. citizens in the intimacy of their own
homes. Americans had to face endless television images not only of what
their own boys were doing in the furtherance of national policy but of
what was being done to them. The first real "digitized war"[5] was in
Kuwait, but by then the U.S. military had learned something about the
power of television images to undercut national policy and worked hard
to control the package of images that reached the living rooms back
home. Electronic images of the day's action, culled for favorable impact
and presented as updates by Coalition military leaders daily, were transmitted not only to newspaper readers but, via satellite coverage, to a
global television audience. Ironically, the other side just as fully understood the power of live-action images generated on the spot, and allowed
U.S. reporters from the Cable News Network to broadcast from within
the bombarded enemy capital; these full-color, vivid depictions of the
enormous price paid by Iraqi civilians became as much a part of the Iraqi
propaganda war as the Coalition briefings were part of that side's strategy.

Arthur Clarke, the British scientist who in 1962 gave the world the
technological capability to place geostationary communications satellites
in orbit, optimistically predicted that the almost immediate coverage of
world events they offered would be a boon to mankind, striking a blow
for freedom and humanity:

No government will be able to conceal, at least for very long, evidence
of crimes or atrocities—even from its own people. The very existence

of the myriads of new information channels, operating in real time and across all frontiers, will be a powerful influence for civilized behavior. If you are arranging a massacre, it will be useless to shoot the cameraman who has so inconveniently appeared on the scene. His pictures will already be safe in the studio five thousand kilometers away, and his final image may hang you.[6]

Alas, just the opposite seems to be happening, according to Fred Ritchin, a former director of photography for the *New York Times Magazine* and now professor at the Tisch School of Arts of New York University: "readers are no longer saying, 'The photograph tells us something different about the world than what we thought. Therefore, we have to rethink our position about the world.' Instead, they say, 'The photograph must be wrong, it must have been manipulated by those computers of yours because we disagree with it.'"[7]

The irony is that just as we have developed a way to deliver anywhere in the world an image we thought to be more truthful than the written word, or at least more objective, we have also uncovered a technology that permits us to reconstitute those images in a manner to suit our various purposes, beneficent or nefarious. Before photography, the bias of a painter or an artist rendering a newsworthy or commemorative moment factored into our perception of the message. When the photograph replaced the painting as the visual chronicler of such moments, the public (assumed) that it was finally being shown the unvarnished, unadorned, undistorted truth. Indeed, according to Ritchin, the reason we were slow to give photographers credit for their work as artistic product was that for a long time the tendency was to attribute the image to the camera rather than to the photographer. But with the arrival of computers and their image-processing capability, the "imager" gained control over what the photograph tells us: "Now we need to know who made the picture, which in a sense is very good. Now the photographer becomes the author of the image, because we have to know whether we can trust the photographer to have actually made the photograph."[8]

Rights to Photographic Images

The first excursion into the legal treatment of photographic images came upon the heels of the introduction of the new technology.[9] The legal issue was conceived with the intrusion of the camera, which, unlike the painting, could create a likeness of people and the events they had been part of whether or not they wanted to sit still for it—literally or figura-

tively. The famous Brandeis and Warren law review article that introduced the concept of privacy law in 1890 was prompted by a concern
about photographic images invading the privacy of individuals:

> Recent inventions and business methods call attention to the next step
> which must be taken for the protection of the person and for securing to
> the individual what Judge Cooley calls the right "to be let alone."
> . . . Instantaneous photographs and newspaper enterprise have invaded
> the sacred precincts of private and domestic life; and numerous
> mechanical devices threaten to make good the prediction that "what is
> whispered in the closet shall be proclaimed from the house-tops."[10]

The authors predicted that the legality of circulating portraits would
come before the courts shortly and that the desires of private individuals
to prevent the sale and publication of photographs of them without their
authorization would receive favorable consideration.[11] They were right.
An early-twentieth-century case in New York held that the use of a photograph in an advertisement without the consent of the subject was
actionable,[12] and the New York legislature shortly thereafter passed a
law prohibiting unauthorized use of photographic images.[13] A few years
later, the use of a plaintiff's name and picture in an advertisement was
declared to be an invasion of privacy in a Georgia court.[14] By 1967
thirty-five states had enacted privacy laws,[15] and by 1984 every state
except Rhode Island had created protection for the right to privacy that
would prevent commercial exploitation of photographic images without
the consent of the subject.[16]

The legal control of photography has culminated in a case in which
the judge's decision described with precision how close a photographer
might approach his nonconsenting subjects. The landmark case involved
Jacqueline Kennedy Onassis, widow of the assassinated U.S. president
and wife of the famous shipping magnate, and Ronald Galella, who
numbered among the *paparazzi*, that swarm of free-lance photographers
who seem prepared to violate any standard of decency in their attempts
to get candid shots of public figures that always find a ready market
among gossip tabloids.

When Mrs. Onassis requested that Galella allow her and her children
some privacy, he flaunted his perceived First Amendment power to do
anything he chose to get his shot, jumping around and posturing while
taking pictures of her party and even threatening her life by coming per-
ilously close to her in a power boat while she was swimming.[17] Galella
received several court injunctions ordering him to stop "harassing,
alarming, startling, tormenting, touching the person of the defendant . . .
or her children . . . and from blocking their movements in the public

places and thoroughfares, invading their immediate zone of privacy by means of physical movements, gestures or with photographic equipment and from performing any act reasonably calculated to place the lives and safety of the defendant . . . and her children in jeopardy." He was enjoined from approaching within 100 yards of her home, within 50 yards of her, within 100 yards of either child's school, within 75 yards of either child, and from using her or her children's name, portrait, or picture for advertising.[18]

Galella appealed, and in a manner the dissenting judge called irrational and without justification, the Court of Appeals reduced the distances from which Galella could photograph Onassis and invade her privacy by 84 percent and 87 percent.[19] However, the court did confirm that such protection from intrusive photography was now well within the expectation of citizens:

> There is substantive support today for the proposition that privacy is a "basic right" entitled to legal protection. . . . There is an emerging recognition of privacy as a distinct, constitutionally protected right. . . . While the Constitution provides protection for specific manifestations of privacy . . . the protection of a person's general right to privacy—his right to be let alone by other people is like the protection of his property and his very life left largely to the law of the individual states [citation omitted].[20]

New York, in which a great number of such cases are filed, has not recognized the right to prevent intrusion explicitly by statute, beyond the pioneering statute prohibiting the use of photographs for commercial purposes without the consent of the subject. Still, the courts have liberally applied a theory of freedom from emotional distress as a protectable interest. There can be, of course, legitimate social needs and public priorities that may override this reasonable expectation of privacy and freedom from harassment. Yet even in such cases, the interference should not exceed a level necessary to achieve the purposes of the more important public interest[21]—similar to the need for unfettered political debate encountered in the case of whether John Silber's videotaped outburst of indignation could be made part of the political advertising campaign of his opponent.

Rights of Photographers

More important to most photographers than the right to intrude on the privacy of their subjects is protecting property rights in their work product. To professional photographers the philosophy of Ayn Rand seems most compelling: "Without property rights, no other rights are possible. Since man has to sustain his life by his own effort, the man who has no right to the product of his effort has no means to sustain his life. The man who produces while others dispose of his product is a slave."[22]

Photographic images come under the protection of copyright law and are the legitimate property of their creator, except "work for hire," which belongs to the employer. Professional photographers further seek to protect their economic interests in their photographs by having subjects of their photos sign releases acknowledging the proprietary rights of the photographer to the negatives and the images. The American Society of Magazine Photographers (ASMP) recommends that all photographs bear an imprint of the copyright claim. They also recommend that these copyrighted photographs be licensed, not sold, and for particular uses only. This means that the photographer will retain control over all subsequent uses of his or her work products.[23]

This practice has given rise to frustration when embarrassing pictures confront a subject later in life. In other situations, it means that the subject must return to the photographer to replicate the portrait-quality rendition of the original photograph. It does not foreclose the possibility that the subject may have the image rephotographed, rendering a less than perfect copy despite the copyright notice. Indeed, there is a thriving business in copying old photographs, which most people would consider to belong to them, not to the professional photographers who took them. Many photographic houses turn a profit on reproducing passport-sized copies of portraits or refurbishing treasures from family albums.

New techniques of electronic imaging facilitate such misappropriation of images because both professionals and amateurs can capture them—using inexpensive digital scanners or downloading from database files—then manipulate them on their own computers. While there are three traditional sources of protection of property rights—ethics, technology, and law—the new electronic imagers may have to rely primarily upon creating an ethical environment in which their labors are appreciated and compensated accordingly. Unfortunately, the various methods of technological protection, such as embedding identification marks within the image itself, can be edited out by the very technologies that make it easy to reproduce the images in the first place.[24]

The law always lags behind technological advances and cannot, in any event, precede a consensus based upon ethical concepts the community is willing to support and sanction. Unfortunately, some photographers are so apprehensive about the ease of piracy and loss of proprietary rights in the new electronic environment that they are unwilling to release electronic rights.[25]

However, computers may be able to provide technological solutions to verify that the recipient of an image delivered by an on-line telecommunications line accepts and honors the financial arrangements. Furthermore, it is anticipated that images marketed in digital form could have the "artist's identification throughout the coding of the entire image and to make the image indecipherable without buying from the artist the mathematical key that renders it intelligible."[26]

To tackle the revolutionary influences on photographic imaging, especially in the electronic environment, the ASMP is organizing a licensing agency designed to serve the emerging markets for electronic images. By this action the ASMP hopes both to promote the use of its members' images and to establish trade practices in the electronic markets that will be acceptable to its members.[27] If the first phase is successful, ASMP hopes that it will be able to offer the image to publishers on-line, so that they can browse for the images they require.[28] Picture Network International (PNI), a consortium of five major stock agencies with archives of still pictures, is moving more rapidly to on-line access of images.[29] PNI is the brainchild of two *National Geographic* photographers, Benn and Cary Wolinsky, who established the company in 1990 with the goal of expanding the market for photographs and increasing protection of owners' rights, using the most up-to-date technology to supply images directly to desktop computers.[30]

Another service is planned by CD Stock (a consortium of four stock agencies coordinated by the 3M Company).[31] It will not have an archive of images but will act as a clearinghouse through an electronic and facsimile mail system. PNI planned to begin sometime in the fall of 1993 to offer images users can view and download through a computer equipped with a modem, while the 3M offering will be embedded in four compact discs offering some 5,000 images each.

As the photographic images migrate to on-line access and compact discs from which images can be easily copied to a computer's hard disk for later manipulation, lawyers begin to worry about new questions: Is the mere display of an image a technical violation of the copyright law? What rights of adaptation and reproduction exist for users who download images? Does the right to display travel with the individual image and, if so, to what size audience? Must a subsequent composite picture acknowledge its components? Does the "first-sale" doctrine apply to an image embedded in a compact disc? What constitutes fair use?[32] Some intellectual property lawyers believe that displaying a copy on the video monitor probably falls under the exception in the copyright act for copying for use intended and would not constitute an infringement.[33] Technology has raced far ahead of the law with respect to electronic images, and the law cries out for clarification.

Rights to Broadcast Video

The advent of the videocassette recorder confronted the courts with a new and more difficult copyright issue. As recently as the early 1970s, network programs did not carry a copyright notice, because the law presumed that broadcasting a program on television was not a "publication" but a private performance to be governed by the contract negotiations and agreements reached between two parties, the network originator and the station that aired the program. There was no conceivable way at that time for a viewer to record and resell a performance, so there was no "copy" to become the subject of copyright infringement.

All that has changed. Some 4 million to 5 million VCRs are now purchased annually,[34] (75 percent of the American public owns one).[35] The sale of video*tapes* was slow initially, but 500,000 copies of *Raiders of the Lost Ark* were sold in less than a month after its Christmas 1983 release,[36] and it seemed for a while that a new box office had been created. Over the years, however, people started renting tapes for viewing, much as people once went to rental libraries to get the best-sellers they wanted to read. But while books are no longer rented in any great numbers, home viewing of tapes does not yet seem to have reached its peak, with more than 14,000 videotape-leasing outlets now operating nationwide.[37] By 1992 rentals were earning $8.2 billion annually over purchases—almost as much as theatrical revenues ($4.6 billion) and sales ($3.7 billion) combined.[38]

It may be that the practice of renting books established a precedent more useful for books than for videotapes. Under the doctrine of "first sale," which grants a copyright owner the right to transfer ownership but not to control any uses thereafter, the receipt of royalties from book rentals and the millions of video rentals has long been prohibited by law.[39] Even if a video becomes an enormous hit with the renting public, those whose artistic and creative efforts went into producing the movie do not reap a dime of that money.

While still small compared to rental revenues, video sales have been growing steadily, especially certain kinds. Disney's Oscar-nominated animated feature *Beauty and the Beast* sold a record million copies in the United States on the first day it was for sale in October 1992, with an expected market of 20 million, or about one cassette for every twelve U.S. residents.[40] *Fantasia,* which sold only a fifth as many copies on its first day of sale, eventually sold more than 14 million.[41] With such a healthy market for sales developing, the movie industry may become less concerned about the loss of royalties on rentals due to the first-sale doctrine.

If producers could force themselves to accept that movies for which they received only one sales price were being profitably rented as videos again and again, they had much more trouble accepting that copies of their work product were being taped and circulated without even that first sales price being paid by the user. Thus it was that most of the litigation over VCR technology arose over taping off the air of television-distributed programming. Since the programming is offered free to the general public, how can the public be told how they might use and enjoy it? And if large parts of the general public obstinately refuse to accept limits in the ways the product could be used, how can such limits be enforced?

It took almost a decade to resolve these questions. The first lawsuit, *Sony Corp. v. Universal City Studios,* was filed in 1976, but the Supreme Court's decision was not issued until 1984. Although the lower court did not see a violation of the copyright act in the taping at home of television programs, the Ninth Circuit Court of Appeals agreed with the complainants that their rights had been infringed and that they deserved relief. The Supreme Court disagreed, admonishing the appellate court for enlarging the scope of "an article of commerce" that is not the subject of copyright protection and beyond the power authorized by Congress. In addition, the Court found that the widespread primary use of VCRs was for "time-shifting," viewing at a later time a program the VCR owner had been unable to see at the time it was televised. Thus the respondent was unable to "show that the practice has impaired the value of their copyrights or has created any likelihood of future harm." As to attacks on the VCR as an inducement to illegal activity, the Court determined that VCRs were used for legitimate purposes and would not enjoin the public's widespread use of the product to protect the complainant from the nefarious use alleged.[42]

Taping television programs in their entirety for personal use appears to have become accepted as fair use. This is not in accord with the historical interpretation of fair use, which severely limits the amount of copyrighted material that can be reproduced. Even the intended use is different: in the past, fair use had been restricted to protecting citations of parts of the work "for purposes such as criticism, comment, news reporting, teaching (including multiple copies for classroom use), scholarship, or research;"[43] here the copying was to achieve the very enjoyment offered by the original product. The court's rationale must have been based on the fact that no commercial use of the tapes had either been alleged or documented. The case might have been decided differently if there had been allegations that the video recordings were being offered for sale.

The holding was consistent with an earlier Supreme Court decision in a photocopying case.[44] There the Court had to reckon with the difficulty of trying to hold back a technology that had produced countless street-corner copying houses all over the country—a development making it possible for any citizen to become an information provider. Furthermore, that case involved the photocopying by the National Library of Medicine and National Institutes of Health of scientific articles (many of which were taken from plaintiff's thirty-seven professional journals) in single copies for distribution to the NIH staff of 12,000, plus satisfying thousands of requests from their affiliated libraries around the country.

In both the taping and photocopying case, the Court was concerned about dealing with a new technology in a judicial context, rather than leaving the remedy for Congress to fashion as part of its legislative function. In both cases the justices were divided in their opinions. The motion picture producers did take their case to Congress, seeking repeal of the first-sale doctrine that prohibits earning royalties from videotape rentals, but were unsuccessful. However, they pursued their legal rights diligently in the courts against all potential defendants in the videotaping industry who sought to derive income from videotaped material. They no longer seek redress against users whose videotaping is only for personal use in the home.[45]

There are several lessons to be learned from these experiences. When dealing with a new technology whose effects are unknown, one may rely upon the technology itself to curb its excesses, enact legislation to delineate the environment in which it is to be deployed, or rely upon litigation to resolve particular disputes. Legislation offers advantages of open discussion of all issues and equities, but it is difficult to obtain, unless there are clear objectives of the producers and users of the new technology. Litigation has the advantage of solving only those parts of the problem that are currently crying out for solution, leaving other parts of the problem to be resolved through nonlegal strategies if possible. Litigation must also limit its considerations to those raised by the particular litigants and to the specific factual situations in which their dispute arose. The legislative process is more likely to air the full range of possible future conflicts and policy alternatives to deal with each, relying on a societal consensus to support the remedies it fashions.

The Integrity of the Image:
Colorization and Other Computer "Enhancements"

Most photographers or producers of electronic images (called imagers) have a strong desire to protect the integrity of their work product and to be identified with it. However, the remarkable capability for manipulation of these electronic images leads to the temptation to scan an image and see what more can be made of it. Such manipulation may offend the originator or may create something to enhance its value.

A tempest in a teapot raged, if only briefly, early in 1988, over the transformation of black-and-white movies to color by Turner Network Television (TNT), which had acquired major archives of old motion pictures. Famous actors, including James Stewart and Burt Lancaster, joined the producers George Lucas and Steven Spielberg in lobbying Congress to enact legislation establishing "moral rights" of writers and producers to protect the integrity of their intellectual works from "mutilation."[46] Ted Turner's release of such classic black-and-white films as *Casablanca* and *It's a Wonderful Life* in computer-colorized versions precipitated agitation for a change in the law. Such a change, providing a modicum of "moral rights" to the originators, would also serve to bring U.S. law more in line with the Berne Convention, to which the U.S. had never adhered largely because of the lack of a tradition of moral rights in this country.

In his testimony before Congress, George Lucas warned that colorization was just the tip of the iceberg concerning changes that engineers would soon be able to make using emerging technologies: "Tomorrow more advanced technology will be able to replace actors with 'fresher faces,' or alter dialogue and change the movement of the actor's lips to match. It will soon be possible to create a new 'original' negative with whatever changes or alterations the copyright holder of the moment desires."[47]

Despite protests that colorization is "morally wrong" and threatens the "cultural heritage" of the movie pioneers,[48] the motion picture, broadcasting, cable, and advertising industries all lobbied against protective legislation.[49] What resulted was a compromise. Congress passed a law establishing a National Film Preservation Board with authorization to designate up to twenty-five films a year for registration as classical films.[50] This label would denote that these films had not been materially altered in any way.[51] Nonetheless, the U.S. Register of Copyrights decided that the colorized version of the film was sufficiently new and different to deserve its own copyright.[52] The purists won by establishing the official recognition of "classics" to be viewed in their original form;

the industry and younger viewers, unfamiliar with the virtues of black-and-white films, also won approval for colorized versions to enter the marketplace.

The colorization of old movies is just one example of the ability of the computer to manipulate and enhance images. The new technologies of cutting and pasting and reformatting images and sounds make it easier to distort someone else's work while making it more difficult to ascertain what pieces have been used for what purposes, what can be used without compensation, or even who should be compensated. The borrowing of tunes in the making of music videos is rampant, as digital recording equipment permits easy mixing of sounds from several sources. A regrettable miscarriage of economic, if not legal, justice is found in the use without compensation of a rare Nigerian drum sequence by the jazz drummer David Earle Johnson in the theme song to the television show "Miami Vice." Johnson claims the sequence was played "for a friend" who recorded it and incorporated it into the song. Without a written agreement on which to sue, the musicians' union was unwilling to press Johnson's case for misappropriation of an intellectual asset.[53]

Although the United States has joined the Berne Convention in recognizing moral rights of the creator to protect the integrity of the creation, such rights are tenuous at best. The U.S. copyright statute does not recognize moral rights as such, and scant court decisions can be said to have helped establish any recognized rights. The U.S. entered the Berne Convention only in 1991; prior to that, intellectual-property lawyers argued that U.S. legal practice did provide many attributes of moral rights despite not having changed the statutory law to make these rights explicit.[54] In other countries, artists have a legal right to protect the integrity of their works in later renditions, even where the copyright has passed into other hands. In the United States, to the extent that any such rights can be said to exist, they are largely ignored. Tom Lord-Alge, a rock-music recording engineer, has confirmed that pandemonium reigns in his field: "We're all blatantly stealing from everyone else. That's just the way it's done."[55]

Raymond H. DeMoulin, a former vice president of the Eastman Kodak Company and director of the Center for Creative Imaging in Camden, Maine, summarized the problems that arise as the ability to manipulate images becomes easier and easier:

> The concern is not that we are going to change the image and that changing an image has never been done before. It is that we can change it more easily. And who now owns the image? Who has the copyright? Then comes the "bottom line": is it more profitable with new technology? Does it add something to your business? These

answers are "yes." Does it make money for you where other images haven't? The answer is, "yes, it does." We are going to have to balance ethics and the bottom line and certainly we have to look at copyright. . . . These issues are important to us because we are teaching people to change images and we want to protect the image makers.[56]

The versatility of the computer version of "cutting and pasting" became apparent when the respected photographic publication *National Geographic* transformed the landscape surrounding the pyramids near Cairo for aesthetic purposes in its February 1982 issue. Readers were shocked. How could the highly respected photographic journal move one of the great pyramids?

In 1984 the *New York Times Magazine* published a picture showing off the capabilities of computers: the imagers transformed the familiar view of downtown Manhattan.[57] They inserted the Statue of Liberty and the Eiffel Tower from Paris, replaced the Chrysler building with the TransAmerica building from San Francisco, moved the Empire State Building uptown a few blocks, turned the Citicorp Building to face the opposite direction, and generally reconstituted the way New Yorkers were accustomed to seeing their city.[58] According to Fred Ritchin, who supervised the transformation:

The technology is amazing. . . . You have this impulse to say make it bigger, make it smaller, make it pink, because it is so easy. This is what some people have called the God Complex. You see yourself rearranging skyscrapers. It is sort of the Superman Complex. You can leap buildings in single bounds. You can make them shorter or you can make them taller. You can do whatever you want to do. This is just a cautionary tale to say that this is what can happen in magazines, just as there is a tendency to manage text, there is a tendency to manage imagery. . . . Basically, what photographs then get used for is to prove the point of view of the writer, of the text editor, or an art director, and not to discover the world. Not to see the world. Not to see great things. Not to go back to 1936 when we were still interested in exploring things. Now we are more interested in illustrating things.[59]

National Geographic's and the *New York Times Magazine*'s entries into the computer graphics sweepstakes were only two of many. *TV Guide* followed suit with a cover of Oprah Winfrey's face attached to Ann-Margret's body.[60] Of course, photographic manipulation already spans generations. Back in the 1930s, *U.S. News and World Report* used a sharp blade, retouch paints, gluepot, and airbrushes to move microphones on FDR's desk, while more recently it used a Scitex computer to remove dirt from the fingernails of Prime Minister Benazir Bhutto of Pakistan.[61] Of course, assembling composite pictures once required highly skilled artists and more than a few minutes. A computer operator and the proper software can accomplish the same feat in seconds.

The desire to achieve artistic unity or to reconstruct reality is not a new phenomenon. There is a monumental painting in the eighteenth-century Schönbrunn Palace on the outskirts of Vienna in which the artist, working before the days of photography, achieved a composite reconstruction of history by assembling in the city square many famous people who were not contemporaries. This was not an unusual occurrence and did not provoke criticism, even though some viewers might come away with a somewhat distorted view of the historical event supposedly being recorded.

Ritchin also points out that photographs are used to verify accusations, as, for example, in the use of the Zapruder film that records the assassination of John F. Kennedy by Lee Harvey Oswald. Or the government-filmed videotape of District of Columbia Mayor Marion Barry using cocaine in a hotel room. Or the privately filmed videotape of Rodney King's beating by Los Angeles policemen. But this power of images to substantiate charges rests on old presumptions about the integrity of pictures. As the public becomes more aware of the new capabilities for manipulation and computer simulation, all images may come to suffer a loss of credibility, as people begin to question exactly what it is they are being asked to accept as the truth.[62]

Blind reliance on the power of pictures to tell the whole story will find itself more frequently under attack in the courts, and the rules of evidence will be challenged to come up with new ways to challenge the evidentiary value of a raw photograph. Indeed, it is not necessary even to "doctor" a photograph to produce false evidence. The computer may reconstruct an image from the descriptions of observers or even the imaginations of interested parties. For example, when a Swedish airplane crashed in Finland and there were no cameras to record what happened, a computer image was reconstructed from the comments of three eyewitnesses and published as a news photograph.[63]

The Challenge of Virtual Reality

All the current activity in electronic imaging is child's play compared to what is in store for us in the area known as virtual reality—defined as "almost reality; it is virtually a reality."[64] The 1992 motion picture *The Lawnmower Man* makes use of virtual landscapes in which two people in different locations have "virtual contact" with each other. Museums are beginning to offer the ultimate magic carpet ride—a computerized peek into the landscapes, flora, and fauna of the various geological regions of the world: jungle habitats, mountain ranges, tundra, or wherever the viewer might like to be transported.

It has been predicted that when virtual reality reaches a point "when virtual objects can barely be distinguished from real objects, it will be nearly impossible to tell if someone has 'copied' or 'prepared a derivative work' from a protected virtual object or even an entire virtual world."[65] Philippe Queau, from the Institut National de l'Audiovisuel in Paris, has seen a vision of the future of computer imaging and found it daunting: "We are currently witnessing the end of an artistic world. Artists of tomorrow will no longer produce works but something yet to be named. They will no longer create objects but rather micro-universes in perpetual evolution."[66]

Once that occurs, many established legal shibboleths may crumble. What can be copyrighted as a finished product if an artistic work is in perpetual evolution? The courts have confronted this possibility in the case of computer games, each of which can be different, and still found the video game both "original" and "fixed," and entitled to copyright protection because someone conceived of the vision of the audiovisual display and how it would function.[67] The same may become the rule of law in protecting the underlying software and the visual display in virtual realities. However, this does not resolve the question of what happens to video images stored in databases, such as those described in the advertisement on page 76, nor does it address the practice of taking a snippet here and there, as in the theme song of "Miami Vice." If there appears to be a "derivative work," then it will be covered, but snippets are merely derivative uses of portions of the original work, which may be deemed to be fair use.

Yet if each image (or its constituent components) has to be separately licensed, the difficulty in obtaining individual consent may inhibit use. What about the rights of the enhancers? Should they have ultimate control over the composite? Is the situation of the enhancer any different from a motion picture producer who ultimately orchestrates the final product? J. W. Burkey, a Dallas photographer who has been combining photographic images and computer graphics for a stellar group of corporate clients, is confident that the proprietary rights issues can be resolved satisfactorily. He is adamant, however, that joint copyright in a composite image would be unworkable. Willing to recognize the proprietary interests of the originators and to have them paid a fair price for their enhanced images, he asserts nonetheless: "But the new picture has to be completely mine. There's no time to keep negotiating for each new use of that picture."[68]

Those who have created the components may not agree, especially if, like the bongo drum sequence incorporated into the television-show theme song, the enhanced version earns substantial income in future years. Some form of licensing arrangement similar to the provision for earning residual royalties based upon the number of re-uses may be more equitable if arrangements for the collection and allocation of earnings can be devised. There is much to be done before reasonable accommodations of video images to the global information marketplace via on-line access can be clarified.

Because of the special malleability of visual images, the law will have to support greater freedom for the user to take advantage of the very characteristics that make the software attractive. This does not mean that all forms of legal protection to ensure compensation must be abandoned just because it is inconvenient to determine who owes what to whom. Methods already exist for creating a simultaneous billing upon the downloading of a video image from a centralized commercial data base, but this does not protect against unauthorized and uncompensated further use of the image in its altered form. Technical experts continue to believe that for every technological lock placed within the work product, there will be a pirate locksmith ready and willing to break in, if not for the financial reward, then merely for the joy of accomplishment.[69]

Conclusions

It is too early to predict how the law will deal with electronic images. New electronic art forms are being generated every day on the frontiers of computer imaging, and they will continue to challenge lawyers to come up with new forms of protection to guarantee fair use, to prohibit misuse, and to assure adequate compensation.

It is not too early to ascertain what the areas of concern will be. First, what do we call this new computerized digital landscape? We need a new name for an electronically created photograph. Norwegians use the letter M for *montage,* a word that goes back to the earliest days of photo manipulation.[70] Perhaps *construct, composite,* or *recompilation* might be more accurately descriptive. *Electronic imaging*[71] seems to be emerging as the term of first choice, but perhaps an elision to *electrage* or *computrage* will emerge.

Second, whatever nomenclature comes to be adopted, it is clear that the result of all this technological ferment is that we can no longer trust a photograph to tell the truth. Rather than relying upon the image itself to validate what appears within it, the artist who makes or manipulates the image will become more legally responsible for its contents and also more recognized and acknowledged as its creator. Whether and how each contributor to a composite electronic image will be compensated remains clouded with uncertainty, but the details of contractual arrangements should be no more difficult to develop than those involved in producing a motion picture with its many components.

Third, subjects of electronic images are going to seek more control over the use of their likeness. Assuming that the photographer has unquestioned rights to the image simply won't do when it can be manipulated into something damaging, embarrassing, or even more valuable than the original. We must be able to share in the decision of how the images and modifications are used.

Fourth, what will be the rights of users of electronic images? Will society follow the video-image model and leave personal use acceptable but proscribe redistribution? How about parodies or cartoons? Will the purpose of the distribution determine the legal nature of the publication or distribution? Will it be permissible to make a private copy and circulate it among friends? After all, we don't think twice about copying a cartoon and placing it on an office bulletin board or circulating copies among our acquaintances. But in today's world of electronic bulletin boards, a copy can reach thousands of viewers.

Finally, what will the future hold for photographs? The new technologies emerge helter-skelter one upon another. Will the future be limited for photographers who do not master such software packages as Adobe Photoshop, Aldus Photostyler, Fractal Painter, or Publishers' Paintbrush, as some predict?[72] One observer has likened the present apprehension among photographers about the future to that of fifteenth-century monks who wondered what would happen to their carefully hand-crafted illuminated manuscripts with the arrival of Gutenberg's printing press.[73]

What has happened, of course, is that illuminated manuscripts have become priceless with the passage of time. So may the realistic chemical images of the present day become priceless relics as electronic images replace them as the medium of choice. However, at least some of us may relish the opportunity to spiffy up the image of our faces that appears on the screen of our videophonic access devices. We may even divide into two camps—those who prefer virtual reality and those who prefer the real thing.

5

Who Owns Your Electronic Messages?

One morning in January 1990, Alana Shoars, who had been administrator for the electronic mail system of Epson America, Inc., for a mere ten months, walked into her boss's office and noticed a batch of printouts on his desk. They looked suspiciously like the contents of the electronic mail messages she supervised, which were protected by passwords: "I glanced over at some printouts, and a lot of warning bells went off in my head. As far as I'd known, as E-mail coordinator, it wasn't possible to do such a thing."[1]

Ms. Shoars was appalled, since she had informed employees whom she trained to use the E-mail system that their messages were private.[2] When she criticized her manager for reading what she considered to be private messages, she was told in no uncertain terms to mind her own business. Supervision of the E-mail system was, she thought, her business. If anyone should know the rules governing its use, she should. The right to stand up for ethical values she considered important was first and foremost in her mind: "You don't read other people's mail, just as you don't listen to their phone conversations. Right is right, and wrong is wrong."[3]

That moral was not so clear in the minds of her employers or other employers. Along with many of its corporate colleagues, Epson America, a Japanese-owned company of computer printers, believed it had a right to monitor the use of the electronic mail systems and to expect them to be used for company purposes only.

Ms. Shoars was dismissed from her job the day after the altercation over the E-mail incident, allegedly for insubordination and "gross misconduct." Epson America, whose corporate headquarters are in Torrance, California, denied that the dismissal was related to her questioning the E-mail procedures.[4] It acknowledged that it reserves the right to inspect its E-mail systems but claimed that it did not abuse this privilege.[5]

Ms. Shoars filed a million-dollar wrongful termination suit[6] and has been joined by several other former Epson America employees in a class action suit questioning the invasion of privacy.[7] According to the manager of Hewlett Packard Computer Operations and Data Communications for Epson, the company has installed a tap on the electronic gateway where the Hewlett Packard mainframe computer interfaces with the outside MCI E-mail Communications Service, systematically printing and reading all the E-mail entering and leaving the Torrance site.[8] The lower court agreed with Epson's lawyer that neither state privacy statutes nor federal statutes address confidentiality of E-mail in the workplace and dismissed the case. But this is not the end of the controversy. Neil Shipman, Ms. Shoars's lawyer, vowed to take the case all the way to the U.S. Supreme Court if necessary, championing the asserted rights of employees.[9]

The incident precipitated an uproar among users of electronic mail systems and their managers. There is no consensus on reasonable expectations of privacy. A recent *Macworld* survey of "electronic eavesdropping" reported that 21.6 percent of the 301 participating companies admitted searching employee files, including electronic work files (73.8 percent), E-mail (41.5 percent), network messages (27.7 percent), and voice mail (15.4 percent). Only 30.8 percent of the companies gave advance warning to employees.[10]

The notion of the privacy and sanctity of "mail" comes from the moral tradition and relatively recent legal sanction prohibiting opening someone else's letters transmitted through the United States Postal Service (with quite limited exceptions).[11] But does this tradition, either in custom or in law, carry over to the private electronic mail systems commonly used in many of the largest corporations worldwide? According to Rex Heinke, a Los Angeles attorney specializing in privacy issues, tradition is of no help in this instance: "This is a classic example of a technology that doesn't quite fit any prior mold."[12]

The question of corporate responsibility to provide privacy in the workplace environment and the government's role in assuring such privacy is a hotly debated issue on "The Law of Cyberspace," an electronic conference linking several network providers, in which lawyers hold forth with a marked lack of consensus.[13] The event that generated this debate was the introduction in May 1993 of a bill by Senator Paul Simon (Dem.-Ill.), The Privacy for Consumers and Workers Act, that would require employers to notify employees when they are monitoring their communications.[14]

There was a lead article on this topic in the first issue of *The DataLaw Report,* a new newsletter for lawyers specializing in legal issues related to proprietary rights in information.[15] The newsletter report estimated that E-mail users of corporate local area networks would climb 60 percent that year, to 15.1 million users, and to 38 million by 1995, while E-mail messages transmitted within Fortune 2000 firms in North America are expected to surge from 6.1 billion in 1993 to 14.3 billion in 1995.[16] How should such messages be regulated?

Corporate E-Mail Systems

Federal Express, American Airlines, Pacific Bell, and United Parcel Service all have internal electronic mail systems that automatically inform users when they log on that the company reserves the right to monitor messages and that the system is intended for business and not personal use.[17] International Business Machines also notifies its employees that the E-mail system is intended for business use only. Citicorp presents its E-mail users with a one-line reminder of its policy that they should limit their messages to Citicorp business and that all messages are the property of Citicorp.[18] Michael Simmons, chief information officer at the Bank of Boston, has stated what many believe to be the correct corporate policy: "If the corporation owns the equipment and pays for the network, that asset belongs to the company, and it has a right to look and see if people are using it for purposes other than running the business."[19]

In 1993 over 10 million people logged on to their E-mail systems regularly, sending more than one and a half billion messages.[20] For many, it was their primary means of business communication.[21] Given this fact, it is perhaps irresponsible, as Mitchell Kapor, developer of the popular spreadsheet Lotus 1-2-3 and founder of the Electronic Frontier Foundation, concludes, for companies not to have policies governing their E-mail systems.[22]

Because civil liberties issues arose over the use of public electronic messaging systems, Congress enacted the Electronic Privacy Act of 1986 to ensure that electronic messages on telecommunications transport and information systems offered to the public would receive the same protection from disclosure as telephone voice messages.[23] The Act makes it a felony for unauthorized persons to tap or break into electronic communications systems. However, this law would not be applicable to corporate messaging systems where authorized managers enter what may be perceived as personal electronic files. And here is where the law and the expectations of employees became muddled.

The confusion is not unexpected, as many of the corporate messaging systems do have electronic gateways to public messaging systems. Thus is it not always clear to the users when they enjoy privacy protection and when they may be operating in a corporate fishbowl. According to David Atlas, an E-mail analyst at the International Data Corporation: "When you send a message, most people think it's as private as sending it through the U.S. Postal System. But in some companies it can be as private as writing it on the bathroom wall."[24] The dividing line between public and private is not crystal-clear in a digital environment unless the network provider has an established policy stating clearly what kind of electronic service is being offered.

In fact, it has been standard practice for many years for corporations to monitor the use of their internal messaging systems. The Communications Workers of America (CWA) estimates that 15 million U.S. workers are subject to such monitoring daily,[25] but this is a means for clocking, measuring, and recording employee performance. In the telecommunications and telemarketing industries as well as in ticket reservations for entertainment and travel services, listening to voice messages is the primary measure of performance. But monitoring employee performance is different from monitoring electronic messages between employees to determine whether they are related to business purposes, although the electronic surveillance may appear to be the same.

According to CWA spokesmen, Northern Telecom, against whom they filed a suit on behalf of the employees, had been monitoring voice, video, and data communications of employees for over thirteen years. Under pressure, Northern Telecom became the first major company to ban such electronic eavesdropping.[26]

Civil rights lobbyists have urged Congress to pass a federal ban on such alleged electronic misbehavior, but the problem is that it is not entirely clear what constitutes electronic misbehavior. A congressional task force headed by Senator Patrick Leahy concluded in the spring of 1992 that no action was necessary at that time.[27]

The Diversity of E-Mail Messages

There is a remarkable diversity of message environments evolving on today's electronic networks. John Armstrong, former vice president for science and technology at IBM, and his colleagues have analyzed the different forms of electronic dialogue on the internal IBM network.[28] Armstrong argues, quite persuasively, that electronic mail is truly a new form of communication, unlike any that has existed previously. It removes many of the barriers of face-to-face communication, providing access across language, time, geography, race, color, and religion.[29] It is both less intimidating for those transmitting the message and less intrusive to those receiving it. It is easily accessible at a time and place of the receiver's choosing. Perhaps its most startling difference is the ability to exchange messages within a large group.

Whereas the letter posted in eighteenth-century England might reach Japan in a few months or years, today an electronic message can travel the distance with the speed of a laser beam. The reply can be returned as rapidly, or with a time delay of whatever length pleases the sender. Thus it may curtail time for thoughtful analysis, but there is an immediacy that says someone out there is watching—"listening" or "reading" and perhaps "absorbing" the message.

Armstrong has found multiple levels of electronic messages on the IBM corporate network with a taxonomy to identify the differences. *Electronic briefings* permit senior executives to send on-line messages to hundreds of thousands of employees and at the same time to invite their on-line replies. *Electronic conferencing* affords a group of any size to address on-line any subject matter in which they share an interest. *Computer-mediated queries* are tightly controlled, information-oriented forums. Answers are intended to be brief and without chitchat. *Lightning rods* are forums designed to draw off discussion that would clutter up or be a distraction for other forums, so they are less rigid in requiring that contributors stick to the subject matter assigned. *Metaforums* are aimed at the administrative problems in organizing the electronic environment, and TEMPMISC is a catchall corner where discussions with no other home can reside. If such discussions do not "catch on" within a reasonable amount of time, they disappear into the ether from whence they came. WHYCONF is dedicated to the benefits and philosophy of conferencing, while additional electronic areas are devoted to on-line seminars, voluntary newsletters, on-line user groups, and focus groups.

Usually self-selected in the corporate environment, employees might be assigned by their job descriptions to participate in a particular conference. Some conferences are mediated by a conference chairman or leader. Others are freewheeling ones in which anyone can contribute or "append" a comment. New discussions often evolve into separate "forums," called "SIG's" for Special Interest Groups on CompuServe and GEnie. Such computer conferencing is a pioneering area of the electronic frontier that has not yet developed its own set of rules. There is a tension between those who feel that such conferences should be the equivalent to the chitchat at the water fountain or coffeepot and others who feel that the subject matter should be tightly controlled. In some electronic environments a certain amount of profane language is tolerated, whereas in others it would be considered ill-mannered at least, if not downright prohibited. Some feel that such "telecommunities" should be left to devise their own rules of behavior.

In short, what is generically called E-mail is really a wide variety of forms of communication, some of which closely replicate their nonelectronic counterparts and others of which are pioneering new forms of their own. The users of these services or inhabitants of these electronic spaces often assert proprietary rights and express a strong desire to make their own rules of behavior.

New Forms of Communication

Aside from the rich variety within the IBM network, there are new forms of electronic messaging systems developing in telecommunities around the country. The sheriff's department in Maricopa County, Arizona, started an electronic bulletin board some years ago, designed to encourage computer users to report information about criminal activity. It developed into something far more diverse than a posting of notes about crime, however, as it permitted access to the weather, open discussion groups, and chitchat.

Residents of Santa Monica, California, and Colorado Springs, Colorado, have enjoyed municipal electronic messaging systems for a number of years, providing them with better public access to the workings of the city government. Senior Net is a new network organized to permit senior citizens to share their experiences, using computers to enrich their lives. These are but a few of the thousands of computer communities that are developing as the personal computer invades more and more households and offices.

Armstrong concludes that the E-mail systems have a dramatic impact on the social and political interactions of those who use them: "The immediacy of conferencing is one obvious way in which conferencing allows new possibilities compared with many other forms of communications within large, geographically dispersed organizations: the dramatic speed with which communities of interest can exchange information, come to conclusions and take action has little precedent."[30]

However, the responsibility for policing this new environment is not so obvious when you move outside the place where corporate policy prevails. In the more publicly available networks, there is some confusion over the providers' responsibilities for the content of the messages. These providers range from individuals who invest a few thousand dollars in computer equipment to permit them to offer a bulletin board for messages from their friends and acquaintances to companies like CompuServe, a subsidiary of H&R Block, and Prodigy, a joint venture between Sears and IBM, which offer dozens of different types of electronic communication to several million subscribers nationwide.

Many computer users agree that it is too early to begin drafting laws regulating behavior on electronic networks, because we are not sure what this new form of electronic communication really is or what its potential might be. Some have likened it to a form of electronic soapbox. Indeed, this is the first mass medium in which people who have no other contact with one another can talk, as in New England town meetings, where all citizens can come together and speak their minds.[31] In fact, what is called E-mail on networks such as the Internet, the largest collection of interconnected work stations, originally used primarily by educational institutions but now more than half by commercial users, is a mishmash of many different forms of electronic communication, some of which constitute what we consider mail—for example, a confidential "letter" from one person to another or, in the case of direct mail marketing, of one person to many others—but much of which is electronic discussion in forums of special interest groups, more like "rapping" in the company lunchroom.

Questioning Applicable Laws: Prodigy

The law applicable to electronic mail or electronic forums has never been more confusing than in the electronic services offered by Prodigy. This information network provider has been criticized by some users for being too paternalistic and censoring mail and/or discussion, and by the Anti-Defamation League for being too libertarian and permitting anti-Semitic hate messages to be transported in public forums.

Prodigy has been accused of being a Peeping Tom, peering into its subscribers' private messages. Prodigy vigorously denies this charge, stating its policy to comply rigorously with the privacy protection required of electronic mail systems and the ethics of personal privacy. Prodigy allows subscribers to list their names and electronic addresses in its directory but does not require them to take action if they want their names removed, as most suppliers of telephonic services do, or even to pay for the privilege of having an unlisted number. Indeed, this policy of permitting subscribers to "opt into" the directory system is forward-looking in offering users personal autonomy over the use of information about themselves.

Nonetheless, Prodigy has been thoroughly criticized through the media, first for exerting too much editorial control over its public forums—a right Prodigy claimed as a "publisher" of information services[32]—then for reading private correspondence and terminating subscribers who were using the service to protest a rate increase.[33] After that controversy subsided, it was accused by the Anti-Defamation League of permitting libelous statements to be dispatched on the public forums.[34]

In the first instance, Prodigy shut down a public forum on homosexuality, called Health Spa, in which there had been some harsh confrontations between religious fundamentalists and gay rights activists. Prodigy made no effort to compromise what it felt to be its right to curtail services that many of its users found overly contentious. In the second incident, Prodigy did not anticipate the enthusiasm with which some of its users would rely upon it. Having announced, like telephone service, a modest monthly flat rate ($9.95) for access to the system, its managers had assumed that users would send a modest amount of mail through it. Finding instead that some users were sending thousands of letters monthly, Prodigy announced a rate increase for the larger quantities of mail.

There followed a voluminous heated discussion on-line about the rationale for such an increase. After a couple of months of debate, and still a couple of months before the increase was to take place, Prodigy executives decided that the arguments had been exhausted and declared a moratorium on any more discussion of this issue in its public forums.[35]

Undaunted by this dictate, some of the determined opponents took to the private mail mode to continue their lobbying efforts to force Prodigy to change its decision. Through some clever manipulation of the technical capabilities of the mail system, they were able to generate an enormous amount of traffic on the system, stuffing electronic mailboxes in the process. Some participants were sending as many as 40,000 messages a month! Several of the most blatant offenders lost their rights to use Prodigy.

According to Prodigy sources, no monitoring of the private mail system took place, but recipients of the solicitations to support the drive complained. A number of them were Prodigy employees or advertisers who were protesting mail urging them to boycott their own employer or client. As a consequence, Prodigy revised its standards of conduct, prohibiting the use of "macros" and other technical devices for generating mass mailings on the network. All of the terminated subscribers were invited to rejoin the network if they were willing to abide by the new rules.

In all the charges and countercharges, Prodigy did not reckon with the fact that sophisticated computer users were accustomed to a freewheeling electronic messaging system with no parietal control exercised by the manager of the system. Such computer-literate subscribers were appalled at the regulatory environment imposed by Prodigy. For its part, Prodigy maintained its position that most of the information sources it offered were like a publication for which the publisher selects those items to be included and those to be excluded.

Prodigy, unlike systems such as CompuServe, GEnie, and America Online, claimed to be serving middle America. It likened itself to the Disney Channel, offering family fare that appeals to a large spectrum of users. Thus it claimed a legal responsibility for the content of the public forums but insisted that no effort had been exerted to limit the discourse on the electronic mail.[36]

Although admitting that there were technicians who could read mail in "mailboxes" that had not yet been collected by recipients, Prodigy maintained strict rules prohibiting its employees from voyeurism, warning that it could constitute the commission of a felony under the Electronic Communications Privacy Act of 1986. From a legal standpoint, private communications are not considered to be published and cannot be the basis of a libel action. On the other hand, archives of public forums or bulletin boards are maintained for a reasonable amount of time to permit replication should there be any question of legal liability resulting from the content.

This practice permitted Prodigy technicians to review thousands of entries into the public forums when Prodigy was accused by the Anti-Defamation League of transmitting hate mail. They admitted that some of the less objectionable messages were permitted and stoutly defended by Prodigy management under the rubric of free and unfettered discussion of issues. The most vociferous and objectionable speech was uttered only in the private messaging systems.

Prodigy management came to learn the nature of that speech because it had been sent to a Jew who sought to have it retransmitted into a public forum to demonstrate the prejudice of its originator. Prodigy rejected this request fifteen times according to its count,[37] because it would be deeply disturbing and "grossly repugnant to community standards" to broadcast messages that are "blatant expressions of bigotry, racism and hate."[38] Prodigy made its position abundantly clear: it did not intend to "play bulletin board thought police."[39]

New York Newsday published the story under the huge headline HIGH-TECH HATE, even though it had been notified the night before by the Associated Press, where the story originated, that a computer search had found no anti-Semitic notes on Prodigy's public bulletin board. AP's denial appeared as an insert in the same issue.[40]

Eventually the establishment press came to the defense of Prodigy, complimenting this fledgling electronic information service for stoutly defending First Amendment rights to a free marketplace of ideas. The *New York Times* published an editorial giving its stamp of approval to Prodigy and denouncing the Anti-Defamation League for jumping the gun ill-advisedly.[41] Mitchell Kapor, president of the Electronic Frontier Foundation, dedicated to defending constitutional protections in the new frontier of cyberspace, found it "heartening that the *New York Times, Washington Post* and others had editorials telling the Anti-Defamation League to back off because Prodigy was within its First Amendment rights in deciding what to carry and what not to carry, even if one believes that Prodigy's editorial policy about what it selects is in need of improvement."[42]

Brian Nielson, a computer scientist writing in *Online*, held a distinctly different view, suggesting that there should be complete freedom on the part of the users to choose their subject matter and mode of expressing it:

> Is removing a bulletin board message censorship? Well, the service is Prodigy's "publication," and a publisher does have the right to select from the many letters to the editor which ones it will print. On the other hand, such bulletin messages are in the nature of personal messages, and it is clear that Prodigy exerts no real editorial judgment about what is published and what is not—the users themselves are doing the publishing, and Prodigy is subsequently unpublishing the material it does not like. With a service that is simply "there" for users to shape and modify as they wish . . . , does Prodigy have the right to decide after the fact that it doesn't like certain topics discussed? If electronic communication is to become widespread in our society, does the public deserve protection to engage in whatever topical discussions people may choose to participate?[43]

At the first conference to explore the ramifications of computer networks, there was no unanimity about the legal environment in which they would choose to operate. Some participants, like the print publishers, praised Prodigy's claim to the rights and responsibilities of publishers. Others preferred a model in which the provider of the information transport medium has no liability for the content. Yet others sought to impose a hybrid model, while a few wanted to explore new constructs.[44] Such lively analogies as homesteaders, saloon keepers, and sheriffs colored the conversation of conference participants, but the legal eagles turned to more contemporary models such as kiosks and bookstores. Many of the seasoned computer experts and cyberspace residents bemoaned the fact that their electronic wilderness was on the verge of becoming civilized, or at least legalized. Like the cowboys of the golden west, they feared that their freewheeling days might be numbered.

The WELL (Whole Earth 'Lectronic Link) is a pioneering bulletin board for free discourse operated out of Sausalito, California. It serves widely disparate users all over the country and has encouraged many of the most vocal protesters to seek solace in existing legal constructs. Users of the WELL are warned when they log on to the system: "You own your own words. This means that you are responsible for the words that you post on the WELL." Cliff Figallo, WELL director, warns in addition: "The WELL is a saloon on the electronic frontier, and I am the bar-keeper. . . . There is no way we can patrol the boundaries of a multiple-gigabyte territory."[45]

If network participants post messages at will, it becomes virtually impossible for anyone to assume the obligations and liabilities of a publisher. This was the error that Prodigy made, according to some thoughtful observers:

> The misjudgment by Prodigy management can be stated simply: They maintain (in good faith, I'm sure) that their ownership of the service gives them the right to censor what's being communicated on their private network. Users feel differently, legal niceties aside.
>
> Ahead of the law, perhaps, the citizens feel that Prodigy cannot be treated as purely private property. Prodigy is an electronic forum. On a forum you trade, you talk freely. The freedom, as with any freedom, has limits. But the point is: On a forum, you feel free. Expectation and reality should match.
>
> Ironically, what Prodigy saw as an abuse of the medium, both in the volume of E-mail and its contents, was a sign of success, or at least strong interest. Had the people who run Prodigy watched more closely what happened with similar networks in this country and overseas (prodigious consumption of E-mail and hot debates), they would have cheered instead of reaching for the electronic garrote.[46]

Jerry Berman, director of the Information Technology Project of the American Civil Liberties Union, speculated that information services like Prodigy should be likened to a shopping center, which under some court rulings on free speech have been treated as public forums.[47] But even this analogy may not be accurate. Electronic pen pals have evolved into very cohesive electronic enclaves, and they want to govern their own electronic environment. The Reverend Paul Milner, system operator for Lutherlink, a computer network of the Lutheran church affiliated with Ecunet, has observed that participants on his network want to police their own behavior. They do not tolerate outside interference any more than they tolerate user behavior that is objectionable to the user group.[48]

William Louden, general manager of General Electric's GEnie system, agrees that self-policing is best: "We let the user post what he wants. If we get a complaint, we respond. We act not as a censor; we see our role as closer to that of an editor. I don't think messages should be screened first. Just like you can't yell 'Fire!' in a crowded theater, customers learn that they have responsibilities here."[49]

However, both CompuServe and GEnie, for instance, immediately zap from public view any obscene or illegal message and agree to remove other messages if members complain that they are offensive. Anyone who repeatedly sends messages violating these guidelines loses membership and access to the system. Such supervision does not sit well with many of the new homesteaders of the electronic frontier, such as Russell Singer, a California management consultant and one of the Prodigy members disconnected for his role in the rate protests: "To me, it's an electronic neighborhood. I'd log on at night, and all my friends would be there. . . . It's better entertainment than sitting and watching reruns of Laverne and Shirley. . . . If you look 20 to 30 years out, and you think what will happen to political debates, this is where they will occur."[50]

New Case Law: *Cubby v. CompuServe*

The only case to confront some of these issues head-on involved CompuServe, one of the earliest of the electronic mail and conferencing services sponsored by a computer company that offered time sharing. Over a decade the company has developed a dedicated following of aficionados, numbering 838,000 at the time of the litigation in 1991. CompuServe offers a wide variety of topics on which users may offer their comments and observations, including CompuServe Information Service, which is more like an electronic library than a mail service. The forums involving special topics open to discussion number more than fifty, and users may enter what is called a chat mode, in which they encounter other users on the system at the same time—an interactive discussion in real time rather than messages entered at various times to be retrieved, as in a computer conference or forum mode.

The forum that was the subject of litigation was called Rumorville USA, part of the Journalism Forum. Rumorville, for most purposes a daily newsletter, was operated by Don Fitzpatrick Associates of San

Francisco, which assumed "total responsibility for the contents," according to its contract with CompuServe. CompuServe thus claimed no responsibility for the alleged defamatory statements.

The trial court agreed with CompuServe that it operated solely as a distributor and not as publisher and, therefore, could not be liable for the contents of material placed in the system:

> CompuServe has no more editorial control over such a publication than does a public library, book store, or newsstand, and it would be no more feasible for CompuServe to examine every publication it carries for potentially defamatory statements than it would be for any other distributor to do so. . . . Technology is rapidly transforming the information industry. A computerized database is the functional equivalent of a more traditional news vendor, and the inconsistent application of a lower standard of liability to an electronic news distributor such as CompuServe than that which is applied to a public library, book store, or newsstand would impose an undue burden on the free flow of information.[51]

This decision cheered the providers of electronic mail and information services, since most, other than Prodigy, prefer not to assume responsibility for the content of the many forms of communication passing through their systems. The cheer may be short-lived, however, as the decision pertains only to messages that look more or less like "publications" and for which there is a responsible party upon whom liability can be placed. There is still no decision on what protection will be provided for other forms of communication over electronic networks or, alternatively, what responsibilities will be imposed upon users and providers. Providers of existing messaging and electronic information services have also been reluctant to assume the nomenclature of "information utility," which might insulate them from liability for content as a "common carrier" but would expose them to a right of access to anyone prepared to pay the price of admission.

Conclusions

There are many proposals afoot to regulate the new realm of electronic messages, including a full-fledged constitutional amendment guaranteeing First Amendment rights to all electronic systems.[52] Several legal issues need to be resolved, as First Amendment rights can include both the right of a "publisher" to publish without government censorship and the right of privacy of the individual to control access to personal information. Moreover, it is not clear to what extent the right of anonymity will be preserved, a right that has firm legal roots.[53]

Furthermore, it is becoming more and more difficult to identify the nature of the various messages embedded in a digital electronic stream in which the signals are all ones or zeros without spelling out whether they purport to be news, mail, book, conference call, or private conversation. Thus it is not easy to determine what legal rubric would be appropriate to cover them. To draft all-encompassing legislation or regulations would run the risk of too much uniformity imposed upon an electronic landscape that is, as Armstrong has documented, richly populated with varying seedlings pregnant with new and exciting growth possibilities.

More significant, the users of these various forms of communication and the inhabitants of what is coming to be known as cyberspace want to be left alone to manage their own affairs. It is estimated that there are between 30,000 and 40,000 computer bulletin boards in the United States alone, fewer than 10 percent of them operated commercially.[54] How to reconcile the jurisdictional authority of geopolitical entities with the ad hoc jurisdictional reach of these telepolitical entities is a legal nut waiting to be cracked.

To apply the same rules to all E-mail would inhibit the development of new forms of communication that might bring rich new dimensions to the marketplace of ideas. Budding entrepreneurship is pushing the envelope in many diverse directions, some of which are irritating and disturbing to established information providers as well as users. There will be confrontations at the borderlines between electronic communities and geopolitical communities. If the cybernauts behave irresponsibly, transgressing established territorial laws of the politically defined areas where they live, they will be dragged into the local courts. However, as they begin to police their own electronic territories and define acceptable behavior within the electronic environment, jurisdictions are more likely to defer to them to set their own standards of behavior.

6

Who Owns Video Entertainment?

At 12:32 A.M. on the morning of April 27, 1986, East Coast subscribers to HBO's cable channel were surprised to see the opening scenes of *The Falcon and the Snowman* fade from their screens, replaced by a color bar pattern on which appeared the following message:

> Goodevening HBO From Captain Midnight
> $12.95/month? No way!
> (Showtime/Movie Channel beware!)[1]

The HBO studio in Hauppauge, Long Island, went into a tailspin as engineers struggled to restore the movie transmission. For four and a half minutes the signal wavered as the interloper who called himself Captain Midnight and the HBO engineers waged their own Star Wars, each trying to overpower the other's signal. When the movie signal was finally restored, it was not clear whether the HBO people had over-whelmed the intruder's signal or whether Captain Midnight had completed his message of warning and decided to beat a strategic retreat.[2] Although flamboyant, this was only one more salvo in a war that had been being waged for years between the cable television programmers and the satellite dish industry.[3]

Captain Midnight's prank sent a shiver through the cable television industry. Cable programmers were concerned that the consumer press would turn him into a folk hero. David Pritchard, vice president of HBO, declared his action "a criminal, willful interference of a government-licensed satellite broadcast."[4] It was the first confirmed deliberate interference with a satellite signal, according to William Russell, speaking for the Federal Communications Commission, who claimed that it was a violation of the Communications Act and could lead to a $10,000 fine and a year in prison. The FCC and the Justice Department were already considering whether there might be a way to seek even more severe penalties.[5] Martha Donovan, staff member of the House Communications Subcommittee, called the stunt "a strange event, indicative of the frustration some people feel," and announced that the issue of satellite jamming had already been included as a topic of hearings planned for May 21 by the committee.[6]

Captain Midnight: Pirate or Champion?

Captain Midnight described himself as "a champion of the satellite dish owners,"[7] and some journalists applauded his efforts: "Star wars, of sorts, have started—luckily in a nonlethal fashion. The battle line is drawn in the sky, where the satellites fly; the conflict is down here on earth, where more than 1.5 million American households depend on direct satellite reception for their television watching. They are in arms over the scrambling of their favorite channels by the originators of satellite-relayed programs, and their protests have stirred political passions."[8]

Congressmen in states with large rural areas, such as Timothy Wirth (Dem.-Colo.), Wendell H. Ford (Dem.-Ky.), Dale Bumpers (Dem.-Ark.), Barry Goldwater (Rep.-Ariz.), and Nancy L. Kassebaum (Rep.-Kans.), came to the aid of the satellite-dish owners. Matt James, Bumpers's press secretary, explained: "An awful lot of folks out there in the rural areas of Arkansas, when they bought these satellite dishes, were seeing television signals in their own homes for the first time. The senator feels these people have the right to receive the signals, and after they've put out $2000 to $5000 to buy a dish, that they have a right to receive the signals at a reasonably equitable cost, as the people in the cities can with cable programming."[9]

In addition, television viewers had always expected that any entertainment sent out over the public airwaves belonged to whoever had the equipment to pick it up. After all, that was how radio and network television came into being. Originally the manufacturers of radios had provided free programming in order to stimulate the purchase of radio sets. AT&T had conceived the notion that individuals would pay a fee to broadcast messages to the public, but this pattern did not become popular. It was soon displaced by stations that organized regular programs according to well-published schedules.

Although the radio-station owners pledged to Congress to use this new electronic wonder in the public service, the industry soon came to be dominated by advertisers eager to pay the station owners in order to reach radio and, later, television audiences. Viewers able to pick up

satellite transmissions to cable television systems via the same public airwaves (and often with the same commercials) thought themselves entitled to entertainment without having to pay a special compensation.
Indeed, some dealers relied upon the wording of the Communications
Act of 1934 to the effect that the airwaves were a public resource, and
concluded that anything transmitted over the public airwaves should be
available without charge—especially since the technology that permitted
the satellite transmissions had been developed using U.S. tax dollars.[10]

The legal rationale for federal regulation of broadcasters was that the
radio spectrum, through which the signals were transmitted, was a finite
public asset. Thus broadcasters were licensed by the Federal Radio
Commission and its successor, the Federal Communications Commission, as public trustees to use assigned bands of the public's airwaves in
the public interest. By the 1980s a burst of enthusiasm for deregulation
had left the public interest less in the forefront of consciousness than
reliance upon private enterprise and the natural forces of marketplace
economics. However, the widely held belief in "free TV" remained fixed
in the public mind. A charge to the viewer would be difficult to collect
unless the signals were delivered through a cable that could be disconnected at the source. Thus it was natural that viewers, via satellite
dishes, would be confused by a medley of new signals available to them,
some of which were designated as pay channels but were only figura-
tively part of a cable system and some of which were still free.

In the early days of cable television, the only signals transmitted via
cable were broadcast signals that were difficult for local viewers to see,
because they lived beyond easy reach of the signals. The satellite dish provided the technological capability to extend reception beyond the areas
easily served by cable systems. The situation was complicated by the addition of cable-originated programming that was supported not by advertising but by subscriber fees, thus serving a public preferring to pay primarily for motion pictures without advertiser interruptions. However, the
satellite-dish owners were able to receive both the advertising-supported
programs and the subscription-supported programming by the same electronic device. Until the advent of encryption—the scrambling of the
image so that it could not be viewed without purchasing new equipment
and a subscription—the cable programmers were without a feasible mechanism for charging satellite-dish owners for their programming. Moreover,
the number of viewers via direct satellite reception was small enough that
most programmers did not perceive them as a threat to their economic
viability. Thus it was that Captain Midnight struck a sensitive nerve in the
cable television industry, whose lifeblood was retransmission of broadcast
signals.

The Satellite Boom

For years, backyard satellite receivers had been cropping up all over the countryside, taking these signals from the air without compensation either to the programmers or to the local cable company that had paid for the right to sell them to the owners of signal converters within their area. There was nothing overtly illegal about building or buying satellite-receiving dishes, but it was never conceived that private television owners would be capable of receiving signals meant only for paying customers.

However, there is no reckoning with creative entrepreneurship. An entire new industry that had grown up in the intervening years was now selling satellite dishes to customers wealthy enough to pay the hefty fees and hungry enough for increased channel capacity to put up the cash to correct their faulty reception. Many were farmers in rural areas who were far beyond the reach of broadcast signals and had no cable television companies to service them. But many others well within the broadcast reception area were buying into the satellite reception system too, because they wanted more variety than local broadcast systems offered without having to pay a cable company for service.

As well, television markets were being successfully invaded because customers could, with an admittedly high up-front investment in a dish, dial through more than a hundred different satellite-delivered services at no further cost, while local cable television services, costing $20 a month or more, rarely offered more than fifty to sixty. In fact, some of the older systems were still limited to ten or twelve. And, as monthly rates for cable service were going up, the price of backyard satellite dishes was going down, to less than $1,000. More and more buyers were looking to this alternative, and many saw it as a financial decision, not a legal one.

By August 1984 some 510,000 private satellite dishes were in place, not including an additional 400,000 households served by private cable television systems "that used dishes to serve apartment complexes."[11] A lobbying arm had been organized to represent the interests of the private dish owners in Congress. Called SPACE, the Society for Private and Commercial Earth Stations, its purposes were to ensure survival of the satellite antenna business and those it served.

SPACE was surprisingly successful in getting the attention of Congress and protecting the interests of its clients in the newly proposed legislation to regulate cable television. In the writing of the Cable Communications Act of 1984,[12] a section of convoluted wording was inserted[13] to clarify the legal status of satellite reception by private dish owners.

The new arrangement legalized reception for private viewing[14] of any "satellite cable programming"[15] so long as the signal was not encrypted and the reception was not for private financial gain.

In the debate presenting the consensus legislation, H.R. 4103, to the 100th Congress, Congressman Wirth from Colorado, who chaired the Communications Subcommittee proposing the bill, called it "a major milestone in the decade-long effort to update the Communications Act of 1934."[16] Congressmen Albert Gore from Tennessee and Charlie Rose from North Carolina also supported the legislation. All three congressional leaders were from states with substantial rural populations. Not by accident was the proponent in the Senate, Barry Goldwater, from Arizona, a state with wide expanses of territory unserved by either broadcasting or cable systems. Goldwater was himself an owner of a satellite dish.[17]

Consumer Backlash

As a consequence of the Cable Communication Act, cable programmers immediately made plans to encrypt their signals. Decoding equipment that would enable dish owners to restore the signal sold for about $395. In addition, viewers owning satellites dishes would have to pay the programmers, such as HBO and Showtime, an additional monthly subscription fee of $12.95 for viewing their programs. On January 15, 1986, HBO became the first of the programmers to encrypt. However, both Showtime and the Movie Channel planned to scramble their programming beginning May 27, 1986.[18] Captain Midnight's message, inserted into the HBO signal on April 27, was a strong electronic protest against encryption and subscription fees.

According to HBO spokesmen, they had received many threats warning of disruptions that would occur if they did not reconsider their plans to scramble the signal.[19] But they had not reckoned with the ingenuity of owners of the satellite-dish companies, who had seen a drop in sales from a high in 1985 of 60,000 dishes sold per month to a low of 10,000 by the end of April 1986.[20] There is nothing like a marketing success spurned to spark one into action.

Most engineers had not dreamed it possible that a private person could overpower the HBO signal. According to experts, it would have taken at least 4,000 watts of power and a dish 30 to 40 feet wide, a giant antenna compared with the 6- to 8-foot dishes of backyard owners.[21] For this reason the search for the culprit was originally limited to the Dallas–Fort Worth area, where especially sophisticated equipment was known to be available. However, Captain Midnight turned out to be John R. MacDougall, a twenty-five-year-old employee of the Central Florida Teleport, a satellite uplink facility in Ocala, Florida, that transmitted the strong signals necessary to send programming to satellites for distribution to the cable television systems subscribing to the service.[22] He also happened to be the owner of MacDougall Electronics, which had enjoyed a successful business selling satellite dishes.

The Central Florida Teleport was the only facility the FCC found to have the type of equipment required to interfere with the HBO signal and that could have pulled off the stunt at that time. MacDougall was the operator on duty at the time. Experts warned that an interloper who left no calling card or identifying mark would have been more difficult to trace. Satellite signals cover the entire nation and the satellite could be reached from any location within the signal footprint with equipment capable of disrupting the signals.[23]

Not surprisingly, MacDougall was prompted to lash out at HBO because encryption was hurting his business. He had taken the name Captain Midnight from a television show about high school students running a pirate radio station.[24] (The original Captain Midnight was the hero of a popular television series in the early 1950s.)[25]

MacDougall eventually entered a guilty plea and was fined $5,000. He was given, in addition, a year's probation, and his radio operator's license was suspended. He apologized to HBO, conceding that such businesses had a right to make a fair profit. Nonetheless, he justified his rash act by calling attention to the plight of others like himself, whose livelihood had been threatened by the scrambling of the cable television signals.[26]

But the satellite-dish industry is still alive and healthy, joining forces with the cable television industry that it could not defeat. Many satellite marketers sell subscriptions to programming packages, and programmers may now sell their own signals or packaged combinations of programming channels directly to dish owners. At least one major magazine, *Orbit,* has been developed to help dish owners find the programs they want to watch. By mid-1991, the satellite-dish industry claimed some 3.5 million owners accessing over seventy-five unscrambled channels, seventy-five audio services, and eighty-three subscription services. The monthly sales of satellite dishes, although recovering from the low volume in the mid-1980s, are still less than half the top levels, before signals were encrypted.[27]

The dish industry blames the media for almost destroying their enterprise by hyping the "blackout" of the skies through encryption. The fact of the matter is that there are still quite a number of signals that can be received without payment. These include the two C-SPAN channels, at least one transmission of the public broadcasting service, numerous religious services, the Canadian Broadcasting Company, and a variety of marketing services such as Home Shopping Channel and Quality Value Convenience. All of this programming is supported by means other than a direct charge for access.

More Pranks and Protests

The satellite programming technology is proceeding apace to make decoding boxes more efficient and user-friendly, permitting the presetting of specific channels. Nothing with the national attention or flair of the Captain Midnight incident has recurred, but there have been a number of pranks of the "hacking" or joyriding variety.

On November 22, 1987, someone wearing a Max Headroom mask interrupted a newscast on WGN-TV, a Chicago superstation, and also appeared on WTTW-TV, the local public broadcasting station. The WGN appearance lasted only about twenty-five seconds during the 9:00 P.M. news program, and was not carried on the satellite feed. WTTW's incident was ninety seconds long and occurred during a "Doctor Who" episode. The Max Headroom impersonator bobbed around in front of the camera, threw away a Pepsi-Cola bottle, and mooned the audience with his bare buttocks, which were whacked with a flyswatter by someone offscreen.[28]

Two and a half months earlier, both the Playboy Channel and the Exxxtasy Channel (identified as soft-porn channels) were interrupted by a religious message urging viewers to repent of their sins. Engineers did not anticipate any greater difficulty in identifying the perpetrators of these pranks than they had in finding Captain Midnight, as the equipment required to make such intrusions is so sophisticated that it can be found in only a small number of hands.[29]

Indeed, an engineer at the Christian Broadcasting Network (now called the Family Channel) in Norfolk, Virginia, was apprehended and charged with three counts of satellite piracy and three counts of violating FCC regulations. He was convicted on one felony count of interfering with the operation of a satellite and another for violating his radio license. The proceeding brought vehement protestations of innocence by the defendant, Thomas Haynie, who was a deacon in his church, and by Pat Robertson, founder of the Christian Broadcasting Network, who insisted that the network could not be implicated. The defending lawyer claimed that his client was a "moral man of 'old-fashioned' values."[30] The lawyer also challenged an FCC survey of 300 possible uplinks capable of sending the intercepting signal as being insufficient to convince a jury beyond a reasonable doubt that investigators had exhausted all potential uplinks in the Western Hemisphere, or that an unlicensed perpetrator could not have succeeded in bringing about the deed.[31]

The trial almost ended in a hung jury, but the prosecutor's arguments finally convinced the jurors that the message must have been sent by someone with a profound interest in proselytizing against "unchristian" viewing. The message definitely incriminated a religious fundamentalist: "Thus sayeth the Lord thy God. Remember the Sabbath and keep it holy. Repent, the kingdom of heaven is at hand."[32] Haynie was the only technician on duty at a religious station capable of producing the pattern transmitted.

The convictions of MacDougall and Haynie stand as strong messages, one against using electronic means to protest how information is transmitted and the other indicating that no tampering with the information content would be permitted regardless of how sympathetic one might be with the tamperer's message.

Haynie was the first person convicted under the Satellite Home Viewer Act of 1988.[33] This legislation elevated satellite piracy to a felony and doubled the fines for unauthorized reception of satellite signals by private citizens, from $1,000 to $2,000. Repeat offenders, intercepting the signals for commercial gain, could be fined up to $100,000, and $500,000 could be imposed upon manufacturers and distributors of equipment designed to facilitate the "unauthorized decryption of satellite cable programming."[34] Haynie, who could have been imprisoned for as much as eleven years, was given only a three-year suspended sentence and a fine of $1,000. He was put on probation for three years and required to perform 150 hours of community service. According to the federal judge, the felony sentence alone was punishment enough for the deacon.[35] By the end of the year, he had also lost his job with the Christian Broadcasting Network.[36]

Signal Piracy

The sophisticated pirating of transmission to and from a satellite is not so much of a problem for cable television systems as the far simpler pirating of a signal from the cable to the subscriber. The cable television industry has been plagued, almost since inception, by youngsters with a modicum of electronic skill making black boxes that, with access to the cable, can siphon off the signal and direct it to nonpaying viewers.

The problem is manageable, however, thanks to the naïveté of many of the culprits. The story is told by the operators of the computer bulletin board serving the Maricopa County sheriff's department of how handily they captured one culprit. The computer bulletin board made it convenient for people to report crimes and facilitated the apprehension of lawbreakers. It was also a popular method of obtaining weather reports and local news and of exchanging electronic mail. Discovering this bonanza, an unwitting cable TV pirate who marketed black boxes advertised his expertise on the bulletin board, forgetting, surely, that it was the sheriff's very own. It was not very difficult for the powers that be to set up a "sting" operation to bring him to justice.[37]

Programmers delivering their signals via satellite continue to be plagued by pirates using descrambling devices that can be replicated for use by another viewer. "Signal theft is a cancer that is killing us," warned Rik Hawkins, a retailer of satellite dishes. Many dealers were hawking illegal contraptions out of the backs of vans and charging premium prices for the illegal computer chips, promising purchasers that they were paying a "lifetime" fee for access to the premium pay channels.[38] Many retailers tried to entice customers with the same promise.[39]

There are essentially two methods of modifying the descrambling equipment to enable it to decode signals. One, called the Three Musketeers, gives the user access to almost all the scrambled programs while purchasing the viewing rights to only one. The procedure requires replacing the integrated circuit within the descrambler with one of similar functionality, which fools the unit into believing that it is authorized to descramble all the scrambled channels responding to that particular technology. The other technique, Cloning, duplicates the identity of one descrambler to a similar unit. This can be replicated many times, producing an entire family of descrambling units with only one identity code. The viewing rights purchased by one "master" can be shared with all members of the family.[40]

The manufacturers of the descrambling devices were one step ahead of the sellers, having developed an electronic means of disabling the descrambler once they were able to ascertain the codes contained in the illegal boxes. The descrambling device, a tiny computer chip embedded within the electronics of the Videocipher, has a twelve-digit code that can be addressed via satellite, thus authorizing the equipment to permit the subscribers access to whichever programming services they have agreed to pay for the privilege of viewing. If an authorized code is copied and later identified, all equipment using the same code can be deactivated by the same mechanism required to activate it. By buying or confiscating pirated equipment, authorities could often identify codes that were being used illegally and deactivate many illegal descramblers for each modified descrambler identified.

A cottage industry has grown up around the sale of tampered chips, and as many as half the companies selling dishes have been reported to have sold illegal chips in some areas.[41] Indeed, around Roanoke, Virginia, the market for illegal descramblers was so aggressive that as many as three-fourths of the retailers of satellite antennae were estimated to be equipping their new dishes with the modified microchips.[42]

In the Caribbean, Mexico, and Canada, where the microchips cannot legally be marketed because of restrictions against the export of the technology, offshore seminars were openly held to instruct skilled technicians in the art of installing illegal chips.[43] The tiny chips were embedded deep within the electronics, so customs officials attempting to stop the importation of the tampered equipment into Canada had no way of determining whether a box was illegal.

The Cable Communications Act of 1984

By 1984, when the Cable Communications Act was passed, it was generally agreed that any unauthorized interception of services from a cable system or satellite transmission should be prohibited. Thus the state laws, which the industry had assiduously lobbied to have enacted, were reinforced. Armed with a federal law with teeth, the cable television industry and the earth satellite industry set up Anti-Piracy Task Forces"[44] and assigned an 800-number hot line for reports of questionable activities. Both industries are highly disaggregated but have organized strong industry organizations to represent their common interests. Each industry association allocated a substantial amount of its income to public relations to call attention to the problem, to lobby state legislatures to enact prohibitory legislation, and to identify and bring the perpetrators to justice.

Even with the cooperation of the FBI in tracking down illegal activities, there was a question about what to do with the customers who had bought illegal decoding equipment without realizing they were breaking the law. Since the cable television programmers and legal equipment suppliers were both eager to turn the illegal owners into paying customers, an amnesty system was devised: suppliers offered to exchange modified decoders for legitimate ones, with an understanding that the customer would sign up with a program subscription package within thirty days.[45]

A two-pronged strategy was tested in Roanoke, a community known to be rife with illegal decoding equipment.[46] The FBI descended upon two satellite equipment stores thought to have sold modified devices. At the same time General Instrument zapped the offending descramblers by sending out a signal (or electronic countermeasure) using the ciphers that the hacker had added to the equipment he had sold to his customers.[47] This action rendered the machines brain-dead by wiping out the original identification number, making it impossible for a repairman to reactivate the equipment.[48] Owners of illegal units would see their investment wiped out instantaneously. The electronic offensive was accompanied by a full-page ad in the local newspaper, warning: "If you're stealing subscription satellite TV . . . your number is up."[49]

The local FBI raids and electronic countermeasures, widely publicized by the press, were a strong prod to accept the amnesty offer with no questions asked. One Roanoke housewife took her unit in and, breathing a sigh of relief, said she would no longer need to warn her children to keep their descrambler a secret.[50]

Coincident with the FBI raid, the local distributors of satellite dishes mounted a multicompany effort with Viacom Satellite Networks, a New York producer and packager of satellite TV programming.[51] This Satellite TV Fair, mounted in a local mall, alerted citizens to the potential liabilities of using illegal decoders and offered a centralized location where they could turn in their modified descrambling units.

In other parts of the country, U.S. customs officials got a piece of the action. Because new equipment, the Videocipher II, used encryption technology forbidden to be exported under the export control regulations, customs officials took a special interest in the problem. In San Diego, two distributors of illegal descramblers were arrested on suspicion of illegally exporting descramblers to Mexico.[52] In Plentwood, Montana, agents of the U.S. Customs Service, Canadian Customs Service, U.S. Border Patrol, and the Sheridan County, Montana, sheriff's department all cooperated to curtail the activities of Radial Satellite Systems, one of the largest pirate operations in the country.[53] These are but two of several raids conducted by both the FBI and the customs service around the country, many of which were in border states.

Much of this effort has been successful. But the problem, although markedly abated, has not been solved. With the advent of the Videcipher II Plus, which General Instrument touted as 99 percent foolproof, it was anticipated that the number of illegal decoders would drop precipitously. But people who trafficked in the illegal decoders bragged that within twelve months they would catch up with the technological advances of the equipment manufacturer.[54]

In April 1991, two men from Manassas, Virginia, entered guilty pleas in response to charges arising out of one of the largest satellite-signal-theft seizures ever conducted by the FBI. Michael Neal and Terry Crigger of T&M Communications agreed to forfeit more than $85,000 in cash found in their business offices and $15,000 found at Crigger's residence. According to the affidavits filed, the two had allegedly modified some 3,000 decoders and realized revenues of $900,000, buying three houses and two trucks to be used to further their illegal activities. Deppish Kirkland, general counsel of the Satellite Broadcasting and Communications Association, whose antipiracy investigative staff assisted with the case, said the association would seek a percentage of the $100,000 seized in order to bolster the efforts of their antipiracy task force.[55]

Conclusions

The most important lesson to be drawn from the experiences of the satellite-dish industry is that self-help may be the only route to survival for the cable television programmers and manufacturers of descrambling equipment. The failure to address the problem in legislation until very late in the development of the industry allowed the satellite-dish industry to grow up in a legal vacuum, during which time it was not clear whether the activity for which it sold equipment was legal or illegal.

The presumption certainly was that planned interception was illegal pursuant to former section 605 (now 705) of the Communications Act, which prohibited the unauthorized interception of radio and wire communications not intended for the general viewing public. But there were many people who had bought dishes to pick up public broadcasts originating at signals too distant to allow reception with a garden-variety roof antenna. If the dish owner now discovered that simply by turning the dish tuner he could pick up transmissions not intended for the general viewing public, had he slipped across the line into illegal activity? And how was the innocent viewer to tell the difference between types of broadcast signals? Had the people who sold him the antenna to help facilitate the reception of broadcasts intended for the general public now become criminals, not through any action on their own part but through the fact that their customers, innocently or not, had used their equipment to gain access to property not rightfully intended for their use? The situation was ambiguous at best.

Eventually the FCC officially ruled that the unamended section 605 prohibited the unauthorized reception of satellite-delivered programming, since the signals were intended for a specific audience, not the general public.[56] But far too many consumers had purchased equipment based on the assumption that what was found in the public's airwaves and technologically available was theirs for the taking.

Congress agreed that it was inequitable that Americans should have openly purchased satellite dishes in the uncontradicted belief that they were legal and now be prohibited from using them. This benign and sympathetic approach was in sharp contrast with the Canadian policy in early years of actually destroying private satellites. This practice was quickly ended after loggers retaliated to protect their dishes in the back-woods of the Canadian Rockies, where they could not have obtained broadcast signals otherwise. Likewise, eleven Canadian officers of the Atmospheric Environment Service in Mould Bay, 76 degrees north latitude and 900 miles from the North Pole, relied upon their 10-foot dish to remind them that they were "part of the world."[57] Clearly, there are pockets of people all over the world who cannot be reasonably served by either broadcast signals or cable television systems.

Arthur Clarke, the British scientist (and science fiction author) who pioneered the research that led to the use of the geostationary orbit, never sought to patent his product. Perhaps it was an oversight, as scientists usually seek their rewards through attribution and recognition. Perhaps it was a belief that this was a resource that belonged naturally to all of us. Certainly the technology of information distribution has revolutionized access to information for many millions of viewers all around the globe.

Nonetheless, the ethics of access remain clouded in controversy. The satellite-dish industry has made great strides with strong legislation, vigorous efforts at enforcement, and a reasonably effective technological means of controlling access. Still, it is estimated that approximately half the viewers of satellite signals in the U.S. are using illegal decoders, representing a loss of subscription revenues of at least $100 million annually.[58] Clearly the territorial rights of satellite information providers have not yet been conceded, despite enabling legislation, and poaching on what are considered private proprietary domains remains a thriving industry.

7

Who Owns Religious Information?

On September 4, 1991, the Biblical Archaeology Society (BAS) of Washington, D.C., announced a stunning technological achievement. It would publish a portion of text from the Dead Sea Scrolls—the oldest and most important religious documents ever discovered—reconstructed by a computer from Hebrew writings contained on manuscript fragments. These fragments had been held for more than forty years by scholars who had laboriously pieced together thousands of bits of manuscript by hand, not permitting other scholars access to the fragments or to photographs of them. But Dr. Ben Zion Wacholder, professor of Talmudic Studies at Hebrew Union College in Cincinnati, and his research assistant, Martin G. Abegg, Jr., had accomplished the unprecedented feat of computer reconstruction.

For decades a controversy had raged over the value of the scrolls, their origin, their translations, their dates, and who should have ultimate control over their custody and the distribution of information they contained. The scrolls lay hidden in caves near Jerusalem from the first century A.D. until the spring of 1947, when they were discovered by nomadic Bedouins.[1] Eventually the largest number of fragments were collected under the auspices of the Palestine Archaeological Museum (PAM), now known as the Rockefeller Museum, in East Jerusalem. PAM appointed a team of seven internationally recognized scholars, informally known as the International Committee to Edit the Scrolls of Cave 4 Qumran (hereafter the Scroll Team), with the responsibility of overseeing the reconstruction, translation, and interpretation of the fragments. Forty years later, examination and publication of the scrolls were still restricted to this one officially recognized body of scholars.

Hershel Shanks, president of the BAS, explained to an astonished audience how a team of two scholars at the Hebrew Union College, with the aid of a desktop computer, had, it seems, literally reconstructed the

text word by word from the scant information available to them in a concordance—an alphabetical listing of every word of text and the words
that precede and follow it—prepared for the Scroll Team.

Shanks was not looking for congratulations for the Hebrew Union
scholars whose technical virtuosity led to this breakthrough. He was
more concerned with the stranglehold a small group of scholars had had
on these documents. "We've broken the monopoly!" he announced.[2]

The custodians promptly denounced the unauthorized scholars, calling them pirates. John Strugnell, former editor-in-chief of the Scroll
Team (he had been fired a few months earlier for indiscreet remarks
about Judaism),[3] observed, "What else would you call it but stealing?"[4]
But shortly after the announcement of the computer reconstruction, the
Huntington Library in San Marino, California, opened to all scholars an
archive of photographs of the fragments in its possession,[5] and two
months later the BAS published two volumes of facsimiles of the fragments procured from an unrevealed source.[6] Dr. Lawrence Schiffman,
professor of Hebrew and Judaic Studies at New York University, was one
of the most enthusiastic proponents of these disclosures: "Most will
regard those who make this material available as Robin Hoods, stealing
from the academically privileged to give to those hungry for the knowledge secreted in these texts."[7]

Discovery of the Dead Sea Scrolls

The story of the Dead Sea Scrolls raises fascinating questions about legal
rights to information. The documents that were the subject of this controversy were some 800 leather and papyrus manuscripts found in caves
and among ruins of a communal settlement that was destroyed by fire in
A.D. 68.[8] Their significance lies in their age—they are the most contem-
poraneous historical record of early pre-Christian and Judaic history we
have. The documents we know as the Bible come from manuscripts dating probably from the tenth century A.D.

The first scrolls were discovered in the early spring of 1947 by two
Bedouin shepherd boys searching for a stray goat while tending their
flocks in an arid and uninhabited region adjacent to the springs at 'Ain-
Feshkha, on the northwest corner of the Dead Sea. This area is near
Khirbet Qumran in the disputed West Bank territory that has been
occupied by Israel since 1967 but claimed by Jordan. At the time of their
discovery, the territory was still under British jurisdiction, although it
was claimed as grazing lands by the Bedouins.[9]

In this area, along the shoreline of what was once a single large lake, caves are so numerous and complex that it is easy for objects, and even people, to remain hidden in them. According to the Bible, King Saul took 3,000 men to caves such as these to search for David and was unaware of David's presence until David chose to reveal himself.

Thus it has been conjectured that the scrolls may have been brought there to keep them from falling into the hands of the Romans during the war that resulted in the destruction of Jerusalem in A.D. 70 and crushed a Jewish revolt.[10] Some years after the discovery of the scrolls, the ruins were excavated, revealing a building about 111 feet long and about 90 feet wide containing a dining room, kitchens, a dormitory, workshops, a lavatory, two baptisteries, and a scriptorium in which the scrolls might well have been written.[11] The ink in the scriptorium was identical to the ink on the fragments. However, it was later learned that such ink was widely used throughout the area and could not clearly be identified with the particular site.

The Bedouins exploring the caves in 1947 found large storage pots that they hastened to open. Perhaps they were hoping to find gold or incense, but these pots contained only smelly old decaying cylinders of leather and papyrus, scrolls that appeared to them to be in the Syriac language. They carried the scrolls to the market at Bethlehem, hoping for a sale. They offered them to a Ta'amireh sheik, who acquired them and sent them on to a merchant in the Syrian Orthodox community, who passed them on to another merchant in Jerusalem. Four scrolls and fragments of a fifth eventually turned up at the doorstep of Metropolitan (a title) Athanasius Yeshue Samuel, who cared for ancient Syriac manuscripts in the St. Mark's Monastery in Old Jerusalem. Metropolitan Samuel recognized that the manuscripts were in Hebrew, not Syriac. He burned a small piece of the scrolls to see whether they were made of leather, which would determine their worth. Many months went by before he was able to strike a deal. In the meantime, some the of scrolls were sold. Metropolitan Samuel attempted to get many eminent authorities to appraise his purchases, and some (who were later criticized by their peers) pronounced them worthless.

During this period Palestine was in a state of turmoil, and it is quite remarkable that the manuscripts survived at all. By February 1948, matters had settled down sufficiently for some of the scrolls and fragments to be assembled and taken to the American Schools of Oriental Research (ASOR). There they were photographed by John C. Trever, an American scholar, who recognized their value and sent prints to Professor William F. Albright, of Johns Hopkins University. He was able to confirm that they were from the Old Testament book of Isaiah, most likely written in the second century B.C.,[12] and declared that they were "the greatest manuscript discovery of modern times."[13]

In 1949 further searches were made of the caves where the manuscripts had been found. Archaeologists were seeking additional fragments for their religious and historical significance, Bedouins for their commercial value. The archaeologists were under the leadership of Father Roland de Vaux from the École Biblique et Archéologique Française, who also served as president of the board of trustees of the PAM.

The search for more fragments went on with some fury during the early 1950s, with archaeological scholars trying to beat Bedouins to each new find. They were not entirely successful, and some of the fragments are reported to be held today by wealthy Jordanians, who value them as a "better investment than anything on the Israeli or the New York Stock Exchanges."[14]

In February 1952 a large cache of fragments was discovered in what has been identified as Cave 4 Qumran (portions of which were the subject of the controversy over the delay in publication). Neither the PAM nor the Jordanian Department of Antiquities had sufficient funds to buy these fragments from the Bedouins or their agent—a Syrian cobbler and antiquities dealer, Khalil Iskander Shahin of Bethlehem, known as Kando—so they sought financial assistance from foreign institutions. The universities of Heidelberg, McGill, Manchester, and Oxford, as well as the McCormick Theological Seminary, All Soul's Unitarian Church, and the Vatican Library, provided funds. The price was about $2.80 per square centimeter.[15] A second gift from McCormick and the All Soul's gifts were made subject to an agreement that the scrolls purchased would remain in the Rockefeller Museum, and that rights to publication would be granted only to the national schools or their designated editors. This agreement was contrary to those of previous gifts, which had provided for fragments to go to donor institutions after publication. However, all the prior agreements were superseded by a decree of the Jordanian government on August 5, 1961, revoking all past agreements and claiming absolute ownership and control over the scrolls.[16]

The outpouring of pieces was so great and the progress of piecing them together so slow, however, that Father De Vaux and his board of trustees, with the agreement of the Jordanian authorities, under whose geographical jurisdiction the fragments were then placed, decided to assemble a team of biblical scholars to assume responsibility for their recompilation and transcription. An accomplice in this effort was an Englishman, G. Lankester Harding, who was curator of the PAM, secretary of the board of trustees, and also director of the Jordanian Department of Antiquities. Thus he represented both public and private entities, obscuring the source of ultimate legal authority over the scrolls but facilitating the effort to collect and archive the valuable archaeological acquisitions. His position was important, as he was also one of the last British colonials left in positions of authority in Jordan.

The PAM was under the direction of a board of trustees representing the participating foreign academic institutions that supported its work, with half of the members being composed of scholars from these institutions (from France, England, Germany, and the United States) and the other half being represented by diplomats from their countries. In 1952 this board approved the selection of seven internationally known scholars who were nominated by the participating European and American schools.[17] First to arrive in 1953 were:

- Professor Frank Moore Cross of Harvard University, who had trained for the Protestant ministry, nominated by the ASOR;
- Abbé Jean Starcky from the Centre National de la Recherche Scientifique of France;
- Father Jozel T. Milik, nominated by the École Biblique et Archéologique of France, a Polish priest who later left the priesthood and resettled in France;
- John Allegro, an agnostic Englishman, nominated by the British School, from the University of Manchester, England (who had studied for the Protestant ministry).

They were joined the following year by:

- John Strugnell, an English Calvinist (who subsequently converted to Catholicism), the youngest of the scholars at age twenty-three, representing the British School of Archeology, now a professor at Harvard University (Strugnell later became the chief editor of the Scroll Team);
- Claus-Hunno Hunzinger, a German scholar and Lutheran pastor, of the Deutschen Evangelischen Instituts für Altertumswissenschaft des Heiligen Landes. (Hunzinger was soon to be replaced by another French priest, Father Maurice Baillet);
- Monsignor Patrick Skehan from the ASOR.[18]

Although the Jewish Palestine Exploration Society nominally was entitled to representatives on the PAM board of trustees, its representatives were not permitted to enter Jordan.[19] Of the original appointees, only three are still on the Scroll Team: Cross, Strugnell, and Milik (although Milik has not been active for some years). The others passed their custodianship on to their protégés and graduate students (with the approval of the remainder of the team), a practice condemned by other biblical scholars, who considered themselves at least as competent and deserving as these younger academics to undertake the remaining work.[20] The team was expanded over the years to include some younger scholars picked by the existing team with the approval of the Israeli Antiquities Authority (IAA). What irked outsiders was the lack of access to the materials in order to pursue independent or parallel research on their restoration and interpretation.[21]

The appointees were given no formal title; neither was there any formal agreement, set of bylaws, or mandate for performance. As Professor Cross observed, "We knew what we had to do!"[22] The task was formidable: retrieved from more than a meter of debris accumulated in Cave 4 were at least 15,000 fragments of more than 500 texts, only 98 of which had been published by the early 1990s.[23]

The members of the Scroll Team were presented with the largest puzzle in history. According to scholars who worked on the pieces, many were indecipherable. Others were damaged by Scotch tape that had been used to attach pieces that appeared to go together, or by castor oil used to moisten the illegible fragments to make the script readable on infrared photographs.[24] Many pieces had darkened from exposure to contaminants during the centuries they lay in the cave. For the researchers, the task was not only a professional challenge; it was also a labor of love. Progress was slow because both money and time were limited. Only three of the scholars were in residence in Jerusalem, the others joining them only while on sabbatical or during summer vacations.

According to the professional ethics of the archaeologists, a major manuscript would be assigned to a scholar for reconstruction and translation, granting a right to first publication of the work in progress.[25] As in other similar academic circles, such proprietary rights would be recognized among peer groups. The sanction for jumping the claim of a colleague is ostracism from professional circles. Proprietary allocation of research resources, such as cuneiforms and fossils as well as shards and manuscripts, was respected within the academic community. According to Professor Cross: by and large, "it is material in which they have invested 10 to 20 years of their life and hence simply don't want to give it away to other scholars to publish and take the credit . . . and one must understand the human desire to have some credit for work done."[26]

Custody and Control of the Scrolls and Their Information

Some of the scrolls and their fragments were in frequent transit for a few years. The five scrolls purchased by Metropolitan Samuel, for example, were taken to the United States in January 1949 and offered for sale after his monastery came under shellfire. But for a while it seemed that they would have no takers. Major universities and libraries either did not have the financial resources to buy the scrolls or did not see their purchase as a priority, given the fact that the scrolls found in Cave 1 had been taken to the ASOR and photographed for preservation of the images. Access to the original leather and papyrus seemed a luxury they could ill afford.

Museums and other collectors who could afford to buy and preserve the originals were apprehensive on the grounds that they could not obtain good title. The Department of Antiquities of Jordan claimed that the scrolls had been removed from Jordan without permission, so legal title could not be acquired by a purchaser in good faith.[27] Metropolitan Samuel allegedly tried, without success, to sell the documents to the Department of Antiquities before sending them to the United States. That the Middle East was in a state of turmoil did not help clarify the legal question of who had a right to claim an interest in the preservation and custody of the scrolls.

At the time the five scrolls were removed from the caves in 1947, the territory was still in the hands of the British. Under British law, treasure trove (usually gold or silver) could be legally claimed by the Crown, but artifacts embedded in the soil could be claimed by the landowner unless they were of such significance that they were entitled to the trusteeship of the entire nation. The notion that the government had a duty to assure the preservation of artifacts of historical importance had emerged in nineteenth-century legal thinking. In France, Victor Hugo campaigned against the destruction of historic monuments; the U.S. government established Yellowstone National Park in 1872; and the Danish archaeologist Jens Jacob Asmussen Worsaae issued his seminal report on the preservation of antiquities in 1877. Still, no one in the Anglo-American world articulated a legal rationale prior to the introduction on February 7, 1873, by Sir John Lubbock, a member of Parliament, of "A Bill to Provide for the Preservation of Ancient National Monuments." What might have seemed an innocuous legislative proposal introduced an element of trusteeship, burdening a landowner with a duty to recognize that artifacts—insofar as they contain historic and scientific value—belong to the nation,[28] as expressed in a recent article:

> The idea was that the history of England, though it might in part be embedded in a physical structure, could hardly be said to belong to some individual. In preventing the destruction of its history, the nation was not taking something away from the owner, but was safeguarding something of its own. Whether the claim was put in propri-

etary terms, as something "belonging" to the nation, or in some less legalistic form, the concept was the same: The nation as a collectivity had a preexisting interest in many objects that had always been considered entirely private.[29]

Perhaps it is poetic justice that an Israeli patriot, General Yigael Yadin, a renowned archaeologist as well as a military man, borrowed a quarter of a million dollars to purchase the five scrolls, adding to the collection of fragments that his father, Professor E. L. Sukenik of Hebrew University, had purchased late in 1947 from an antiquities dealer (not Metropolitan Samuel). General Yadin, responding to an ad in the *Wall Street Journal*,[30] acquired the scrolls, with their cultural connection to the ancient Hebrew sects. Yadin had to scrounge the funds from several sources and purchase the scrolls through an intermediary, as Metropolitan Samuel could not knowledgeably deal with a Jew.[31] Eventually a generous benefactor, D. Samuel Gottesman of New York, provided the bulk of the funds, and the treasured manuscripts were donated to the new state of Israel in 1955. It was determined that a special museum would be built to house them. Today these scrolls from Cave 1 are on display in the Shrine of the Book in Jerusalem.

A copper scroll, later found broken into two pieces, became the property of the government of Jordan. The scroll was lent to the University of Manchester, where scholars achieved the superhuman feat of dissecting and deciphering the inscriptions without being able to unroll the scroll. Most of the remaining scroll fragments eventually came to reside in the PAM, which remained a part of Jordan until 1967, when Israel occupied the land upon which the museum stood.

With Israeli occupation of this part of Jordan in 1967,[32] overall supervision of the reconstruction process passed to the IAA. The Jordanian government had already repudiated the claims of the foreign institutions that refused to transfer physical possession to the participating research institutions, but reconfirmed the Scroll Team appointed by the Jordanians.[33] The legal status of the collection was made more complex by the nationalization of the PAM by the Jordanian government in 1966, repudiating any outstanding claims of foreign institutions to the scrolls. Once the area became occupied by the Israelis, custody of the museum and its contents came under the jurisdiction of the IAA as a national institution.

Legal claim to the underlying original fragments has never been brought to court, although it has been assumed that Israel has at least a presumptive right to control the disposition of the scrolls in its possession as "spoils of war," as de facto, if not de jure, occupier of the territory in which they are now found, or as the appropriate source of cultural patrimony. The existing protocols and resolutions of the United Nations and UNESCO concerning the treatment of "cultural property" and its proper return to its rightful owners did not come into existence until after the discovery of the scrolls, and it is not clear who the rightful owners might be even if they were in effect.

There are also rules concerning what cultural property may not be removed from a country claiming it.[34] However, nations in which there is a flourishing economic market for such cultural objects, such as Germany, France, Switzerland, Japan, and the United Kingdom, have not hastened to subscribe to these treaties.[35] The United States acceded to the UNESCO convention on cultural objects only in 1983[36] and restricts its applicability to countries that have a strong policy prohibiting pillage of cultural objects and a high motivation to protect their own national treasures. A prior existing convention adopted the principle of universal ownership on the theory that such treasures are the "common heritage of mankind."[37]

Indeed, many economists would argue that the highest and best use of the cultural treasures would be obtained by a free marketplace in such objects, and that third world countries rich in much-sought-after artwork and classical manuscripts would be better off encouraging rather than prohibiting a sale. The great ancient Greek temple of Pergamon, which originally stood near what is now Bergama in the modern state of Turkey, was returned by the Soviets from the Hermitage in Leningrad to the Pergamon Museum in East Berlin, from which it had been removed in World War II. Greece and Turkey might also have had a legitimate claim to it. The Parthenon Marbles (often called the Elgin Marbles) have not been returned to Greece either, despite much urging from the Greek government. The most recent refusal by the British government was in 1984.[38] Therefore, it is not surprising that little controversy has arisen over the physical possession of the scrolls.

The information contained in the documents themselves can now be studied and obtained from thousands of photographic images. The issue of custody and access to these images has piqued the interest of researchers as well as the general public.

Photographic Images and Their Disposition

There has been a great deal of controversy over the preparation of photographic images of the intact scrolls as well as of the many fragments. A complete set of photographs is unlikely to exist, as some of the fragments may remain in private hands and others have deteriorated or remain hidden in the sands of the Middle East.

The best photographs of the Cave 4 fragments were made by Najib Albina, a superb photographer, between 1953 and 1960. Each of the negatives contains a PAM number indicating its source in the Palestinian Archeological Museum.[39] It seems likely that Albina kept a copy of the photographs in his personal archive, as this is a common practice among photographers.

During the years of unrest in the Middle East, the custodians of the scrolls and fragments feared that the originals might be destroyed inadvertently, so sets of photographs were entrusted to Oxford University's Centre for Postgraduate Hebrew Studies and Hebrew Union College in Cincinnati. Both sets were transferred with instructions that they were to be preserved but not put on view or made available to scholars other than those on the Scroll Team or approved by the supervisory authorities at the IAA.

The earliest distributed set of images is the one at Hebrew Union College, which employed Wacholder and his assistant, Abegg. Being denied access to the photographs in the library of their own institution was one of the motivations that prompted them to turn to the computer and concordance for assistance in unraveling the fragmented Hebrew text. They did have access to photographs for the final comparison of the computer-generated text with the images of the original text—but not from the Hebrew Union Library, which continued to honor the agreement of nondisclosure. Another set of Albina's photographs was obtained from sources in Jerusalem.[40]

In 1980, Elizabeth Hay Bechtel, philanthropist and founder of the Ancient Biblical Manuscript Center (ABMC) in Claremont, California, arranged and paid for the Huntington Library photographer, Robert Schlosser, to go to Jerusalem to duplicate the Albina photographs with the intention of storing them in the Claremont institution. She also financed the construction of a vault at the ABMC to safeguard the film. The ABMC had successfully negotiated an agreement with the Department of Antiquities and Museums (now the IAA) whereby that institution would keep custody over the work under the same restrictions imposed on the other depositories. In her capacity as president of the board of trustees, Mrs. Bechtel was a signatory to the agreement as well as financial contributor to accomplish its purpose.

However, before Schlosser's work reached the ABMC, Mrs. Bechtel had a falling-out with James Sanders, director of the Claremont museum. Its board, siding with him, voted Mrs. Bechtel out of the presidency, relegating her to the role of an ordinary trustee. She then withdrew her financial support for the ABMC, and it never received the full set of photographs intended to be deposited there.[41]

Additional photographs (including new shots at both the Rockefeller Museum and the Shrine of the Book) were made by Schlosser in 1984 on a second trip to Jerusalem, funded once again by Mrs. Bechtel.[42] She entrusted a full set of his photographs to the Huntington Library solely for safekeeping, without imposing any restrictions. The deposit was made strictly as an accommodation to Mrs. Bechtel, who was a generous donor to the Huntington (as she had been to the ABMC).[43] Knowledge of this deposit of scroll photographs at the Huntington was not made public, and the acquisition was not listed in the library's catalogs of its holdings.

In July 1991 the Huntington Library decided to make its collection of photographic negatives available to all scholars, on the same basis as the remainder of its collections. According to officials of the library, this consisted of 3,000 master photographic negatives of the ancient manuscripts, which they believed to be of the entire collection of published and unpublished scrolls as well as duplicates of the photographic archives at the Rockefeller Museum and the Shrine of the Book in Jerusalem.[44]

The Huntington's action followed the announcement of the computer reconstruction but was not triggered by it.[45] The two announcements, coming one on the heels of the other, precipitated intense media coverage that attracted wide public interest in the controversy. The director of the IAA denounced the action of the Huntington Library as an unethical "violation of the agreement that we had with the people allowed to have the films," and threatened legal action.[46] Members of the Scroll Team, now headed by Emanuel Tov, also expressed their outrage. But the Huntington Library had not signed that agreement. The IAA never took legal action, either realizing that its case rested upon weak legal grounds or recognizing that the weight of public opinion was leaning too heavily on the side of its opponents. It agreed in principle to an open-access policy.[47]

The IAA was facing substantial criticism itself over its policy of tight control and secrecy. For years, numerous scholars had sought and been refused access to the scroll materials, and the BAS had taken up the challenge, waging a concerted publicity war urging release of the photographs and free competition among scholars.[48]

Huntington officials relied upon the proposition that only the original authors of the manuscripts could retain a copyright to unpublished material. Since the authors were long since dead, they argued, the information contained in the scrolls was already in the public domain.[49] Scholars lauded the decision to provide access to the Huntington's photographic copies as the "scholarly equivalent of breaking down the Berlin Wall."[50] Editorials in major newspapers echoed this approval.[51] A resolution adopted by the convention of biblical scholars at Mogilany, Poland, two months before had urged making facsimiles or photographs available.[52] In addition, the Israeli Knesset's education committee, under the leadership of the historian Michael Bar-Zohar, recommended that access to the unpublished scrolls be made available to all scholars.[53]

On October 27, 1991, a joint announcement was released by Tov and Amir Drori, director of the IAA, that outside scholars would be permitted access to the photographic collection in Israel, but only if they signed an agreement not to publish the texts.[54] On November 19, the BAS released what was claimed to be the largest single collection of photographic images ever published of the Dead Sea Scrolls from Cave 4. The collection was preceded by an introduction written by two biblical scholars, Robert H. Eisenman of California State University, Long Beach, and James M. Robinson of the Claremont Graduate School.[55] The source of the photographic images was not disclosed, and scholars are remaining quiet about their speculations.[56] A set of the Albina photographs could have been available to the BAS.

In late October, Hebrew Union College announced that it too would open access to its photographs of the Dead Sea Scrolls. The university's president, Albert Gottschalk, lauded his faculty members as "pioneers" in reconstructing the text by computer and said the IAA could not restrict scholars from publishing once they had viewed the scrolls.[57] Wacholder and Abegg were planning four more volumes of their computer-reconstructed texts. In April 1992, E. J. Brill of the Netherlands announced publication of an edition, authorized by the IAA, of photographs on microfiche of the collection maintained in Israel, thus ending the forty-year ban on their release to unauthorized scholars.[58]

What the Computer Accomplished

What exactly was the technological accomplishment of Professor Wacholder and his student assistant that precipitated such a flurry of public interest in opening access to the photographs of unpublished Dead Sea Scrolls? Neither Wacholder, a Hebrew scholar, nor Abegg, a doctoral student specializing in an historical interpretation of the Hebrew Bible, was a computer-scientist. Both were, however, computer-literate. In 1988, based on work done in the 1950s by four young scholars, a concordance, combining approximately 60,000 entries, was finally published, and an authorized copy was obtained by Professor Wacholder in December 1990 to facilitate his work.[59] As previously described, it listed all words appearing in the original manuscripts together with the words that appear on either side of them. Phrases were also identified by the source of the particular scroll or segment from which they were taken. According to Brian Hayes, editor of the *American Scientist:* "It might seem at first that a concordance would not provide enough information for a complete reconstruction of a document. Only the local context of each word is given, and so one is left with a jumble of disconnected phrases, which have to be assembled like the pieces of a jigsaw puzzle. Because the pieces of the puzzle overlap, there is a method of assembling them that requires no guesswork or intuition and quickly converges on a correct reading."[60]

Because many of the connecting words are the same prepositions and connectors used over and over, it defies the limits of human persistence to achieve such a feat. A computer, never tiring or despairing, can continue making comparisons until some sense comes out of the reconstruction. Wacholder and Abegg used no supercomputer but a modest desktop Apple Macintosh and standard word-processing software, Microsoft Word.

According to computer scientists, the process involved "a particularly easy instance of a technique that has uses in many other fields, from navigation to molecular biology to seismology."[61] Linguistic skill was needed to sort out ambiguities the computer could not handle. In other words, the reassembly of the text was computer-aided rather than computer-automated.[62]

Although what Abegg did was not very complicated, it was very laborintensive. He had to type all of the words in the concordance into the computer's memory. This may sound like a straightforward exercise, but Hebrew is written from right to left, while ordinary computers assume that one is writing from left to right. Today, computer software programs that accommodate such languages are available, but Abegg had to enter each and every line backwards.

It took many hours "knee to knee," as Abegg describes the process, for Professor Wacholder and his computer-skilled student to read and check the integrity of the resultant text against their more accomplished human brains, whose judgment far exceeded that of their electronic servant.[63] They were able to reconstruct twenty-four manuscripts of the Qumran Cave 4 Scrolls within several months.[64] None had yet been published by the Scroll Team. It seems obvious that this same method could have greatly facilitated the job of organizing the original fragments even where no concordance existed. Because much of the material was similar or even identical to existing Old Testament texts, a computer comparison of photographic images with known manuscripts could have been achieved in a fraction of the time it was taking the Scroll Team. Where the sources of the manuscript are completely unknown, computer-aided reconstruction would not be as effective.

Thus the computer is not a substitute for the expertise of the scholar, but only an aid in expediting and verifying what the scholar believes to be true. The computer could not have accomplished the task without Wacholder and Abegg, confirming that the manuscript made sense. According to Professor Cross, computers are useful aids, but "[t]he human brain of a scholar is still the best device to solve the most difficult problems and is faster than a computer program in solving the obvious problems."[65]

The newly expanded Scroll Team of fifty-three biblical scholars (forty men and thirteen women), headed by Emanuel Tov, has moved rapidly to endorse computer technology to facilitate and accelerate publication of the texts.[66] The opportunities go far beyond the conventional data-processing applications currently in use. Computer imaging will allow photographs to be converted into electronic images that can be displayed and manipulated on the screen, enlarging and enhancing images that are faint and indistinguishable. Eventually the entire collection of Dead Sea Scroll images may be collected and offered to one and all on a CD-ROM.

The ABMC, the Oxford Centre for Postgraduate Hebrew Studies, and the Oxford Forum for Qumran Research are leading the way into the new age of electronic imaging.[67] The Annenberg Research Institute in Philadelphia, which targeted Dead Sea Scroll research as a priority, was given a full microfilm set of the photos from the Huntington Library to be used by the dozen scholars assembled there in 1993 for full-time research.

Stephen A. Reed of the ABMC has completed an inventory and catalog of all scroll materials. ABMC, the recipient of a grant of computer-imaging equipment from Apple Computer that will permit all of its photographs to be turned into electronic images, is also rephotographing both the original negatives and some of the original scrolls maintained by the Shrine of the Book in Jerusalem.[68] However, Professor Lawrence H. Schiffman of New York University warns that such computerized reconstructions, involving personal judgment on the part of the scholar, must be verified by comparison with the originals before being assumed to be correct, so the tedious process of checking and cross-checking may be eased but not eliminated.[69]

Content of the Dead Sea Scrolls

In its strict sense, the term *Dead Sea Scrolls* applies exclusively to those fragments discovered between 1947 and 1956.[70] Many of the scrolls pertain to Old Testament books, including the entire book of Isaiah, today displayed in the Shrine of the Book. The Isaiah scroll appeared to be much the same as the versions dating from medieval times. While some scholars expressed a concern that the scrolls might undermine the authenticity of the Bible and question extant versions of early Christian history, in fact, most of the revealed text confirms the later versions as more or less the same as the earlier ones. Overall, the published biblical scrolls contain little that questions accepted Christian theology.[71]

There were more than 190 biblical texts, most of which have been published. Only the Isaiah Scroll from Cave 1 was complete, but fragments of most of the other books of the Old Testament (with the exception of Ezra and Esther) were identified. These fragments go back as far as the third century B.C., bringing knowledge of their contents much closer to the time of their writing than the copies from the Middle Ages, the only text available until the Dead Sea Scrolls were found.

There are a large number of sectarian texts, including one that appears to be a rulebook of established codes of conduct for the community usually identified as the Essenes. They produced a vast body of their own literature, most of which has already been published. The group from which the scroll came was a highly disciplined and, indeed, ascetic society, not unlike a strict sect of Essenes, one of three major Judaic groups known to be in existence at the time Jesus of Nazareth was living and teaching. The predominant view remains that the prescribed rules of order were possibly those of the Essene community described by Pliny the Elder in his *Historica Naturalis* (as well as by Josephus and Philo) as residing in the vicinity.[72]

A third group of texts contains Jewish compositions from the Second Temple period, written by various Jewish groups outside of the Khirbet Qumran area, whose origins have not been determined but which appear to be from the Apocrypha and Pseudepigrapha. The remaining thirty or so fragments are from nonliterary texts whose source and content have not been identified.[73]

The fact that the entire contents of the Dead Sea Scrolls have still not been revealed to the world has led to widespread rumors, ranging from a conspiracy to suppress the contents, because it might undermine the foundations of Christianity as a unique and messianic religion, to more outlandish claims of historically accurate prophesies from the popular supermarket tabloids. According to the *Weekly World News,* "a famed biblical scholar," a Dr. Felix Bonjean, identified as one of only six men permitted to examine remnants of some of the scrolls allegedly kept under lock and key by the Vatican, claimed that they revealed that a group of "bulb headed" extraterrestrials in UFOs landed on the earth 2,500 years ago, that God has "fiery green eyes, flowing brown hair, and stands 9 feet tall," that Jesus Christ would be reborn in 1994, and that the world would end in 11991. The scrolls also supposedly revealed prophesies of an antichrist who resembled Adolf Hitler, a "horrifying plague in the late 20th century" (thought to be a reference to AIDS), and the election of a daughter of a slain president to the presidency of the United States in 1996.[74]

A popular publication by two Australians has highlighted the controversial theories of Robert H. Eisenman, of the California State University at Long Beach, who certainly holds more prestigious credentials than the tabloids but who claims that the Scroll Team has been dominated by Dominican scholars with an intention to suppress any evidence that does not conform to accepted Catholic theological doctrine.[75] However, Hershel Shanks, in reviewing the book, pronounced it "hogwash," echoing the sentiments of most biblical scholars.[76]

Appealing to Copyright Law

The discovery, custody, and control of the Dead Sea Scrolls constitute a classic controversy over religious dogma as well as posing an interesting question of legal rights to information. Many different claims of proprietary interest in the scrolls could be asserted. The Bedouins who discovered the scrolls had presumptive rights in their possession. Some purchasers had made their acquisitions in good faith. The nation-state within whose bounds the scrolls were found had claims of historical and cultural rights to their archaeological treasures. Nations to which the scrolls have been transported also have viable claims to legal custody. The libraries that have maintained either originals or copies of the texts have a vested interest in their protection. The elders of the religions whose historical roots were in question have the most at stake. In addition, the scrolls have attracted interest from the public, which has a justifiable curiosity about the provable historical circumstances surrounding the life of Jesus.

The two scholars who wrote the introduction to the BAS publication of photographs reflected the concerns of scholars that overall quality of scholarship would be diminished if equitable access were not accorded to peers: "Arrangements that initially seemed reasonable need, a generation or so later, to be supplemented by some mechanism by means of which scholars who were beginning their careers when the discoveries were made (not to speak of scholars then not yet born) can gain full access to them before their careers have been completed. It is under this higher claim of the academic community and society at large that the present edition has been initiated."[77]

The claims of the academic community, of the national community, and of the cultural heritage of mankind cannot recompense the scholar who toils long and hard for years over often indecipherable fragments only to have his work product published by another. As Professor Elisha Qimron,[78] a member of the expanded Scroll Team, protested in a letter to the editors of the *Biblical Archaeology Review:* "A major achievement of my professional career has been stolen from me."[79] To protect his proprietary interests in the 121-line Hebrew text he reconstructed, Qimron filed suit, seeking $250,000 for infringement of copyright in a photograph of his work product that was published by the BAR. He was able to obtain an injunction prohibiting use of his reconstruction in "Israel and elsewhere," even though he had distributed numerous photocopies himself to many of his colleagues throughout the world.[80] Qimron won a judgment in the Jerusalem District Court for $7,250 in damages, $29,000 for mental anguish, and $18,125 in legal costs.[81]

The Israeli professor contended that his reconstruction of the fragmentary material contained in the manuscript known as MMT, an acronym for *Miksat Ma'ase HaTorah* ("Some of the Precepts of the Torah"), was not just a translation, but included his conjectures about the missing pieces of text.[82] Judge Dalia Dorner agreed. While piecing together thousands of scroll fragments with 50 percent of the scroll still missing would not qualify for copyright, researching areas beyond his own expertise in order to reconstruct the missing half rendered the text an original work that Judge Dorner found qualified for copyright protection under the laws of both the United States and Israel.[83]

Scholars on the expanded Scroll Team also sided with Professor Qimron. In a signed statement, circulated among those attending a special conference on scroll research organized by the New York Academy of Sciences and the Oriental Institute of the University of Chicago in December 1991, the researchers charged "unethical appropriation" of their work products exchanged informally at scholarly meetings because "all scholars have a right to see their work appear in print for the first time under their own name."[84] This protest was directed to two scholars, Robert Eisenman and his co-author, Michael Wise, assistant professor of Near Eastern languages and civilizations at the University of Chicago. Wise capitulated and publicly apologized to the assembled scholars, regretting that "I did not more fully express indebtedness to colleagues whose work I consulted."[85]

Lawyers for the defendants in the Qimron suit, all of whom reside in the United States, filed a counterclaim in a Philadelphia court seeking a declaratory judgment that the subject matter was not capable of copyright protection. It was later withdrawn, since the same issues were being litigated on appeal in an Israeli court.

Wacholder and Abegg, however, who are planning to publish four more volumes of their own reconstructions of the Qumran texts, filed for a declaratory judgment in the Philadelphia court. What they seek is an advance ruling that their own work will not be considered an infringement of Qimron's claimed proprietary text.[86]

The *Biblical Archaeology Review* has not budged from its support for open access to all scholars, decrying Qimron's efforts to enforce copyright protection, giving him exclusive rights to use of the two-thousand-year-old text of which he was not the author, but conceding that Qimron has filled in letters that had not survived the ravages of time.[87]

Emphasis on Ethical Standards

In order to avoid such litigation and controversies, the scholarly community interested in the Dead Sea Scrolls is attempting to reformulate a code of ethics. Professor Robinson, who with Professor Eisenman wrote the introduction to the recently published photographs, suggests establishing a Commission on Future Manuscript Discoveries, to be entrusted with establishing policies and procedures that would provide insulation from and supervision over the scholars actually performing the work.[88] In his estimation, one of the problems has been that the members of the Scroll Team have been supervising themselves. The assigned editing scholars would be entitled to publish the first edition, the *Editio Princeps,* but not to include any of the editors' own scholarship beyond that needed for the first edition itself.[89]

Such individual scholarship would be reserved for a successor volume. This first publication would be limited to translation of the text and technical notes and accepted for what it is: a prompt transcription made available to the entire scholarly community. Within one year the editors would be under an obligation to supply photographs of the text and a preliminary transcription with a computer disk that other scholars could acquire and read on their own word processors. If the scholars failed to meet the one-year deadline, the work would be assigned to another scholar. If they did meet the deadline, they would be permitted another four years to complete the work of preparing the first edition. Thus, it is hoped, both the scholars and the public would be well served.[90]

Conclusions

Whatever the outcome of litigation and the efforts of the biblical scholars to establish ethical norms for their own professional environment, it is clear that they will no longer have the luxury of working in an ivory tower. They will be operating in a fishbowl, carefully observed by press and public. Aggrieved members of their profession, like Professor Quimron, will seek redress in the courts of law in their own territorial jurisdictions, where their appeals will stress the limits of established legal domains.

The slow pace of the past will not be tolerated by the court of public opinion. The *New York Times* pronounced its benediction upon the accomplishment of the computer team, which led the march toward a more open policy:

> Some on the committee might be tempted to charge the Cincinnati scholars with piracy. On the contrary, Mr. Wacholder and Mr. Abegg are to be applauded for their work—and for sifting through layer upon layer of obfuscation. The committee, with its obsessive secrecy and cloak and dagger scholarship, long ago exhausted its credibility with scholars and laymen alike.
>
> The two Cincinnatians seem to know what the scroll committee forgot: that the scrolls and what they say about the common roots of Christianity and Rabbinic Judaism belong to civilization, not to a few sequestered professors.[91]

The mysteries of religious dogma have throughout history been managed by various tightly knit priesthoods of custodians, regardless of time, culture, or place. What this computer-aided analysis has done (along with the release of the photographs) is to strike a blow for accessibility and freedom of access to religious information. The silent electronic servant may be as potent a religious force as the Protestant reformer Martin Luther, who posted his 95 Theses "for the purpose of eliciting truth" on the door of All Saints Church in Wittenberg on October 31, 1517.[92]

8

Who Owns Computer Software?

In 1987 an irate reader wrote a letter to the editor of *Computerworld* expressing his frustration over litigation initiated by the Lotus Development Corporation. Lotus had gone into court claiming copyright infringement of its highly successful spreadsheet program Lotus 1-2-3. The defendants were several software companies offering "clones," look-alike programs that purported to be able to do precisely what Lotus 1-2-3 did, but at a lower initial cost. The reader wrote: "Lotus Development Corp.'s suits against 1-2-3 look-alikes may make good business sense but are little more than attempts to pull up the gangplank now that they are on board the ship. The problem is that they are trying to make it appear that their products are islands in a sea of unrelated personal computer products."[1]

The writer was by no means alone. Computer scientists at the prestigious Massachusetts Institute of Technology thought the issue important enough to picket the Lotus offices in Cambridge, Massachusetts. The picketing was led by two giants in the field: Marvin Minsky, founder of MIT's Artificial Intelligence Laboratories and a professor of electrical engineering, and Richard Stallman, developer of EMACS, a popular programming editor. In a style harking back to 1960s protests, the group chanted: "Put your lawyers in their place; no one owns the interface." A spokesperson for Lotus called the protest "silly," and said it represented an "ignorance of the realities of the marketplace."[2]

At one level, the suit was nothing more than one more step in the legal process refining exactly what aspects of software programs are entitled to copyright protection. In this case, Lotus claimed that three components of its program were so entitled: its interface, command structures, and source codes. But at a second level, the strong public response to Lotus's legal action suggests that thirty or so years into the information revolution, the computer community was not yet near a consensus on the protection to which software developers were entitled.

As this chapter will suggest, the tension in such cases is not solely between the interests of the two litigants but also between rights of the party seeking copyright protection and the needs of the society at large. This tension is expressed in the following question: Are certain elements of information technologies so critical to the continued evolution of the information revolution that our courts must think very carefully before agreeing to privatize and protect them, even where a clear case can be made that such protection had been extended in the past to noninformation products?

The story of three electronic spreadsheets—VisiCalc, Lotus 1-2-3, and Quattro Pro—and the efforts of their owners to protect them are instructive in this regard.

The world first heard about electronic spreadsheets in September 1979. An innocuous ad on page 51 of *Byte* magazine announced a new software product called VisiCalc and suggested that it could dramatically compress the time required for managing data. All the user had to do was enter numerical information in appropriate boxes and the program would automatically update all important calculations affected by these figures. VisiCalc was devised by two MIT graduates, Dan Bricklin and Bob Frankston. Bricklin got the idea from his calculator at the Harvard Business School: "I had my calculator, ran my numbers at home at night, and when I made errors, daydreamed about 'word processing' numbers so that I could recalculate them with a new assumption—say, 12 percent instead of 10 percent. My image was based on a calculator with a mouse and a heads-up display like a fighter plane so you could see the numbers."[3]

VisiCalc did not impress its early reviewers. One of Bricklin's Harvard Business School professors scoffed at it. Still, Frankston and Bricklin pushed on. They took their program to a fellow student, Dan Fylstra, who was selling game cassettes. Fylstra agreed to distribute the product through VisiCorp, a firm he set up on the West Coast.[4] He then took a prototype to Apple chairman Mike Markkula, who was less than enthusiastic. He was more interested in demonstrating his own checkbook-balancing program to Fylstra than in hearing Fylstra out about the benefits of VisiCalc.[5]

He was also less than prescient about the future of the electronic spreadsheet. Because of VisiCalc, one of his Burlington, Massachusetts, dealers was to become the most successful Apple dealer in the country at that time. The first copies of the program were shipped in October 1979. The developers of this new phenomenon were apprehensive about calling the new product a *spreadsheet,* the popular name by which such programs have come to be known.[6] The name VisiCalc was coined from its concept as a visible calculator.[7]

VisiCalc hit the market in a big way. In the annals of computer history, it will be remembered for its impact not only on the nascent software industry but on the nascent personal computer industry as well. As a software breakthrough, VisiCalc gave birth to the "what-if" kind of computer considerations,[8] allowing those responsible for business planning to compare a series of contingencies with an ease and facility never before possible. VisiCalc made important contributions to the personal computer industry in two major ways. First, by empowering the personal computer with forecasting capabilities, it pulled back planning functions from the people working on mainframes. Second, by giving a large new group of potential computer purchasers an easily understood reason to take the plunge, it dramatically expanded the overall market for personal computers. According to Frank Rose, a software analyst: "Before Visi-Calc, personal computers were toys—fun for hackers who liked to diddle with electronics but not suited to serious business. VisiCalc . . . was the product that ushered the personal computer into the American office. In the process, it wrested power away from the data-processing managers who controlled corporate mainframes."[9]

VisiCalc also helped jump-start the IBM-PC.[10] Given the fact that many people bought their first computer solely to access this new program, sales of all personal computers—Apple, its competitors, the IBM-PC, as well as its many clones—skyrocketed.

Million-dollar fortunes were made—and then lost—as the product soared in popularity and then sank into obscurity. For some unfathomable reason, possibly the euphoria of surfing on their wave of success, the developers of VisiCalc let an employee, a young Beta test manager named Mitchell Kapor, depart the company with a clearly established legal right to produce his own software that VisiCorp had declined to develop and market. Thus they contributed to their own demise. By 1984, one year after Lotus 1-2-3 was introduced, the price of VisiCorp stock plummeted from its high of eleven dollars a share to twenty cents a share. Over time Lotus 1-2-3 made millions for Kapor and launched the start-up of one of the industry's most productive and successful software companies, Lotus Development Corporation. Eventually Lotus acquired what remained of its predecessor, laying to rest the question of whether any ill-acquired proprietary information might have been transported away from the company.[11]

The fall of VisiCalc—intertwined as it is with the rise of the program that brought it down, Lotus 1-2-3—offers an interesting case study of the proprietary issue in computer software, an issue whose definition would lead to a complex series of court cases. Fortunately, or unfortunately, depending upon your perspective, VisiCalc was developed during the period in which the patent office did not favor patents for software, and it was not unusual for lawyers to steer their clients away from this alternative form of protection for spreadsheet inventions.

Nor was it clear whether copyright law applied to computer software, although the copyright office did accept software for registration with the understanding that there was some question about the legality of providing software copyright protection. Bricklin admitted that he and Frankston would have sought a patent had they thought it possible.[12] If they had, the owners of VisiCalc would have acquired a seventeen-year monopoly (others would have called it a stranglehold) on the development of such spreadsheets; competitors wanting to enter the field would have had to seek a license from them. Later events suggest that this would have severely retarded developments in the spreadsheet field.

Protection of Software Development

Part of the reason there is no certainty concerning legal protection of computer software is historical.[13] When computers first appeared, in the 1950s, the software (the instructions that tell the computer what to do) was sold as a part of the total package of equipment, including installation and maintenance of an operating system. Little attention was paid to the separate value of the software at this early state of development. Many thought that the big powerful machines were so expensive and so specialized in their largely computational function that the industry would consist of maybe a dozen manufacturers at most. As long as you received software when you purchased the hardware, few envisioned a day when software sales would develop into a stand-alone business. Indeed, in those days the operating software was included as a part of a computer's patent.

In the late 1960s, when computer manufacturers were required by the antitrust laws to "unbundle" their software and offer it separately from the hardware, lawyers were not at all confident of how legal rights of ownership and control should be asserted. At first, many lawyers expected the patent law to be an appropriate haven for inventors of computer programs to obtain a monopoly over their innovative work (truly new, original, and nonobvious) for enough time to allow recovery of start-up costs. The patent office shied away from issuing patents, however, in part because of the administrative burden. The copyright office (where only a modicum of originality is needed for protection) was more hospitable, accepting registrations subject to verification by the courts or by Congress that they were within their mandated authority in doing so. At the beginning, therefore, it was not at all certain that software would find protection in patents or in copyrights. So lawyers turned increasingly to the trade secrets law—a body of law designed to permit businesses to protect information that gives them a competitive advantage—but it is an alternative that requires the cooperation of the recipient in keeping the secrecy.

In the early 1980s three things happened that changed the picture drastically. In 1980 Congress enacted an amendment to the copyright law legitimating software copyright;[14] in 1981 the Supreme Court, in *Diamond v. Diehr*,[15] gave the patent office unequivocal permission to issue patents for certain kinds of computer software;[16] and, at about the same time, with PC-1 the IBM corporation entered the market for desktop personal computers, a market that had been dominated by Apple. Apple had encouraged the rather small coterie of users (often called "hackers") to write their own software and exchange disks in an open and collegial manner. This tradition arose in the academic environment, where computer programmers were supported by educational institutions whose primary function was to produce and share the fruits of research.

Thus when software for the personal computer entered the mass marketplace, the only protection available seemed to be trade secret licenses. As the distributors had no real relationship with those who acquired the floppy disks holding the program, however, the concept of an enforceable contract between the two was tenuous. The lawyers then came up with a questionable solution. The floppies were packaged with a "shrink-wrap" license, which purported to include all the provisos that might have been included in a contract negotiated between more or less equal partners; the user was warned that breaking open the plastic wrapping constituted acceptance of the terms of the contract.

Courts have questioned the validity of the shrink-wrap license, but software developers continue to use it.[17] They also claim copyright protection and file for patents where available. Indeed, in such a fluid legal environment, any prudent lawyer would seek all three forms of protection: trade secrets law, with a shrink-wrap license for mass-marketed software; patents, if the software was truly innovative; and copyright, in the absence of assurance that either of the other alternatives would provide real safeguards.

Software manufacturers continued to seek copyright registration, as the copyright office was hospitable. Thus when the Commission on New

Technological Uses (CONTU) asked a group of copyright lawyers whether the law should be changed to apply copyright law to computer software, there was a warm and positive response, as they already had a large investment in this type of protection. Indeed, one of the arguments put forward for retaining copyright as the legal regime of choice is that copyright lawyers have more skill dealing with computer software than do patent lawyers. Patent lawyers do not agree and continue to pursue patents for their clients quite diligently.[18]

Copyright procedures had to change to accommodate the protection of software that was marketed under a claimed protection of trade secret law. Copyright law traditionally covered intellectual work that was fully disclosed through publication (such as books, maps, and magazines) or public display in newsstands and galleries, inviting readers and viewers to see all of the product (such as sculpture and paintings).

Software developers marketed their products with a *source code* (the high-level language used by the programmer) transformed into an *object code* (language understood by the computer) that was incomprehensible to the ordinary user. According to constitutional mandate, copyright and patent protection was not designed to prevent disclosure to the public, but only to ensure a right to compensation in the form of a royalty or patent license fee. But in software design and manufacture, clearly the intent was to impose secrecy about the details of implementation. The copyright office cooperated, by providing that trade secrets could be blocked out in the source code submitted to the office and even, in some cases, that a product could be registered without any identifying material.[19]

Lotus and Look-alikes: The Interface Litigation

Once the dust had settled on the decades-long litigation to establish that object code and source code were well within the copyright rubric, the attention of the legal profession turned to the computer interfaces. There are several types of interfaces: (1) those that define the environment through which the user engages the computer's functions, such as menu commands; (2) those that permit software programs to be deployed by computer hardware; and (3) those that permit software programs to interact with one another. In this litigation Lotus has also played a leading role.

Not surprisingly, when look-alike challengers to Lotus 1-2-3 began to appear, Lotus executives and their lawyers were far more aggressive than their predecessors had been in protecting their interests. One of the early cases against look-alikes involved a competitor that advertised itself as being "designed to work like Lotus 1-2-3 keystroke for keystroke," "a feature-for-feature workalike for 1-2-3"—even advising that "users familiar with 1-2-3 can skip this chapter."[20]

Lotus sued, claiming copyright infringement. The defendant argued that only source code and object code were entitled to copyright protection, and that the user interface of Lotus 1-2-3 was utilitarian—like the functional layout of gears on a standard automobile transmission, the keys of a piano, or the configuration of controls on a musical instrument—and thus not subject to copyright protection.[21] The lawyers for Lotus countered that the intellectual effort and creativity required to create a successful interface was more difficult than converting the design to a code the computer could understand. Judge Robert Keeton acknowledged this valuable information asset, following a line of cases that had already determined that nonliteral elements of the computer software—the sequence, structure, and organization—could be protected by copyright.[22]

Indeed, according to Judge Keeton, were it not so, and the nonliteral elements of expression "merged" with the idea, leaving only trade secret law for protection, then the length of protection would be very short: "merely the time it takes to examine a program and then duplicate the nonliteral elements in a newly written computer program."[23] In a lengthy opinion, Judge Keeton concluded that the defendants had copied a computer interface—specifically, the menu command structure of Lotus 1-2-3—that was capable of being expressed in many, "if not an unlimited number of ways," and was very much a part of a copyrighted work.[24] One fledgling program spawned by the spreadsheet explosion, Microsoft's Excel, was cited in the opinion as a good example of an electronic spreadsheet that avoided infringment by using a different command structure. Judge Keeton rejected the arguments of the defendants that because Lotus's menu command structure was an essential and functional element, thus furthering the utilitarian aspects of the software, it was not qualified for copyright protection:

> It may be quite true . . . that things that *merely* utter work, such as the cam of a drill, are not copyrightable. It is not true, however, that every aspect of a user interface that is "useful" is therefore not copyrightable. For example, Lotus 1-2-3 is surely "useful." It does not follow that when an intellectual work achieves the feat of being useful as well as expressive and original, the moment of creative triumph is also a moment of devastating financial loss—because the triumph destroys copyrightability of all expressive elements that would have been protected if only they had not contributed so much to the public interest by helping to make some article useful.[25]

But there is a strong societal interest not treated in Judge Keeton's argument.[26] In the case of the "user interface" in particular, it is clearly in the interest of society for there to be only one system, or very few. Otherwise, every time an organization changes or upgrades its software, it must factor in not only the cost of the new equipment but the often very high cost of retraining its employees to use an entirely new system, adding to the cost of the product.[27]

Much of the public concern about judicial resolution of these cases is that they militate against industry standardization in the user interface. Unless the similarities are dictated by the restrictions of the particular industry segment to be served (as, for example, cotton growers),[28] judges hearing copyright infringement cases have tended to find for the plaintiff (the copyright holder) when there are such substantial similarities program to program that it could be said by the nonexpert to have the same "look and feel."[29] If a program could be designed so that the user group could access its features in a variety of ways, having the user press the same keys to bring about the same results has led to an assumption that actual copying did take place.[30]

However, users generally desire compatibility of programs, especially in a general category of programs. There is nothing more frustrating in network access, for example, than being unable to remember how you "sign off" from the particular program you have been using—that is, how you turn off the meter charging your account. Is the command QUIT, OFF, DISC (disconnect), SO (sign off),\Q (quit), LO (log off), or some other variation? Much damage can be done by having an icon of a container used as "storage" (save) in one program and "garbage" (delete) in another. One frustrated icon basher described the situation as follows:

Graphical user interfaces were ballyhooed as providing an intuitively obvious and consistent interface.

Yet some consistency breaks down when applications use different pictures for the same functions, even basic ones like opening a file or pasting from the clipboard. Maybe software makers feel compelled to use different icons. They do not want to risk infringing the possibly copyrightable look and feel of another package's icons or arrangement of them. Anyway, someone like me who uses a half dozen software packages could wind up mastering 150 or so icons, the hieroglyphics of the 1990's. I'd be as literate as an Egyptian seven-year-old from the time of the pharaohs. (*The Columbia Encyclopedia* informed me that there were only 604 Egyptian hieroglyphs. Most, it said, could be used in up to three different ways.) I fear that a fluent future user may have to master more than six hundred symbols . . . the latter will begin to make our screens look like Japanese or Chinese typewriters.[31]

By encouraging differentiated user interfaces, the law impedes the adoption of widely shared conventions, frustrating users, unnecessarily requiring programmers to reinvent the wheel, pushing up development costs, and inhibiting the compatibility that encourages a competitive marketplace. The challenge is to devise a legal system that encourages standardized user interfaces while rewarding human labor that leads to innovation and progress.

In attempts to accommodate the needs of PC users and software programmers who wished to design compatible programs, various strategies have been devised to standardize user interfaces. Each has its pitfalls. The most obvious was to convince the courts that the expression used in the interface design was so restricted by the use for which it was intended that it "merged" into the unprotectable "idea."[32] The second strategy is to convince the court that the similarity is due to a limited number of ways to accomplish the task and that the choice of command is dictated by necessity rather than by a desire to copy a competitor's choice of expression.[33]

A third strategy is defensive; companies would seek patents or copyright protection for all of their software in order to be able to cross-license with other companies those products that are needed to serve the marketplace optimally. However, this strategy does not serve small companies well if they do not have a sufficient storehouse of intellectual property rights of their own to offer in exchange at the bargaining table.[34] Another strategy, favored by a group of professors of intellectual property law, is to file *amicus curiae* ("friend of the court") briefs in computer software cases, urging a finding of "fair use" for decompiling[35] a computer code in order to study and understand the underlying uncopyrightable elements of the software (citing the applicability of section 102[b] of the copyright law, which excludes "any idea, procedure, process, system, method of operation, concept, principle or discovery").[36] Further, they argued, since decompilation was the only means of gaining access to the object code, the public would not receive "its fair part of the copyright bargain": the "opportunity to read and be inspired by the work and a free license to copy all of the ideas and processes embodied in it."[37]

A different strategy is exemplified by the efforts of the European Community (EC) to devise a new form of protection dictated by the needs of the marketplace. After much deliberation, the EC decided to recommend to its members changes in legislation to permit decompilation of computer object code for specified purposes when "indispensable to obtain the information necessary to achieve the interoperability of an independently created computer with other programs."[38] The directive specifically warns against such a decompilation right being used for the "development, production or marketing of a computer program substantially similar in its expression, or any other act which infringes copyright."[39] A similar rational and analytical approach has been carried forward in parallel by the U.S. Congress Office of Technology Assessment, with only modest legislative impact to date.[40]

A final strategy is to gamble reaping sufficient rewards from the marketplace to minimize the damage should later litigation not sustain your legal grounds. This was the alternative that Borland International, a competitor to Lotus, must have chosen when it issued Quattro Pro with a similar interface to Lotus 1-2-3, although its own proprietary version of the electronic worksheet was quite different.

When Borland brought out Quattro Pro, with two interfaces, one its so-called native or original interface, and the other an "emulation" interface of Lotus-1-2-3 commands, there was sufficient reason to believe that this simulation might be found to be a copyright infringement. The case was to be heard by the same Massachusetts court where Judge Keeton had made something of a habit of presiding over computer software infringement cases. By then, his decision discussed earlier had been roundly criticized by intellectual property lawyers as ignoring the elements in the software that are excluded by the statute from copyright protection or are already in the public domain.[41] He paid lip service to these exclusions but found sufficient evidence of copying to find Borland guilty of infringing Lotus's copyrights.

By the time Judge Keeton confronted the *Lotus v. Borland* controversy, decisions in other circuits had been rendered criticizing the sweeping precedent enunciated in *Whelan v. Jaslow*, the leading decision in the interface cases. That case involved a software program whose major intellectual contribution was an understanding of the dental profession and its mode of operation. The courts found the user interface designed for the dental profession to be copyrightable.[42] Later decisions determined that computer software must be broken down into its constituent parts before comparing similarities.[43]

In the Borland decision (which was settled for half a million dollars and withdrawal of the infringing product from the market),[44] Judge Keeton modified his sweeping rejection of the Lotus 1-2-3 clone, recognizing the need to filter out unprotected procedures, processes, systems, and methods of operation that are excluded from copyright protection. Nevertheless, he found that Borland had definitely infringed portions of the Lotus 1-2-3 interface but that a jury could find other noninfringing elements. The tests, according to Judge Keeton, were threefold: (1) to filter out the uncopyrightable elements from the copyrightable expression, for example, the idea, system, process, procedure, or method; (2) to determine whether the "expression" chosen to implement the noncopyrightable elements had been so essential that it could not be distinguished from the nonprotectable elements, and thus could be said to have been merged with one or more of them; and (3) having identified protectable elements of "expression," whether they represent a "substantial part of the allegedly copyrightable 'work.'"[45]

Judge Keeton found that Borland had copied the Lotus 1-2-3 menu commands, menu hierarchy, macro language, and keystroke sequences and that such elements were subject to copyright protection. By its own admission, Borland could have differentiated these commands from those used by Lotus, as its original interface was substantially different from that of Lotus-1-2-3. There were other elements Judge Keeton found to be functional and thus not copyrightable. He found his three tests to be consistent with those enunciated by the Second Circuit in a similar case involving user interfaces, and rejected the sweeping protection offered by the Whelan case while recognizing that the precedent it established was still good law in the Third Circuit until the Supreme Court decided to accept a user interface case.[46]

The Third Circuit follows the Whelan decision in upholding that only the idea behind the program belongs in the public domain and all else is expression, which can be protected by copyright. The Second Circuit rejected this approach in *Computer Associates v. Altai*.[47] While admitting that the "essentially utilitarian nature of a computer program further complicates the task of distilling its idea from its expression," the court commended the lower court for breaking the software into its component parts, "since each subroutine is itself a program and thus may be said to have its own 'idea.'"[48] Under this reasoning, it is necessary to sort out which ideas may be replicated while still avoiding replicating the ways in which these ideas are expressed.

The Ninth Circuit has gone even further in freeing the interfaces from copyright protection by determining that disassembly of object code is a fair use of a copyrighted work when used to gain access to unprotected elements, even though the "use triggers a misleading trademark display."[49] Sega Enterprises, Ltd., a Japanese corporation that developed and marketed video entertainment systems, developed a trademarked security system that required a compatible piece of software to unlock access to its Genesis Console, only to discover that the U.S. courts would permit decompilation of its object code by competitors in order to write games that would run on its console without a licensing agreement.[50]

On the West Coast, Apple Computer was pursuing litigation against Microsoft and Hewlett-Packard for use of what it perceived to be a proprietary interest in its popular windowing software. Although the case was somewhat more complicated than the Lotus cases, because it involved a license agreement between the parties to use some of the Apple software, nonetheless, in what has been touted by some intellectual property lawyers as "finally getting it right" the court held as a matter of law that only 4 of 150 or so elements in the software alleged to be infringed were sufficiently questionable to send to the jury.[51] In addition, after filtering out all of the licensed aspects, those residing in the public domain, those specifically excluded by section 102(b) of the copyright statute, and those dictated by the necessities of the functionality or by having become common practice in the industry, what was left would have to be "virtually identical," not merely "substantially similar," to constitute infringement. A 1985 decision predicting that the ultimate fate of software protection would be quite thin was justified.[52] The protection provided in the last series of cases (other than the Lotus litigation) seems virtually transparent. Perhaps after a decade of litigation under the software rubric, the emperor wears no clothes.

The Current Curious State of Litigation

Today the various circuits of the appellate system in the United States are in conflict over what portions of software can and cannot be protected by copyright. It is now well established that both the object code and source code can be protected from literal copying. Yet it is still not clear how much or how little of the visible command structure, the "look and feel" of the software, can be replicated by others in order to appeal to the user's preference for the familiar. Some courts are still struggling with perplexing principles that they find unworkable, while others are working hard to understand both the complexities of the law and the underlying economics of software production and marketing.[53]

No consensus has emerged among either lawyers or software programmers and developers over the optimum level of protection for software or under which legal rubric. It is not surprising that those involved in the original decision of CONTU, recommending the deployment of the copyright law for computer software, have lauded the efforts of the courts to conform the copyright law to the new technology,[54] commending the judges trying these cases for their increasing "computer literacy."[55] However, other lawyers find the case law over the last five years "collectively a mess."[56] Anthony Clapes, a leading proponent of copyright as the law of choice for software,[57] has roundly criticized the Altai case as a "legal Chernobyl," finding that "the court has tortured the copyright law into an unrecognizable unusable *sui generis* form of protection for software."[58]

The underlying problem is that the courts, while trying to address one of the major concerns of software programmers and users—achieving a compatible interface—have led the law into a corner where the "expression" left to be protected by the existing copyright law is *de minimis*.

By the time the courts have sorted out and excluded all ideas, processes, systems, procedures, and functionality dictated by the hardware or compatibility with other software, or derived from public domain, there may be little left to be protected under the copyright statute other than the right to decompile the object code. If that is arguably permissible under the doctrine of fair use or excluded from contract restrictions by virtue of preemption under the copyright statute,[59] then what remains are only those innovations that are so truly revolutionary, new, and nonobvious that they qualify for patent protection or that expression so different from any other that it is incompatible with common usage. This state of affairs may portend the end of an extended period of judicial ferment attempting to tailor existing legal concepts to an elusive and undefinable technology.

As I have noted, many in the software industry criticized Lotus when it first started filing infringement suits. Bricklin, who created VisiCalc, called the litigation "[t]he worst thing to happen to software, ever."[60] He found the use of compatible interfaces far too important for the health of the software industry to permit a monopoly over the functionality of popular programs: "We all borrow from the best of others. . . . That's what progress is all about."[61]

Scott Davis, a consulting engineer at the Digital Equipment Corporation, agreed, seeing an awful lot of waste in program writers trying to create variations on what have already been established as workable components. He preferred a situation in which the best interface came to be established as a standard, with programmers then free to direct their energies forward rather than backward: "What you want to do is build on what somebody else has built and not reinvent what was on the bottom."[62]

The concept of each generation standing upon the shoulders of previous generations is a long-standing tradition in the sciences. But scientists compete in a different environment, nurtured in research institutes and university laboratories, where salaries are more or less assured and professional rewards and recognition are meted out through an elaborate system that includes literature citations, research grants, and prizes. Software professionals work in a myriad of small and large software houses that rely for their financial health, if not their very survival, on the reactions of the marketplace to their most recent innovation.

The Special Importance of Computer Software

The legal controversy might have remained of small interest to the public at large, except for the substantial impact that computer software has upon our economy, our politics, and our social lives. Computer software, as essential today as steel production was to early-twentieth-century industrial states, constitutes the crown jewels of an information economy.[63] The healthy functioning of an information-based economy relies heavily upon computer software, not only for publishing manuscripts (the traditional province of copyright) but for running computer-aided manufacturing (traditionally the province of patent law), as well as our national transportation system, national defense, education, and a myriad of other national and local enterprises. There is hardly an aspect of modern life that does not depend heavily upon computer software.

A strong computer software industry is a major asset of the U.S. economy. Japan and the European Community, as well as Singapore and Australia, have targeted the software industry as critical for broadly based economic development. The American competitive advantage continues; over the last twenty-five years, the number of U.S. domestic software firms has quadrupled, and income has grown from $250 million a year to well over $100 billion in 1990, accounting for more then 40 percent of the global market for mass-marketed software.[64]

Because computer software is essential to most other sectors of the economy, it is considered a "driver technology."[65] It is software that makes possible computer-aided design of manufactured goods. Robotics, the brightest promise for increased productivity and quality control in manufacturing, can function no better than its software. Computerized communications systems facilitate the transfer of instructions, orders, inventory control, even diagnostics—not only for manufacturing firms but for service institutions as well. Such rapid and sophisticated communications permit us to deal effectively in an increasingly global marketplace. Computer software is critical to the takeoffs and landings of air carriers. News and entertainment are enhanced by complicated computer-assisted graphics. Administrative processes are expedited by computerized records systems; and administrative decisions improved through the use of modeling techniques.

The world economy, as Walter Wriston has observed, now operates on a twenty-four-hour "information standard" that disseminates data continuously to millions of computer terminals worldwide, which are used to make financial and market decisions. These decisions, in turn, through the magic of computers, almost instantly become part of the data stream circling the globe and informing the world economy.[66]

The stock market, long computer-dependent, is now computer-vulnerable as well. The precipitous drop in the stock market in the fall of 1989 was attributed primarily to selling waves dictated by widely used computer-driven analyses that automatically triggered sell orders when certain predetermined price levels were reached.[67]

Many of us have become personally dependent on our computers to help us manage our daily lives. We use WordPerfect, Microsoft Word, Ami Pro, or some other word-processing software for our correspondence. Quicken writes our checks, and Lotus 1-2-3, Excel, Borland's Quattro Pro, or some equally efficient spreadsheet, manages our financial affairs. We keep our calendars on Sidekick or Windows. We use electronic paintbrushes. We relieve our tensions with screen versions of solitaire and mah-jongg, Dungeons and Dragons, or Amazon. We may even have an F-15 fighter-pilot simulation on our hard drive.

Those of us who have attached modems to our personal computers may be exploring the frontiers of cyberspace, an electronic environment populated only by the computer-literate and their console cowboy pals. Those whose computer literacy is not founded in the requisite fanaticism may restrict themselves to hopping around on public networks like CompuServe or Prodigy, but millions of us are transporting messages electronically over the Internet to users far and wide across the globe for professional, political, and social purposes.

It is this ability of computers to speak to each other that makes compatibility of software so important. There are so many different protocols for getting into and out of these various software environments that we may be inhibited by technical barriers or just plain user incomprehension. For this reason, broadly based copyright protection seems ill suited for software. Other types of intellectual assets protected by copyright are works of art and literature, for which exact copying would be offensive, if not illegal, and which would lead to dull exhibitions in museums and repetitious readings in libraries and coffeehouses.[68] More important to the user of software is the ability of a standardized interface to access a number of different applications, as well as its ability to fit into a larger universe or networked environment. Compatibility with other operating systems, as well as other software applications, is necessary if the user is to deploy the computer as a gateway to communicate with other machines, telecommunications carriers, and software applications. While an exhibition of artists, each showing different techniques and work products, is pleasing, a cacophony of software programs all bleating out a different set of command structures not only boggles the mind but inhibits the user from migrating to different platforms.

On the other hand, allowing copying of interfaces in computer software leads to customer satisfaction and permits small entrepreneurs to concentrate on building on the platforms provided by major software houses, providing diversity in the marketplace and enhancement of applications for specialized groups of users. Harry Reinstein, former CEO of the Aion Corporation, finds it desirable for all interfaces to be open. Interfaces represent, at least in his view, a competitive point of entry critical to maintaining the competitive environment of the software industry.[69] It may be that the decompilation of code to understand the underlying functionality can be tolerated in the public interest as a necessary social value if some value has been added, improving the general state of the art. However, such a concept of fair use based upon a redeeming-social-value standard ignores the fact that the programmer who improves upon the state of the art has used valuable information assets that, in an information market, should demand and receive market value.

Those who espouse the concept of "freeware" oppose all types of protection, whether copyright or patent or trade secrets, as placing unnecessary burdens upon programmers, requiring them to go back to the beginning and redesign every system to which they would like to make an addition or add a refinement. They consider the legal requirements as excessively restricting developmental work, which must necessarily be expedited by the freedom to tinker with what has already been done, debug the programs, and alter them to improve their functionality for the particular user.

On the other hand, declaring a desirable interface public domain or requiring compulsory licensing at reasonable rates seems hardly fair to developers who have devoted huge amounts of time, resources, and personal commitment to the design of these now very attractive and desirable information assets. The more resources firms allocate to development, the higher the incentive to maintain the assets as proprietary and to derive income from monopoly control of the product. Thus we have the dilemma of trying to allocate fair compensation while assuring that everyone has access to the same building blocks.

In neither patent nor copyright law is the "sweat of the brow" important. Regardless of the amount of human labor invested, it is only the offer for sale of "copies," the payment of the license fee for use of the "invention," or the execution of a contract for the sharing of a "secret" that triggers legal protection for intellectual property. There should be some legally acceptable way to compensate aggrieved parties whose work product has been misappropriated while respecting the Supreme Court's recent reprimand that the "sweat of the brow" cannot be protected under the copyright statute.[70]

Critics of the freeware approach point out that what actually occurs in the sharing or unauthorized acquisition or piracy of information assets is the misappropriation and exploitation of intellectual work products without compensation to those who produced it. No one will challenge the right of gifted programmers who produce valuable information assets to share these assets with whomever they like or, indeed, to donate them to the public domain. But it must be noted that most programmers who do so derive income from other sources.

These are quite different circumstances from software programmers writing for the mass market, whose financial survival depends upon the numbers of disks sold or the number of bytes downloaded from an on-line electronic delivery service. There are many alternative devices for compensating the labor expended in producing information assets. However, in an information society the privatization of these assets in the competitive marketplace demands a mechanism for deriving a fair income from the exchange of these assets in that marketplace.

In the past such intellectual creativity has usually been embedded in a product whose very purchase ensured fair compensation to the person who had conceived such a use for it. In an information economy the intellectual productivity or information asset is often marketed and distributed disembodied from the product that will put it to use. Indeed, computer software can be marketed and distributed in electronic impulses that pass quickly and irretrievably over telecommunications lines to distant parts of the globe. Thus misappropriation law or unfair competition may offer a far better theoretical framework within which to analyze and identify miscarriages of justice than "copy," "secret," or "invention." Certainly there is room for innovation in the law as well as in the realm of manufactured products.

There is no guarantee to the creators of intellectual property or information assets that they will benefit from uses subsequent to that of the first purchaser. Case law currently stands at the point of not permitting unconscionable exploitation of the commercial value of another's work product. However, in our global village, even that legal distinction fails to protect innovators from infringing uses of their work products outside the jurisdiction of courts accessible to the innovator.

Are There Alternatives to the Deadlock?

Merely putting the three types of protection (patents, copyright, and trade secrets) together into a single unified administrative framework would have much to recommend it. Entrepreneurs and their lawyers would not have to seek multiple layers of protection in different agencies, different jurisdictions, and attempts to follow the lead of complex, often indecipherable court decisions. Requiring software innovators to settle on one kind of protection, as some suggest, would not be efficacious. Each system has weaknesses that would leave portions of the software without protection, and each has strengths that if incorporated into a unified system could contribute to a more optimum exploitation of computer software.

On the other hand, an entirely new paradigm might offer a kind of custom-designed protection, with less confusion than reliance upon the existing legal systems designed for the resolution of very different tensions. It might be more appropriate to think in terms of information assets rather than intellectual property. A legal system designed to prevent copying seems an odd model to use in an industry that provides the user with several copying programs as integral parts of every operating system. Indeed, the first thing that software developers recommend their customers do upon opening the package is to make a working copy of the disk, storing the original away in case the copy is damaged or lost. This copying is specifically permitted by the copyright statute.

As a next step we may copy the program to our hard disk. To use the program, we must copy essential parts of it to resident memory. There are programs we can buy that will help us download programs and data from remote data bases, and most programs we use allow easy saving or storing of our work product, in effect copying it from computer memory to a disk, hard or floppy.

In fact, while we can read a book or magazine article without going near a photocopy machine, there is very little that we do with a computer that does not involve copying in one form or another. Thus it would appear to be disingenuous of software sellers to claim shock at the exercise of this basic computer function. It would also appear to be in the interests of an information society to encourage copying rather than discouraging it.

A new paradigm could focus on the uses of information assets rather than the copying of intellectual property. We could avoid using copyright or patents or trade secrets. It would be necessary only to sort out which uses are permitted, which are prohibited, and which require compensation to be made to the originating party. These several categories can be sorted out into the following "uses":

- *Nonuse.* This would preclude literal copying of work product in order to compete with the creator.
- *Authorized Use.* Specifically sanctioned uses, such as for archival purposes referenced in the copyright statute, would be included, as well as all uses licensed by the proprietor of the software.

- *Misuse.* This category would entail all negligent behavior that results in damaging consequences that fairness dictates should be compensable through court action.
- *Abuse.* This category would cover all destructive behavior prohibited by statute and might entail criminal sanctions.
- *Unauthorized But Fair Use.* Such use would likely permit decompilation of code for teaching purposes and for the custom tailoring, for personal or institutional use, of the software by and for the benefit of anyone in lawful possession of the software.

And here are some of the principles that might govern a more coherent legal system for computer software:

1) Ease of registration without lengthy wait for verification that the innovation advances the prior state of the art. This is borrowed from the copyright law. Substantial similarity, as under the present law, would be sufficient to raise a presumption of infringement but would be rebuttable by a showing of independent creation.

2) Full disclosure, which is an underlying principle behind the constitutional origins of both copyright and patent law.

3) Deposit of source code with a receiving office (perhaps the copyright office), where it would be sequestered during the term of protection and released for public access at the end of the statutory period. Such secrecy is borrowed from the trade secrets law but would be available only for a limited period.

4) The statutory period should be long enough to recoup development costs and to provide incentive for innovation as well as reward for "sweat of the brow" that results in utilitarian software. The period should be designed to be short enough that leaving the licensing to the marketplace should not lock or preclude the use of desirable interfaces. A period no shorter than five to seven years and no longer than ten to twelve years would seem appropriate.

5) All actual uses would be subject to compensation during the protected period, except those deemed to be fair personal and noncommercial use or modification of programs to accommodate needs presented in the normal course of business use (using the software for the purpose for which it was intended).

6) Licensing of the uses of the software would be left to the marketplace. If there is sufficient showing of abuse of a dominant position, there are the antitrust laws to fall back upon. Alternatively, some procedure for challenging refusal to license and an appeal to a procedure for compulsory licensing of software interfaces that have become industry standards might be appropriate.[71]

Conclusions

Protecting the crown jewels of the information economy is expensive, time-consuming, and frustrating for lawyers, software programmers, managers, venture capitalists, and users. And it is not easy to determine how to treat computer software in an economy whose well-being depends upon a healthy software industry.

The traditional legal framework for balancing interests between public and private claims on intellectual property has served us well as agricultural and industrial societies. But the advent of an information economy has created tensions between these claims and an imbalance between public and private interests. Recently several interrelated factors have eroded the effectiveness of traditional legal regimes for protection of intellectual property: (1) the development of new communications and information technologies, which increase the number of participants in the marketplace, speed the delivery of their intellectual products and services, and facilitate the rendering of perfect copies; (2) the globalization of the marketplace; (3) the independent sale of information assets separate and apart from manufactured products; (4) the trend toward greater privatization of the information marketplace; and (5) the advent of computer software as a hybrid technology that straddles traditionally discrete areas of copyright, trade secret, and patent protection.

An information economy revolves around the compensated use of information assets. Labor is the value added to facts that are gathered and processed into transmittable data. Arguably, if the labor is not useful, it should not be compensated. If it is not only very useful but, in fact, is used, then it should be compensated by the marketplace or by some socially acceptable alternative, such as tenured professorships, Nobel Prizes, or government- or industry-supported research institutes.

Software programmers and their employers in the private sector are concerned that they will not be compensated for the work they do; venture capitalists are concerned that while no one comes along and offers to share their losses when projects fail, there are many who have claims on the fruits of their successes; users are concerned that the copyright law will push the programmers in the direction of making every system so different from every other one that we will have to decide on a lifetime computer system while still in our teens; even the judges are beginning to be concerned about their ability to cope with the fast-changing technology and the challenges in accommodating the law optimally to the needs of the software industry.

The law may currently be adequate, but adequate may not be good enough. Aside from the problems of harmonizing a global infrastructure for information transfer, it may be no more difficult to modify the present system than trying to persuade the rest of the world to adopt our present overlapping system of trade secrets, copyright, and patents.

Old laws are like hand-me-down clothes. They can be made to make do, but a new suit or dress might fit better, make us feel better, improve our performance. In accord, more than two hundred years ago, was Thomas Jefferson. Inscribed on the marble encircling the memorial to his role in founding the nation is the following:

> I am not an advocate for frequent changes in law and constitutions. But laws and institutions must go hand in hand with the progress of the human mind. As that becomes more developed, more enlightened, as new discoveries are made, new truths discovered and manner and opinions change, with the change of circumstances, institutions must advance also to keep pace with the times. We might as well require a man to wear still the coat which fitted him when a boy as civilized society to remain ever under the regimen of their barbarous ancestors.

Has the role of computer software become so critical to the economic health of the nation and the world that it deserves its own system of legal protection, extracting the optimum practices from existing legal regimes?

9

Who Owns Government Information?

Immediately after the November 1992 election, Scott Armstrong (a journalist), the National Security Archive (a private organization that collects government documents), Public Citizen, and several other public interest groups sought a temporary restraining order requiring the outgoing Bush administration to preserve its computer hard disks intact until the issue of whether it had a right to clear them was decided in court. These groups claimed that the information stored on these disks constituted public records and as such should have been turned over to the national archives for historical preservation. Another claim was that wholesale deletions of computer data by outgoing administrations might destroy evidence of wrongdoing. The injunction was granted and the matter set down for a full hearing.

This issue of who owns electronic data recorded in the act of governance had been going on for nearly two decades, since the revelation that segments of the Watergate tapes had been erased. Only days before Clinton's inauguration, the federal district court for the District of Columbia[1] held that computer records could constitute "public records" and be subject to the Federal Records Act[2] and mandatory disclosure under the Freedom of Information Act (FOIA).[3]

In counterpoint language, the decision also conceded that some of the records stored within the computer could constitute personal records of consultation with and advice to the president, protected under the Presidential Records Act from forced disclosure through use of the FOIA,[4] and that other records might be personal communications of the various staff members not subject to either statute.[5] The decision did make permanent the injunction granted in November, and White House computer hard disks were backed up on tapes before being cleared to make space for the new administration.[6]

What is obtainable through the FOIA is still not clear, but without this permanent injunction future court consideration of just what material had to be supplied could have been made moot by a late-night erasure party. Another issue left up in the air dealt with the form the disclosure must take when information is requested under the FOIA. Normally the cost to the requesting party is the cost of reproduction. For example, when Public Citizen, a consumer lobbying group, sought information from the Occupational Safety and Health Administration in July 1990, the agency supplied six boxes of computer printouts for a fee of about $3,000. But aside from the expense, the material as delivered was much harder to read, organize, and analyze than if it had been delivered on computer disks.[7] Many agencies still contend that the FOIA does not require handing over information in machine-readable media, even though it might be cheaper for the agency to deliver it and more convenient for the requesting party to receive and work with it in this form. The practice of supplying unwieldy rolls of printouts rather than machine-readable diskettes has been described as "the functional equivalent of paying off a $1,000 debt with unrolled pennies."[8] Many agencies still rely upon a 1984 ruling by the U.S. District Court for the District of Columbia that they are free to deliver public records requested in whatever form they find most convenient.[9]

Citizens will likely continue to press for information to be made available in a form compatible with the computers they intend to use in processing and utilizing the information, and it appears likely that the earlier decision will one day be relegated to the judicial dustbin as out of step with the demands and capabilities of new technology. In fact, some legislators may not be content to await the slow erosion of this decision through litigation and appeal. In 1991 Patrick Leahy, Democratic senator from Vermont, introduced legislation requiring agencies to publish in the *Federal Register* inventories of all information processed and stored in electronic form, as well as to make the *Federal Register* itself available to the public on-line.[10] A stronger effort was initiated in March 1993 when identical bills, with bipartisan support, were introduced in the House and Senate requiring the superintendent of documents to provide on-line access to the *Congressional Record* as well as the *Federal Register,* to make both available free to depository libraries, and to encourage all federal agencies to disseminate their electronic publications in the same manner.[11]

Although the Congress failed to act, the new administration sought to achieve the same ends though administrative procedures. On June 25, 1993, the Office of Management and Budget took a major step forward in the quest for improved accessibility to government information in electronic form. Sally Katzen, administrator of OMB's Office of Information and Regulatory Affairs announced that a newly issued OMB Circular A-130 "will help bring the Federal government into the information age," with a promise to both the public and the private sectors to employ all available resources to disseminate government information in a "timely and equitable manner," ensuring that both privacy and security interests would be well protected. However, the mandate is more reassuring that electronic methods will be deployed to improve accessibility on the same basis as other forms of communication and that special efforts will be made to devise tools to facilitate public access to government information.[12]

A related issue involves the way agencies come up with a figure to charge for collecting the requested information and passing it along. According to James P. Love, director of the Taxpayer Assets Project, of Princeton, New Jersey:

> Agencies are now pricing information according to the public's willingness to pay, rather than the cost of reproducing the information. In a period of perennial budget woes, federal information resources are increasingly seen as a source of income for agencies.
>
> This historic shift from a policy of pricing information at reproduction costs to the pricing of information according to willingness to pay, . . . has disastrous consequences for society. It represents a rejection of the principle of universal access to federal information, and it will lead to inefficient dissemination of information that has important social, economic and scientific value.[13]

In the past many agencies disseminated written materials to the public without charge or at a nominal cost. How the pricing is determined has very different consequences for public access to information. High charges can be absorbed by businesses but may be an insuperable barrier to fund-hungry community action groups.

On this most controversial issue, the new OMB Circular A-130 makes clear that government agencies are to recoup only the costs of reproduction of government information and not to derive additional financial resources to recover development costs, thus reverting to the historical norm. However, the circular also warns government agencies not to interfere or attempt to restrict secondary uses of information resources, leaving the private sector to take what it will and reproduce it either as is or with value-added services.

Not everyone agrees that a change to pay-as-you-go user charges that recoup development costs would have disastrous consequences. A substantial argument can be made for transferring the expense for public distribution to the private sector as a more cost-effective way of getting the information into the information marketplace, the idea apparently being that as long as the first recipient is given no proprietary interest in the information, the general public will soon be sharing it. However, the mechanism by which this information will be distributed to those without the financial resources to pay high government costs remains clouded in uncertainty. The fly in the ointment is that often many segments of the general public have no way of determining that released information has political importance until it has been examined and analyzed, and it may often be the case that the first recipient finds after examination and analysis that it is not in its own best interest to encourage wide dissemination of the information. This involves a policy issue not unlike the question of universal access to the public information transport system as more and more common carriers enter the competitive marketplace and the cross-subsidies that characterized the Bell system become threatened.

Reforming how government information is shared with the general public, a promise of the Clinton campaign, was complicated by worrisome communications problems the new administration found in January 1993. For instance, the telephone system in the White House dated back to what members of the computer-literate Clinton election staff saw as the dinosaur age. Clinton himself was heard to exclaim: "There's not even any E-mail. It's a yesterday place, and we need to make it a tomorrow place."[14]

The White House and Electronic Mail

To address the problem of how to make government deliberations more accessible to the voting public, the White House set out to start up an electronic bulletin board on which citizens could register their complaints and suggestions. Not surprisingly, the current inhabitants of electronic spaces were invited to participate in the planning of the new system, and the word spread far and wide throughout the Internet and other electronic mail systems. Groups of researchers formed ranks to try to help the fledgling but well-intentioned new advocates of electronic mail shape the new technology to better serve the needs of citizens.

A message went out over the Internet to multiple recipients, asking for comments about a new White House access through E-mail.[15] As might be expected, the response overwhelmed the electronic messaging system. A staff member attempting to manage the flood was downloading messages several times a day. By mid-March the 600 to 700 E-mail messages arriving each day were still far too many to answer on-line.

They were stored on computer disks and dispatched to the correspondence section of the White House, to be answered by letter, a step that certainly seemed backward. Some progress was being made, as the public had new access to the White House's ear, if not to its responses. Subscribers to CompuServe could reach the White House by the command "Go White House." Subscribers to MCI Mail could type "VIEW WHITE HOUSE," and America Online users could send mail to "Clinton Pz." Prodigy offered a "Write to Washington" E-mail service to enable its almost 2 million participants to reach their elected representatives as well as their president.[16] It must be remembered that all these efforts together reach only a small portion of the computer-literate population, who in turn represent only a small fraction of the total U.S. population.

While the aspirations of the Clinton administration to provide electronic mail service not merely to the White House but to the entire federal government were widely applauded, more experienced minds warned that it would not be an easy task. Andy Grove, the CEO of Intel, maker of the leading technology microprocessors for computer, warned:

> Two years ago we hardly used E-mail. Now we'd be paralyzed without it. It was an enormous and very complicated job to put this thing together. Then, as the traffic grew to 300,000 messages per day, the system got clogged up.
>
> I hear the Clinton Administration wants to create a unified E-mail system for the whole federal government. That's hilarious. We are not particularly incompetent at Intel, and we've been working on our little E-mail system for two years. Saddam Hussein will have free rein while the government tries to get its system to work.[17]

The Clinton White House has made some progress. By July 1993, although electronic messages were acknowledged electronically and still answered by "snail mail," direct electronic distribution of all White House releases was on-line. Furthermore, an opportunity to receive messages of special interest to a particular on-line recipient was also in place.

The Public Access Argument

The definition of information as a positive force in a democratic society can be traced back to James Madison in 1822 as president: "A popular government, without popular information or the means of acquiring it, is but a Prologue to a Farce or a Tragedy or perhaps both. Knowledge will forever govern ignorance, and a people who mean to be their own Governors, must arm themselves with the power knowledge gives."[18]

While Madison seemed to be talking not about the need of the people to be informed about what their government is doing but about the power of information to aid good governance, he saw governance as primarily the function of the people rather than of a remote and insulated bureaucracy. This made accurate information a prerequisite of self-government. Many later presidents who surely agreed with the need for accurate and reliable information in effective governance did not display any particular interest in sharing this information with the governed, in effect leaving the citizenry a disabled if not excluded participant in their own governance.

A later president accused of heading up a highly insular White House, Richard Nixon, would express an early warning about the dangers of an obsessively secretive government: "Fundamental to our way of life is the belief that when information . . . is systematically withheld by those in power, the people soon become ignorant of their own affairs, distrustful of those who manage them, and eventually incapable of determining their own destinies."

Two presidents divided by more than a century have similarly defined a basic philosophy underlying democratic government: free access to information is an essential ingredient of a properly functioning democratic society. Where disagreements have arisen is in whether any government should have a right to keep information about its own workings from the public, either to improve the chances of success for its policies or to protect its members from censure or, worse, for illegal or improper acts.

Producing Information for the Public

Regardless of the questions concerning motivation for withholding information that might affect their own fortunes, government agencies are in the business of producing mountains of information. There are at least four different types of government information: (1) that which is necessary for citizens acting in their roles as voters engaging responsibly in the electoral process; (2) that which is necessary for law-abiding residents in order to comply with the legislative enactments and judicial decisions that are the law of the land; (3) that which is mandated by the purpose for which the agency is established, for example, to provide medical, environmental, commercial, technical, or educational information, and (4) that upon which the very essence of the deliberative process rests, and which cannot be collected reliably and accurately in the private sector, such as census data and sensitive economic data—necessary in the aggregate but damaging or invasive of privacy if disclosed with identifying attributes. Such information assets appropriately fall within the public domain.

The collection of information was a primary concern of the founding fathers and one for which they were prepared to pay a modest amount of money. One of the first acts of the newly constituted U.S. Congress was to organize a census for 1790. The second statute enacted by the Second Session of the First Congress on March 1, 1790,[19] provided for the counting of inhabitants of these United States, commencing on the first Monday of August next and allowing for nine months to collect "accurate returns of all persons, except Indians not taxed."

Two hundred years later the price of conducting the census had magnified many times over, as had the amount of information collected on the inhabitants of the United States. The population had increased from 3.9 million to 248.7 million, and the bill from learning this fact together with others was close to $2.6 billion, to collect basic data from the nation's 250 million residents. More detailed information was obtained from 17 percent of the population, going beyond age, race, and sex to ask residents about their educational levels, how much they earn and spend on housing, and how far they commute.[20]

The information obtained is critical to determining which states gain and which states lose congressional representation as the number of Congressmen remains fixed at 435 in the House of Representatives. It is also critical in determining how much states receive in funding for various federally sponsored programs. Businesses use the data for strategic planning. Direct mail marketers find the census data a valuable resource, as they seek as much information as possible about their potential markets. Thus the news that the 1990 census data would be available at a modest cost on CD-ROM was met with considerable enthusiasm by direct mail marketers.

The 1990 census spawned a new industry, one that allows a cross-referencing of geographic and demographic information. Advancements in information technology and the widening use of computers have made the 1990 census "the first population census that could be manipulated on personal computers." These laser disks provide the detailed information from all fifty states that was provided by each state for the purposes of redistricting.[21] The series provides a computer-readable map and geographic database covering all 3.6 million square miles of the United States.

In the 1960s, challenged by the opportunities provided by the new availability of computer technology, the National Library of Medicine initiated a new service, the Medical Literature Analysis and Retrieval System (MEDLARS), a computerized system for storing, indexing, updating, and retrieving medical bibliographical data. The core of the system consisted of the MEDLARS tapes, on which were stored citations and abstracts of 2 million articles from approximately 3,000 medical and scientific journals published throughout the world.[22] Later, direct access to the MEDLARS database was made available on a subscription basis through Medline, the NLM's on-line terminal reference retrieval system. The MEDLARS tapes were made available for purchase through the National Technical Information Service at a cost of $50,000 each, an effort designed to recoup some part of the approximately $10 million of tax money invested in establishing MEDLARS and to allow private information vendors to compete with NLM if they wished to buy the tapes.[23]

In 1975, the SDC Development Corporation, which neither subscribed to the Medline nor offered to purchase the MEDLARS tapes, sought to gain possession of the tapes through an application under the Freedom of Information Act. The legal question posed for the courts was whether the complete reference library of medical writings and publications accumulated and stored in the NLM database constituted "agency records" for the purposes of the statute.[24] If so, the tapes should be made available for a nominal charge based upon direct costs of duplication.[25] The SDC sought a duplication of the Medline tapes, including "a complete copy of each and every updating tape as soon as each is prepared." For this service, the SDC offered to pay only $500, which it estimated to be sufficient to cover the cost of duplication. After due deliberation in both the U.S. district court and the U.S. appellate court, it was decided that such a comprehensive database was not an agency record for the purpose of the FOIA, and NLM could seek to recover its costs in producing this public service, rather than simply the cost of duplicating it, by charging the $50,000 price it had decided upon as proper.[26]

At the time of oral argument, the lawyer for the NLM admitted that no institution had ever paid the $50,000 charge for a set of tapes, although the NLM had exchanged the tapes with universities and foreign governments for valuable assistance in the cataloging, indexing, and abstracting of medical publications to update the database. Thus MEDLARS was hardly a big money-maker for the NLM. However, it was providing a public service that was not then available in the private sector. Since then a large number of special purpose databases have been developed both within and outside the NLM, serving a vast and rapidly growing health care sector of the economy.

Political philosophers have cited the words of James Madison to justify efforts to obtain more access to information generated by the government. But until the enactment of the FOIA, there had been no statutory mandate offering judicially enforceable procedures for compelling government agencies to release information to the public.

The legislative history of the FOIA reflects this deep concern about the ability of the American people to obtain information about the internal workings of their government.[27] The issue in controversy in the NLM case, however, was not whether the public could be denied access to such information but whether a private-sector competitor could use the FOIA to acquire at nominal cost and in convenient form information to be sold at a profit in the private sector. Clearly, the court found, the public disclosure provisions of the FOIA were directed toward information dealing with the decision-making procedures of the various governmental agencies,[28] whereas the primary purpose of the NLM was to collect medical information, organize it, and make it available to the public. Further, the issue of governmental secrecy, the issue that gave birth to the FOIA, was not involved. The articles and data on the bibliographic tapes all came from published sources, available in print to anyone who wished to compile them.

MEDLARS today offers access, twenty-four hours a day, to over twenty-five databases and more than 13 million bibliographic records.[29] The original Medline contains more than 5 million bibliographic references of research, clinical practice, administration, policy issues and health care services from over 3,500 international journals. Nonsubscribers can request searches at more than 2,000 universities and hospitals across the country. About 6 million searches are conducted on the NLM's computers within the United States and through a cooperating network of international partners in nineteen countries.[30] In 1992, more than 400,000 articles were indexed for Medline, and the access codes available for searching by computer reached 60,000.[31]

The NLM's family of databases covers, among other subjects, information on cancer, toxicology, chemical data, dental research projects, health administration and economics, bioethics, the history of medicine, AIDS, health organizations, population, and its original biomedical service.[32] Sources include journal articles, other serial publications, audiovisual materials, software, technical reports, and monographs.

The concern over the appropriate role for government-disseminated information would not lie dormant for long. In 1986 the criticisms of the private sector were echoed by a congressional committee chaired by Congressman Jack Brooks, who criticized the NLM for licensing use and restricting redistribution of medical research literature.[33] According to

the committee's analysis, there is no disagreement that some information services are "inherently governmental" while others might be better
left to the private sector.[34] The real dilemma, heightened by the advent
of electronic information systems, is to find the middle ground between
the two and to devise some methodology for determining at which end
of the scale various kinds of information rightfully or most efficiently
belong. There is no question concerning the right and, indeed, responsibility of an agency to use electronic means for accomplishing its own
internal purposes. However, according to the committee report, it
should not be tempted, just because it has the ability to provide an electronic service, to engage in competition with the private sector on that
basis alone:

> An agency should take care not to exploit the power that is inherent in
> electronic data systems by providing a nonessential service to the pub-
> lic simply because the capability to provide the service exists. This
> does not mean that an agency must avoid all possible competition with
> the private sector. Rather, an agency that unavoidably competes with
> the private sector in offering information products and services must
> compete fairly. Fair competition means that an agency should limit
> the services that it offers to the public and should leave the private
> sector to provide additional value-added services.[35]

In essence, the golden rule enunciated was that a government agency
should: (1) be certain that it has fully absolved its responsibility to provide for public dissemination of data generated; (2) avoid any arrangement that allows monopoly power over the information; and (3) most
emphatically encourage the private sector to repackage and "enhance
the information so that it can be sold at a profit."[36]

Other Government-Operated Database Access

Many government agencies have a primary responsibility for collecting,
archiving, or distributing information. Still, the arguments for and
against distribution by governments of information they generate continue unabated. By the mid-1980s government databases constituted 20
percent of the top fifty databases, but the government generated only
5.92 percent of the revenue produced from database searching.[37] This
trend toward privatization of information dissemination has accelerated
in recent years.[38] Still, the U.S. government maintains over four hundred
computerized databases.[39] Many of these are also available on-line

through commercial information providers, such as Knight-Ridder and Dow Jones, who turn a profit buying government data on magnetic tapes at modest prices, loading it onto mainframes, and offering it to their subscribers. Some agency files containing classified or confidential information, however, such as social security numbers or household incomes, may be searched only by agency personnel.

Access to only a few of these databases is free, except for the cost of a long-distance modem call; but the free access tends to be to highly specialized PC-based bulletin board systems operated by some highly motivated and computer-literate government worker. Often, one must be among the cognoscenti even to learn of the existence of such bulletin boards.[40]

Researchers can obtain access to vast information resources only if they can identify the right telephone number to call. The available information ranges from meteorological data, for example, from the National Oceanographic and Atmospheric Administration's Climate Assessment Bulletin Board, to the latest figures on housing starts, textile exports, and lumber consumption from the Department of Commerce's Economic Bulletin Board.

Philosophy of Access to Government Information

Electronic access to government information became a major policy issue when the Reagan administration issued a controversial proposal to prevent government agencies from providing on-line access, restricting the federal role to that of wholesaler of information.[41] Under the proposal, agencies collecting data would have to sell their work product to private companies, who could then make it available on-line to the general public—for a fee with a profit margin built into it. As well, federal agencies would be required to forgo developing their own information systems that would compete with private systems.

Members of the public who were aware of the proposal were irate. In particular, PC users with modems saw the policy directive as an outrageous attempt to block an excellent opportunity to use new technology to extend public participation in the nation's business. Hundreds of letters flooded the Office of Management and Budget, the agency that had issued the proposal. The protests came from a wide spectrum of sources—farmers, librarians, patent attorneys. From the nonprofit sector alone came more than forty public interest organizations, ranging from the Consumer Federation of America to the National Education Association, all claiming a public right to inexpensive on-line access to government information. The commissioner of the federal Bureau of Labor Statistics also registered a complaint.

According to Jaia Barrett, assistant executive director of the Association of Research Libraries: "Instead of taking advantage of the technology to improve public access, the administration's approach is going to throw up barriers. If [the proposal] had been in effect when the photocopier was invented, [government agencies] would have been prohibited from selling photocopies to the public."[42]

A coalition of PC users sprang into action to defeat the proposal. They faced a formidable opponent, one of the most powerful lobbying organizations in Washington: the trade association representing the Information Industry Association (IIA). Founded in the late 1960s, the association lobbies for the political interests of more than 500 high-tech information companies, including publishers, database companies, telephone and telecommunications companies, and financial information companies. Two primary goals motivate IIA members: to protect their intellectual property rights to the information they sell and to prevent the government from offering on-line information databases to consumers. In congressional hearings on copyright, Steven J. Metalitz, vice president and general counsel of the IIA, warned that the ultimate losers, were the bill to pass, would be the American public, who would find fewer choices and less innovative options available to them in their search for current, complete, and accurate information.[43]

The optimum policy alternative for marketing government information, whether by directly available consumer access or through private entities, is not entirely clear. The IIA represents a sector of the U.S. economy that is growing at an average of 20 percent per year. Thus it is a prime candidate for special treatment by a government anxious to improve the competitive position of the U.S. in the world economy.

In addition, the IIA claims that government electronic publishing constitutes a subsidy that costs taxpayers too much and that it leads to abuses through the bureaucratic control of information. The debate is far from over, as the IIA's opponents argue that what the government collects belongs to the people and should be made available to them for free or at the cost of duplicating the information, for they have already paid for it.

George Mickelson, governor of South Dakota, is a good example of what an irate citizen can accomplish. He became indignant when a staff member was told that it would cost hundreds of dollars to obtain information from a Department of Agriculture database because it was available only on-line through a contractor (the Martin Marietta Corporation). Mickelson asked South Dakota Senator Tom Daschle why taxpayers, who had already paid for the USDA to compile the information, should have to pay again to retrieve it. Mickelson's office was offered a low-cost account on the Department of Agriculture's database. His actions energized dormant forces on Capitol Hill, where other representatives echoed his concerns over the government's electronic information policies.

In response to the widespread opposition to the Reagan privatization proposal, the new Republican administration under Bush withdrew it. However, privatization of many government databases was already progressing. The only difference in policy was that, although agencies were not prohibited from developing on-line access to their treasure troves of information, most were not encouraged. Nor were they allocated funds for the expensive transfer of paper documents to machine-readable form. Only agencies demonstrating a high priority of access from private commercial interests willing to pay fees for the cost of upgrading the system of delivery were encouraged to transfer their data to machine-readable form.

As examples of the divergent philosophies on pricing policies, consider the efforts of the Securities and Exchange Commission compared to those of the Environmental Protection Agency.[44] The SEC project to provide Electronic Data Gathering, Analysis, and Retrieval, a $50 million system, was designed to sell the record filings of corporate profit statements and ownership at market rates through a private contractor. By contrast, the EPA's Toxic Release Inventory was made available on-line directly from the government, at below-market rates and subsidized by general tax funds. Mandated by the 1986 Superfund law, the EPA system is part of a public education project intended to encourage public access to information on toxic materials. There is an incentive, therefore, to sell the tape at a low cost to private companies in order to broaden dissemination. But the database companies that might be the private-sector distributors of such information claim that the government is providing so much value added that there would be no market for the private sales. Private-sector lobbyists protest that such government-funded efforts undermine entrepreneurial activities.

How can we distinguish those on-line activities in which the government should be providing the product to the end user from those where we ought to rely upon the private sector? In some cases where the agency retains the function to itself, it farms out the work to private-sector contractors. In some cases the private sector simply does not have the incentive or the capability to compel the collection of data necessary to provide accurate inputs—as, for example, in the collection of census data. In some the market is too small or undeveloped to attract private capital.

Under the Clinton administration, the tide may turn to a more favorable consideration of initiatives by all government agencies to meet their statutory mandates by offering on-line access to information. Jerry Berman, representing the views of the American Civil Liberties Union, has recommended that the government should provide an "electronic information safety net."[45]

How President Clinton intends to address the problem lies hidden in an ambiguous statement that purports to satisfy both public-access advocates and private-sector entrepreneurs:

> Government information is a public asset. The government will promote the timely and equitable access to government information via a diverse array of sources, both public and private, including state and local governments and libraries. . . . We are committed to using new computer and networking technology to make this information more available to the taxpayers who paid for it. In addition, it will require consistent Federal information policies designed to ensure that Federal information is made available at a fair price to as many users as possible while encouraging growth of the information industry.[46]

Conclusions

It seems unlikely that proposals to privatize all government information distribution would meet with enthusiastic endorsement. Whether any lessons can be learned from past experience, other than that the gathering and distribution of information is best achieved through a cooperative arrangement between public and private sectors, is not clear. That argument remains to plague us as we strive to become a more efficient and effective information economy.

What is clear is that the public is schizophrenic in its attitudes as voter, taxpayer, consumer, and entrepreneur. Attitudes appropriate for one mode of behavior seem to conflict with those of another. As voter, the public would like greater opportunity to participate in the public dialogue. As the 19 percent vote for third-party candidate Ross Perot in the 1992 election would seem to underscore, the electronic town hall has some appeal. The public would like to reduce the financial burdens it bears, both in its taxes and in the consequences of an ever-growing national debt. But as consumers, the public feels entitled to virtually free access to information that its government has collected and that will help it make intelligent purchases, including purchases of medical services. As entrepreneurs, the public is happy to rely on government agencies to collect economic data essential to national competitiveness and equitable access to markets.

How public information is to be made available to the public and in what form remains a subject for much debate and disagreement as we move more and more rapidly into the information age. Computerized databases offer the opportunity to access information quickly from dispersed locations all over the country—from desktop, laptop, or handheld computer communications devices or public work stations deployed in libraries or public kiosks like telephone booths. Which of these services will be offered by the public sector and which by the private sector requires a delicate balance between the role of the government as a collector and distributor of information and as a regulator of the information marketplace. At the bottom line is the question of how much the public, as voters, is willing to allocate in taxes to public dissemination of information and how much it is willing to pay as purchasers of information in the information marketplace.

The future offers a new level of on-line interactivity, permitting unprecedented citizen feedback. Models of interactive public discussion abound on radio talk shows, television town meetings, and computer conferences. How the information marketplace will evolve with respect to government information is not decided. Some representatives of the people may be less than enthusiastic about deploying a technology that facilitates direct democracy and makes them relics of an age when this country's highly dispersed and disaggregated rural population could not participate directly in government affairs. Representative government is a form of communication system uniquely suited to its historical purposes. How to transform governance in an age of instantaneous and simultaneous information transfer to a population accustomed to having the press distill and process its information is a daunting task.

Many users of electronic network services have found them particularly suitable to democratic discourse. They are not likely to forgo usage of these new tools for democracy. How they will evolve in the future will be determined by what users and voters demand.

CONCLUSION

Information as an Asset: From Personal Autonomy to Public Access

As the previous chapters have suggested, controversy over the owner-ship and control of information is rampant today. Decisions redefining the role of information in our society are taking place in a variety of venues. Many of the decisions are taking place in the courts, where indi-viduals (such as Willis Mog and Scott Armstrong), corporations (such as Lotus and American Express), or groups (such as Public Citizen) are challenging established law governing access to and use of information. Some of the decisions are taking place through exercise of legislative powers by state legislators and congressional representatives (such as Ed Markey and Constance Morella). Many others are taking place through the decisions of state law-enforcement officials (such as Attorney Gen-eral Robert Abrams of New York), state public utilities commissions, and federal administrative agencies (such as the Federal Communications Commission or the Federal Trade Commission). Yet another venue for decision making is within corporate offices of vendors of electronic information services (Prodigy, CompuServe, or America Online), trans-porters of information (MCI, Sprint, AT&T, Bell operating companies, television and radio stations, and cellular services). And finally, the will of individual users is exerted with vehemence in both public and private networked environments.

Since the case histories in this book were compiled, initiatives have continued to proliferate. Most disturbing to designers of multimedia products is the granting of a patent to Compton's New Media of Carls-bad, California, covering what many perceive to be almost all databases using more than just text to retrieve information, entitling Compton to receive royalties from all its competitors.[1] On the other hand, the U.S. government is protesting the efforts of the Japanese to amend their copyright law to permit competitors to "reverse-engineer" (decompile) computer software for the purpose of designing competitive products without paying a royalty.[2] In Europe the EC has issued a directive to its member states to extend the copyright coverage of computer software to seventy years to accommodate the longer lives of "authors,"[3] while John Perry Barlow, a lyricist for the rock band the Grateful Dead and co-founder of the Electronic Frontier Foundation, has written rather persuasively that everything we know about intellectual property law is wrong in the real world and must be changed.[4] Barlow acknowledges the need to find viable ways of compensating creators of information assets, like himself, but some legal scholars are promoting a stronger tilt in the direction of placing information assets in the public domain in order to assure the widest dissemination of knowledge serving the public interest.[5]

In the Library of Congress, where registered copyrighted works are required to be deposited, the librarians have been wrestling with representatives of the Information Industries Association to reach an agreement on how to make CD-ROMS available to public users while still permitting the owners to prohibit electronic downloading of the easy-to-copy, easy-to-reuse data for other than private research and study.[6] Public carriers have also been scrambling to put their own information access policies into place, as evidenced by the groundbreaking effort of Pacific Bell to lead the parade of the Regional Bell Operating Companies into promulgating new customer privacy policies.[7]

Privacy proponents are claiming an absolute right of private citizens to deploy the most sophisticated encryption techniques on the information superhighway in order to deny access to their information assets to any potential intruders, while the U.S. government proposes an encryption standard that will allow its law-enforcement agencies to eavesdrop on all traffic—collecting, aggregating, and comparing the data for evidence of wrongdoing.[8] In the Congress, Senator Paul Simon has introduced legislation to establish a Privacy Protection Commission (something most European nations already have) to serve as watchdog against unauthorized privacy intrusions by the federal government and to provide leadership in the protection of information assets by the private sector.[9]

The Clinton administration did not rest on its laurels after achieving approval of the North American Free Trade Agreement and the General Agreement on Tariffs and Trade, both with assurance of reciprocity in the respect of intellectual property rights. These efforts are major milestones in the international application of protective principles for information trade. Guiding principles have also been announced for the development of a National Information Infrastructure (NII)—thought by some to mean merely the construction of new high-speed data highways[10] and by others to cover all the constituent components of a national information society.[11] In January 1994, Vice President Albert

Gore delivered the policy statement in Los Angeles to the Television Academy, clearly a gesture in the direction of private-sector dominance in the design and deployment of the information superhighways but one that purports to preserve public-sector concerns in its growth and development. The five principles asserted were (1) encouragement of private investment (primarily by removing regulatory impediments); (2) preservation of competition; (3) open access to the network (through uniform standards); (4) universal service (to be assured primarily by the private sector); and (5) flexible and responsive government.[12] Public interest advocates and users of the Internet fear that the emphasis will be on "infotainment" and "edutainment" rather than on social justice and politics.[13] The Commerce Department, through its National Telecommunications and Information Administration, was designated to follow up with a massive examination of how the government could become more flexible and responsive. A special working group was set up to address changes in the copyright and patent laws to encourage traffic on the NII, but geared more toward the fine-tuning of an existing legal structure than the massive overhaul proposed by Barlow.

In the courts, fine-tuning was also taking place to try to fit the many new pieces of information technology into the existing legal maze. In the ninth circuit, the Department of Justice was appealing the success of Ms. Moser, the Oregon chimney sweep who persuaded the lower court to declare unconstitutional the law prohibiting her use of telemarketing technology. The same court upheld the right of the Government Printing Office to refuse free access to its electronic slip opinions of the Supreme Court by a private bulletin-board operator, a service offered for a fee on a federal bulletin board.[14] Microsoft enjoyed a major victory in uncovering and convicting the piracy of 25,000 bootlegged copies of MS-DOS valued at $1.8 million, while a New York State statute governing computer tampering was used to curb the excesses of MJL Design employees, who had used a computer virus to shut down a business with which they had a payment dispute.[15]

The line between the public and the private domains of information is a moving target and will remain so for the foreseeable future, until we begin to see clearly what ethical values we choose to impose and which guiding principles we are prepared to follow. Until then, the legal infostructure will remain an impenetrable and irrational thicket of sometimes irrelevant and often unenforceable laws.

The opportunity to participate in the decisions that will govern uses of information is available to all who are willing to take it. Griping to friends over the dinner table about the intrusions of telemarketing, junk mail, or unauthorized use of one's purchasing habits and medical records will get one nowhere. Speaking out, like Carl Oppedahl and Walter Baer, or expressing outrage, like Justice Brandeis, Judge Bork, and Arthur Ashe, can influence the direction the law will take. More time-consuming is the laborious and deliberative effort to carve out new ways of thinking about information (like the group of intellectual property lawyers filing *amicus curiae* briefs in computer software cases), efforts in the European Community, and working out codes of ethical behavior within user groups and networked communities. These processes are taking place all over the world as we strive to achieve the necessary consensus that serves as the underpinning of a changing legal infostructure.

Three areas of the law—First Amendment rights, intellectual property rights, and privacy rights—have been asked to shoulder the burden thus far in determining when private assets in information are to be recognized, when they are to be offered the protection of copyright or patent law, and when ownership or creator's rights must give way to competing public priorities: the societal need for a free flow of information, the interoperability of a variety of systems, or a personal need for privacy. It is instructive to remind ourselves of the traditional concerns of these three areas of law, so that we can discuss more fully the new concerns they must begin to address.

First Amendment law, which dates back to the founding of our nation, was made part of our Constitution to protect the right of private citizens to criticize their government without fear of punishment. Since the press represented the major nongovernmental source of information for the members of the society, about one another and about their government, it was inevitable that the First Amendment would help establish a flourishing fourth estate. Not surprisingly, First Amendment law inherently tends to favor an unregulated and unrestricted marketplace of information, even in the face of other competing considerations.

Intellectual property law originated much earlier. British copyright law, for example, dates back to the Statute of Anne, enacted in 1709.[16] In principle, intellectual property law was intended to provide incentives to innovators to release their work products to the public in exchange for limited monopoly interests. Copyright law was established to grant monopolies to "authors" for original expression and patent law to "inventors" of innovative ideas with commercial value. These statutes, therefore, restrict the marketplace from appropriating and exploiting the creative expressions or innovative ideas of others.

Privacy law consists primarily in the protection of that private space surrounding one's person into which outsiders should not be permitted to penetrate. Its origins date back to common courtesy and social mores that respected the need for private spaces, reflected in the Fourth

Amendment's prohibition against search and seizure. As a legal principle embodied in statutory law, its underpinnings arise from a concern about the intrusive capabilities of photography in the last decade of the nineteenth century. Although it is not entirely clear that all intrusions into a person's private space are to be forbidden, and if not, under what special conditions they should be allowed, it is clear that there is at least some area of privacy that should be shielded against invasion, in at least most cases. One protected area has been articulated in the old saying that "a man's home is his castle."

Not surprisingly, privacy law generally works against the interests of the marketplace. Those who would invade privacy do not defend their actions by claiming a special thirst for intrusion. Rather, the argument is made that information, to be reliable and useful to the society at large, must be complete. Those who defend privacy argue that the gain is not to the society as a whole but to the commercial interests of those with the skill and imagination to find a market for completely aggregated information on any subject.

Given the fact that these three areas of the law established themselves well before questions about the value of electronic-mediated information arose, they often say little or nothing about many of the most pressing current issues regarding information as property. For example, the First Amendment, concerned as it is with freedom of expression, says little about the right of access of individuals or the press to information sources.

While intellectual property laws offer multiple layers of protection for commercial products that are creative, innovative, and unusual, they offer little or no protection for data that has simply been collected and warrants little more to its purchaser than that it is complete or uniquely organized. Moreover, despite the efforts of some courts to carve out a "sweat of the brow" theory upon which to pin the hopes of information entrepreneurs who have expended great effort and financial resources on developing new uses for data aggregations, and new ways of collecting and organizing the data to best serve those uses, the Supreme Court has rejected this effort to incorporate compensation for "value added" under the copyright regime. Last, efforts to protect computer software, the most useful and utilitarian component of the information revolution, seem to founder upon the judicial efforts to cram it into existing intellectual property pigeonholes. Privacy law offers protection primarily against government intrusions upon privacy, but rarely against commercial interests that intrude upon hearth and home to collect secrets of value in the marketplace.

If we are to continue to rely primarily on a private information marketplace to gather, store, manipulate, process, and distribute information, then it seems we must develop a realistic system of valuing the work involved in these various information functions and fairly compensate those whose livelihood depends upon such endeavors. This conclusion is inescapable, unless one wants to think in terms of a society in which such efforts are the province of the government rather than the marketplace.

There seems less and less question that it is in the interests of society that the wealth of information assets in dispersed locations and in difficult-to-access forms be gathered and organized, especially now that these assets can be accessed, analyzed, and retrieved with the speed and ease that electronic-based media allow. These are costly endeavors. It is a fiction, devised by those whose interests are best served by a more sharing society, that information wants to be free. Users may want it to be free—and in the short run, much can be saved by denying compensation to those who have devised the systems and done the work—but if we as a society do not make sure that providers are compensated for their efforts, the information age may turn out to be a short-lived footnote to history.

As suggested earlier, there are mechanisms other than marketplace economics for distributing information and the wealth that accrues from its use. However, in what we call an information economy, we have chosen, perhaps not entirely knowledgeably, the marketplace as the most desirable mechanism for distributing information in developed economies.

Second, if we are not to place unnecessary obstacles in the path of progress, we must move quickly to deal with the myriad privacy issues that these new technologies raise. The databasing and centralization of medical information, for example, will benefit both patient and practitioner, with a parallel capability for harm to each; the speedy development of a central medical registry is likely to founder if sufficient safeguards are not incorporated in tandem with the establishment of such registries, to reassure us that this information will not find its way to a new market and uses the sources never intended.

Indeed, as more and more centralized registries are created, there may well come a time when the very concept of "public records" is brought into question. In the past we have all willingly disclosed our names and addresses, ages, and social security numbers to obtain driver's licenses; but we may not be quite so willing to do so when such information is stored in databases linked with hundreds of other pieces of information about our personal lives.

It was very disturbing for many to learn that the anti–abortion rights movement, for example, teaches its adherents how to search public records for the home addresses of physicians who perform abortions in order to harass them. Can we be altogether happy knowing that groups with whom we have never had any personal, professional, or economic relationship can buy, sell, or trade lengthy and detailed public records that provide the purchaser with almost instant access to everything about us, from our daily travel patterns to our medical profiles to our financial records? Clearly, we will be unable to attain the potential advantages of a truly networked world unless we start to address questions about privacy that are unique to electronically mediated information centers.

On the issue of privacy, the courts—and Congress as well—are likely to be sensitive and responsive to the mood of society, provided we make our thoughts known. Congressional response was rapid when the public expressed its outrage over the fact that a reporter covering the Bork nomination hearings easily obtained a record of the videotapes the judge had rented. We are frightened by the specter of such personal choices being made part of a public dossier. Cable legislation, as passed by Congress, has for almost a decade included prohibitions against disclosure of subscriber information. The consent agreement negotiated by Attorney General Abrams with American Express represents yet another imaginative resolution of the conflict between sources and collectors of information, providing a more equitable relationship between the two and knowledgeable release of personal information in exchange for negotiated perquisites.

While some may think that one solution to this problem is to expand the scope of privacy laws and to increase the number of activities proscribed, two legal scholars, Arthur Miller and Alan Westin, suggest that the privacy problem might best be solved by giving individuals property rights in all personal information about themselves. Miller writes: "Perhaps the most facile approach to safeguarding privacy is the suggestion that control over personal information be considered a property right vested in the subject of the data and eligible for the full range of constitutional and legal protection that attach to property."[17] And Westin: "[p]ersonal information, thought of as the right of decisions over one's private personality, should be defined as a property right with all the restraints on interference by public or private authorities and due process guarantees that our law of property has been so skillful in devising."[18]

If we grant information—not just personal information—the full protection of property laws, then a law of information assets begins to take form. Let us assume as a starting point that information about an individual is the private property of the individual and that some authorization by the individual, or some overriding public interest must compel disclosure. What legal principles then emerge?

(1) Secrecy: the right to prevent disclosure of information.

(2) Privacy: the right to prevent unwelcome and unauthorized intrusions.

(3) Confidentiality: the right to release information with restrictions, to prevent others from obtaining the information without the subject's consent.

(4) Publicity: the right to release information into the public domain at a time and place of one's own choosing.

(5) Commerciality: the right to sell information for fair value.

(6) Accessibility: the right to obtain information.

(7) Reciprocity: the right to receive value in exchange for value given.

(8) Integrity: the right to control the accuracy and reliability of information.

(9) Interoperability: the right to transparency in the transfer of information.

(10) Responsibility: the duty to act responsibly.

(11) Liability: the right to have grievances redressed.

(12) Commonality: the right to share information in the public domain.

(13) Equity: the right to have no wrong go unrighted.

In the United States, privacy laws have been a patchwork quilt of state variations or federal laws that are sector-specific (cable television, video rental, credit reporting). While abuses by federal agencies were perceived to be a threat early in the history of computer centralization of record keeping, the more pervasive and intrusive uses and abuses of information assets by the private sector are left unregulated or with few sanctions to enforce compliance. Educational institutions receiving federal grants, for example, are required to respect the confidentiality of student records as well as to provide access to the student, but the threat for noncompliance is loss of federal funding without any recourse for the individual student whose rights have been violated.

In Europe, the approach to data protection has been more coordinated and centralized, with national laws and national data-protection officials to monitor practices in the private sector and assure compliance. Moreover, European countries have reserved the right to restrict exchange of personal information with entities in nonconforming countries where the protection offered could not be considered equivalent, thus threatening an uninhibited global marketplace and hamstringing multinational companies. Neither approach has been entirely satisfactory, as a study of European practices conducted by a Harvard Business School student found European companies complying more in the breach than the observance.

The experience in all areas of the law with respect to the use of information assets has differed in Europe from that of the United States. In anticipation of an integrated European economy in 1992, the European Community had initiated a long series of studies designed to harmonize the treatment of information in the twelve European countries adhering to the treaty. The computer software directive is only the most visible of many centralized efforts to conform European practices, but the laws of the individual nations must be revised to assure uniformity. This procedure is long and complex and without teeth to prod the laggards.

In the United States, law reform is a far more diversified activity, the Office of Technology Assessment being the closest clone of the EC directive procedure. OTA responds to requests for guidance from Congress by seeking to reconcile the conflicting views of various stakeholders and to provide alternative paths that congressional committees might follow in the introduction of legislation. A multiplicity of private-sector entities also seeks to provide input, ranging from the American Bar Association's long list of committees of practicing lawyers to the burgeoning nonprofit research institutions and eleemosynary foundations whose primary function is to study and recommend policy alternatives. But the discourse is dominated by powerful vested interests with the human and financial resources to fight for laws favoring their own activities. The Willis Mogs of the world have been heard only rarely.

We are far from viewing information as the valuable asset that it has become—representing a resource as politically significant as oil has been for the last half-century, since the proliferation of the motorcar. Information assets fuel the economies of competing nations in the global marketplace and provide the lubricant for the vehicles that travel on the information superhighways. Regrettably, policy makers express far greater interest in the NII as a conveyance than as a way to establish rules of the road. Access to and exploitation of information assets will dominate political discourse for the foreseeable future. If we as individuals ignore our stakes in these discussions over the deployment of information, our interests will be ignored.

No one is an island of information, cut off from the rest of the world. Information is by its nature intended to be shared. To inform implies transfer from one to another. To achieve complete privacy and sovereignty over personal information, avoiding all outside intrusion, would require life as a hermit. Few of us would opt for such a stringent solution to our information woes. The exchange of information can be accomplished with a more knowledgeable and equitable trade-off of benefits.

Assume that we claim a property right in information about ourselves. What we must decide is whether we are willing to part with it and upon what terms. We must decide whether to deploy an "opt-in" or "opt-out" system of information protection. Businesses prefer an opt-out system, where subjects of the information have a right to withdraw the information obtained about them or prohibit its reuse. Many individuals would prefer to keep a tight control over information and opt in only to those databases that offer some personal reward. We need to decide what information must be disclosed because of a special public interest in its aggregation.

We also need to know what information resides where and how to gain access. We need to know what information about ourselves is valuable to others and what they are willing to provide in exchange for disclosure.

Conclusions

All forms of information are merging into an electronically delivered system. The instrument through which this information is received may be a combination of what we now call a telephone, television, compact disc player, videocassette recorder, magazine, or book. It may be called an "Apple Newton," the new gizmo offered by Apple Computer, the size of a small notepad but capable of accepting handwritten instructions and receiving data in all of its many forms via a radio link with the networked world. It may be the television screen or "infocenter" covering an entire wall of our homes and permitting global access to information resources. It may be a computer terminal or "info-line" in a community communications center with outreach to public information resources the world over. Whatever its shape, the information that flows through its conduits will be governed by the laws and regulations we impose upon ourselves. What legal structures should we devise to protect it?

For personal information, some people want privacy. Others want publicity to enhance their careers or attract new business. Both groups want more personal autonomy over decisions about how information about them is used and when and how it is made public. Some publicly generated information needs to be kept secret in order to be effective— strategic intelligence in times of armed conflict, for example. Other types of information need to be made public because they form the basis of public decisions in a democratic society or because of a threat to public health or safety.

Other information is collected by businesses for their own strategic purposes or to sell. Some corporate information may be protected as a trade secret because proprietary products are manufactured using a secret formula—for example, Coca-Cola. Businesses give away some information because it attracts customers—for example, advertising.

We are promulgating a new body of law pertaining to proprietary rights in information assets. In the agricultural and industrial societies of the past, information had entirely different functions and values than in today's rapidly expanding information economy. In socially integrated agrarian societies or highly disaggregated agricultural economies, shared information about agricultural technology benefited the body politic. Information could be given away without compensation in order to improve and increase productivity of the total economy. In an industrial society, the information was usually embedded in products, such as refrigerators and automobiles, that sustained life and limb for its workers and their corporate bosses. Today we enjoy information products that are produced separate and apart from their agricultural or industrial roots and must be marketed and sold as independent items of trade. And the courts and legislative bodies must adjust to treating information as an asset with legal attributes, not unlike real estate or personal possessions.

The kinds of information we call "knowledge" belong in the public domain, but we must decide which public is the designated owner: a user group, a nation-state, or the global commons. If the "public" is less than global, then network managers must determine how to protect information so that it will be distributed and used only by the user group whose entitlement is appropriately recorded. We are carving out entirely new legal domains—some of them public and some of them private—on the frontiers of information. We must redefine the boundaries between public and private information clearly and unambiguously. We need to establish a global system of electronic signs. Electronic travelers need to know on whose electronic domains they are entering and what rules prevail on these electronic highways. We need warning signs and clearly established rules of "netiquette."

We are schizophrenic about the treatment of information in our society. Although we like to talk about living in an information age and an information society, we have yet to begin to comprehend the consequences of this shift, much less to accommodate it. We spend billions of dollars on the machines that make it possible to access information and billions upon billions to gather, manipulate, distribute, and archive information, but we spend little on understanding the economics of information, less on developing a law of information, and perhaps only a little more on worrying about the ethics of information. That state of affairs is about to change. Every day in our newspapers, on television news, and through E-mail conferences, there is another outcry from someone injured by unwanted disclosure of information, from concerned citizens prepared to do battle with offenders, and from elected representatives motivated to take up the fight for better, fairer, and clearer information laws.

We are in the process of designing a new paradigm for our information society, one that offers room for great economic, intellectual, social, and political growth. It must be based upon the recognition that information is a valuable asset whether the claimant is an individual, a corporation, a national entity, or humanity at large. We are devising methods for placing sources of information and information providers on an equal footing in determining how and when personal information will be converted into commercially viable products in the information marketplace.

We must recognize legitimate rights to withhold personal information and prevent intrusions upon private information environments. We must sort out new rules for information that we are required to make public—such as names and addresses to obtain driver's licenses and birth and death certificates. We must clarify the responsibilities of the public custodians and redefine the circumstances under which third parties are to be permitted access.

When information is disclosed, we must determine how to recognize the legal basis upon which the disclosure takes place. We must clearly establish under what circumstances the person or institution so disclosing should be required to place the information in the public domain (for example, government employees), published with or without compensation. We must establish new mechanisms for transferring rights in information assets delivered electronically, including terms of compensation, sales, royalties (when compulsory licenses are appropriate), and especially what manipulation of video images may be permitted.

We are clearly beginning to expand the boundaries of information abuses that are to be prohibited, beyond the familiar ones of libel, obscenity, theft, and destruction of data. We are also expanding our concepts of negligence in the use of information as well as negligence for failure to use established, reliable sources of information.

We are also rapidly expanding the unauthorized but permitted fair uses of information—those beyond the control of the source. We are moving toward an accommodation to the ability of VCR's and computers to record entire works—videotapes, audiotapes, and computer software—for personal enjoyment and use without intent to commercialize.

We are making giant strides in some venues and small accommodations in others, but we have not yet ventured upon a coherent effort to rationalize the legal infostructure of the information age. The judiciary is a superb instrument for interpreting existing laws and rectifying inequities, but it is not ideally suited to establishing new ground rules for societal conduct.

NOTES

Chapter 1: Who Owns Your Name and Address?

1. Testimony of Carl Oppedahl Before the U.S. House of Representatives, Government Information, Justice, and Agriculture Subcommittee Hearing on U.S. Postal Service Address Correction Activities, Thursday, 14 May 1992. See also U.S. House of Representatives, Committee on Government Operations, "Give Consumers a Choice: Privacy Implications of U.S. Postal Service National Change of Address Program," H.R. No. 102–1067, 24 November 1992 (Washington, D.C.: GPO, 1992), p. 19.

2. Congressman Gary A. Condit, introducing H.R. 1344, *Congressional Record,* H 1261, 16 March 1993. See 39 C.F.R. Sec. 265.6(d)(1) (1991); 56 Fed. Reg. 57805 (1991); see also 39 C.F.R. Secs. 265.8(d)(3), 265.8(g)(5) (1991).

3. Hearing, Testimony of Robert G. Krause, Director, Office of Address Information Systems, United States Postal Service.

4. The U.S. Postal Service estimates its actual costs at 34 cents per piece forwarded or returned for lack of sufficient address. However, the Subcommittee of the Congress addressing this question asked the Postal Rate Commission to review these estimates and found them to be "grossly overstated." See H.R. No. 102–1067, pp. 35–38, and letter from George W. Haley, chairman, Postal Rate Commission, to Representative Robert E. Wise, Jr., chairman, Government Information, Justice, and Agriculture Subcommittee, Committee on Government Operations (24 September 1992), p. 1.

5. H.R. No. 102–1067, pp. 6–8.

6. Ibid., p. 8.

7. U.S., *Statistical Abstract of 1991,* table no. 1285, p. 727.

8. The term *junk mail* was coined by newspapers with the intention of demeaning a service they perceived to threaten advertisements inserted in the newspapers.

9. Patti Doten, "Shopping by the Book," *Boston Globe,* 5 December 1994, p. 45.

10. Reported in Jill Smolowe, "Read This!!!!!!!!," *Time*, 26 November 1990, p. 64.

11. Susan E. Fisher, "What Do Computers Know About You? Personal Information Too Readily Available; Includes Related Articles on Privacy Issues and U.S. Right to Privacy Laws," *PC Week*, 11 February 1991, vol. 8, no. 6, p. 156.

12. U.S., *Statistical Abstract of 1991*, table no. 915, p. 554, Bureau of the Census, U.S. Department of Commerce. The U.S. Postal Service is the single largest civilian agency in the United States, employing approximately 1% of the total work force. The Postmaster General's Report for 1990 suggests that the U.S. Postal Service has reduced its work force to a mere 738,000.

13. Environmentalists estimate that each adult American receives about 41 pounds of "junk mail" per year, representing 3% of the total clutter in the nation's landfills is attributable to direct mail, of which 44% is deemed to end up unopened in the landfills and to produce only a 2% response for the effort. Reported in Smolowe, "Read This!!!!!!!!," p. 64.

14. Ibid., p. 63.

15. Title 5 Section 552(b)(6), Public Law 90–3, 81 Statutes at Large, p. 54 (1967).

16. Several federal circuits have been led to the conclusion that individuals do have a privacy interest in their home addresses that may be asserted in opposition to a request for disclosure under the FOIA; see, for example, *Hopkins v. HUD*, 929 F. 2d 81, 87 (2d Cir. 1991); *Reed v. NLRB*, 927 F. 2d 1249, 1251 (D.C. Cir. 1991); *NARFE v. Horner*, 879 F. 2d 873 at 875 (D.C. Cir. 1989); *U.S. Dept. of Agriculture v. FLRA*, 836 F. 2d 1139 (8th Cir. 1988); *Multnomah Co. Medical Society v. Scott*, 825 F. 2d 1410 at 1425 (9th Cir. 1987); *Heights Community Congress v. Veterans Administration*, 732 F. 2d 526, 529 (6th Cir. 1984) cert. denied, 469 U.S. 1034 (1984); *United States v. Liebert*, 519 F. 2d 542, 548 (3d Cir. 1975) cert. denied, 423 U.S. 985 (1975); *Wine Hobby USA, Inc. v. Internal Revenue Service*, 502 F. 2d 133, 137 (3d Cir. 1974); *AFGE, Local 1923 v. U.S. Department of Health and Human Services*, 712 F. 2d 931, 1932 (4th Cir. 1983) but failed to apply its holding. *AFAGE, Local 1760 v. FLRA*, 786 F. 2d 554, at 556 (2d Cir. 1986) found the privacy interest of the average employee in his address not particularly compelling. In the Wine Hobby case, the third circuit held that names of persons seeking exemption from taxation for wine made at home were exempted under exception 6 but that the court could weigh the public interest requiring disclosure and found none since the information was sought "for private commercial exploitation."

17. *I.B.E.W. Local Union No. 5 v. HUD*, 852 F. 2d 87 at 92 (3d Cir. 1988).

18. *Minnis v. USDA*, 737 F. 2d 78, 787 (9th Cir. 1984).

19. *USDA v. Federal Labor Relations Authority*, 836 F. 2d 1139 at 1144 (8th Cir. 1988).

20. *Federation of New York State Rifle and Pistol Clubs, Inc. v. New York City Police Department,* 73 N.Y. 2d 92 (1988).

21. *Rowan v. Post Office Department,* 397 U.S. 728 (1970).

22. Title 39 U.S.C. Sec. 4009, P.L. 90–206, 81 Stat. 645, 16 December 1967. In enacting the companion statute 39 U.S.C. Sec. 3010 (b), P.L. 91–375, Sec. 14, requiring "sexually oriented advertisements" to be so marked, the Congress stated that it was contrary to public policy to distribute such material to "persons who do not want their privacy invaded in this manner."

23. Title 5 U.S.C. Sec. 552a(b)(3) "for a routine use" and (a)(7) "routine use means . . . for a purpose which is compatible with the purpose for which it was collected"; *FLRA v. U.S. Dept. of Treasury,* 884 F. 2d 1446 (D.C. Cir. 1989) allows disclosure "for a routine use as defined in subsection (a)(7)) compatible with the purpose for which the information was collected."

24. Title 39 U.S.C. Sec. 1707 proscribes the use of any property "used" by the postal service to be appropriated to any other than its proper use, e.g., for receiving the mail delivered by the postal monopoly.

25. Title 39 U.S.C. Sec. 601 and Title 18 U.S.C. Sec. 1696 upheld in *Ntl. Ass'n of Letter Carriers, AFL-CIO v. Ind. Postal System of America,* 470 F. 2d 265 (Okla Cir. 1972).

26. Title 39 U.S.C. Sec. 3621. For a complete history of the transformation of the postal service from a government agency to an independent, more economically efficient organization, see John T. Tierney, *Postal Reorganization: Managing the Public's Business* (Boston: Auburn House, 1981).

27. Testimony of Albert G. Ertel, Hearing.

28. Letter from Charles Hawley, Assistant General Counsel of the Postal Service's General Administrative Law Division, addressed to Albert G. Ertel and quoted by him in Testimony, Hearing.

29. Smolowe, "Read This!!!!!!!!," p. 70; see also Richard Burt and Cathy Cooper, "Bracing for the Coming Sea Change in Marketing," *DM News,* 30 July 1990, p. 25, via NEXIS.

30. H.R. No. 102–1067, pp. 40–41.

31. Smolowe, "Read This!!!!!!!!," p. 67.

32. Statistics attributed to the Direct Marketing Association by Holly Brubach, "Mail-Order America," *New York Times Magazine,* 21 November 1993, pp. 54, 55.

33. Equifax, Inc., is the leading provider of information for consumer financial transactions. Established in 1899 in Atlanta, Equifax has 15,000 employees in 1,100 locations in the United States, Canada, and Europe.

34. By telephone confirmation to Equifax, 2 July 1992.

35. P.L. 98–549, 30 October 1984, Sec. 631(a), (b), and (c), 47 U.S.C. Sec. 551, 98 Stat. 2779 at 2794.

36. Mary Beth Colacecchi, "Lethal Weapon," *Catalog Age,* May 1992, p. 1., cited in H.R. No. 102–1067, p. 39.

37. H.R. No. 102–1067, p. 39.

38. Nicholas D. Kristof, "For Chinese, Lives in Files, Perpetually Open and Overhead," *International Herald Tribune,* 19 March 1992, p. 5.

39. Title 5 U.S.C. Sec. 552.

40. Privacy Act of 1974, 5 U.S.C. Sec. 552a(d) and (e).

41. Robert S. Boyd, "Computers Chip Away at Privacy," *Chicago Tribune,* 4 July 1990, p. 1; zone C, via NEXIS.

42. Lotus Development Corporation, founded in 1982, develops, markets, and supports business software and CD-ROM databases that help users access, analyze, communicate, and share information. The company's first product, Lotus 1-2-3, is the most popular computer software program in the world, with more than 14 million users.

43. Fisher, "What Do Computers Know About You?" p. 156.

44. "Lotus, Equifax Cancel Shipment of Lotus MarketPlace: Households," *Business Wire,* 23 January 1991, via NEXIS.

45. Ibid.

46. Ibid.

47. Boyd, "Computers Chip Away at Privacy," p. 1.

48. Ibid.

49. Ibid.

50. Bob Davis, "Baby-Goods Firms See Direct Mail as the Perfect Pitch for New Moms," *Wall Street Journal,* 29 January 1986, sec. 2, p. 33.

51. Ibid.

52. *Economist,* 18 February 1990, p. 64.

53. The Video Privacy Protection Act of 1988, P.L. 100–618. Sec. 12(a)(2), enacted 5 November 1988, 18 U.S.C. Sec. 2710, 102 Stat. 3195; Cable Communications Policy Act of 1984, P.L. 98–549, 30 October 1984, Sec. 631(a), (b), and (c), 47 U.S.C. Sec. 551, 98 Stat., p. 2794.

54. Fair Credit Reporting Act of 1970, 15 U.S.C. Sec. 1681 (1970).

55. Jeffrey Rothfeder, "The Scoop on Snooping: It's a Cinch," *Business Week,* 4 September 1989, p. 82.

56. Boyd, "Computers Chip Away at Privacy," p. 1.

57. Ibid.

58. Ibid.

59. Ibid.

60. Albert B. Crenshaw, "Credit Card Holders to Be Warned of Lists; American Express Collects, Sells Buying Habits Data," *Washington Post,* 14 May 1992, p. D11; Denise Gellene, "Chalk One Up for Privacy: American Express Will Inform Cardholders That It Sorts Them for Sales Pitches," *Los Angeles Times,* 14 May 1992, p. D1; Arthur Spiegelman, "American Express Agrees to Tell Cardholders It Profiles Them," *Reuter Business Report,* 13 May 1992, Wednesday, BC cycle, via NEXIS. The complete text of the agreement, as reported by PR

Newswire, 13 May 1992, via NEXIS.

Following is the text of the agreement American Express Travel Related Services Company, Inc., today signed with the Office of the Attorney General of the State of New York:

Attorney General of the State of New York
Bureau of Consumer Frauds and Protection
in the matter of
American Express Travel Related Services Company, Inc.

AGREEMENT OF VOLUNTARY ASSURANCES

Agreement made this 8th day of May 1992 between Robert Abrams, Attorney General, State of New York (Attorney General) and American Express Travel Related Services Company, Inc. (American Express), having its principal place of business at the American Express Tower, World Financial Center, New York, New York 10285.

Whereas, American Express is committed to improving the quality of communications with its cardmembers and desires to reaffirm its role in the financial services industry as a leader in protecting the privacy of its cardmembers; and

Whereas, the Attorney General, in furtherance of his interest in protecting the privacy of consumers, has brought to the attention of American Express his concern about whether American Express could provide certain further disclosures in its communications with cardmembers regarding the use of cardmember information to compile mailing lists to enable cardmembers to make informed decisions about whether they wish to receive certain marketing material; and

Whereas, in furtherance of the shared concerns of the Attorney General and American Express for the privacy of consumers, American Express has been cooperating with the Attorney General to voluntarily reformulate the elements of and revise the American Express Cardmember notice regarding the use by American Express of information about cardmembers for mailing list purposes;

Now therefore, in consideration of the mutual covenants contained herein, the parties agree as follows:

1. American Express will revise the contents of the written notification to American Express Cardmembers regarding the compilation and use of cardmember names and addresses for marketing purposes to provide as follows:

(a) In addition to informing its cardmembers that it may use information provided by the cardmember in the application for the American Express Card, as is American Express' current policy, American Express shall revise the notification to explicitly state that American Express uses and analyzes certain information

(i) obtained through the cardmember's use of the American

Express Card which may indicate shopping preferences and lifestyle; and

(ii) obtained from publicly available sources, as bases for the compilation of cardmember lists used for marketing of products and services from American Express and its affiliates and from establishments which accept the American Express Card.

(b) American Express will continue to provide cardmembers with the opportunity to be excluded from cardmember lists used to mail marketing material

(i) from American Express and its affiliates;

(ii) from establishments which accept the American Express Card; or

(iii) from both sources.

(c) American Express will continue to make available to cardmembers both a toll-free telephone number and an address for written correspondence for cardmembers' use in notifying American Express at any time that they wish to be excluded from such mailing lists.

2. American Express shall ensure that the revisions to the notification as described above are communicated to its cardmembers in a clear, conspicuous and understandable manner. The Attorney General acknowledges and agrees that the form of notice set forth in Attachment A hereto is in form and content acceptable to the Attorney General. Such notice shall be in at least 10 point type, and the heading shall be printed in either bold-face type, in a different color than the text of the notice or in some other manner which distinguishes the heading from the text. Such notification may be included with cardmember billing statements or in other mailings to cardmembers.

3. American Express shall begin mailing the revised notice described above to customers who are cardmembers as of the date of this agreement no later than August 1, 1992. In addition, the revised notice, or a substantially similar notice, shall be substituted for the one currently being provided to all new cardmembers and shall be provided within a reasonable time after approval for issuance of the American Express Card. Such notice shall be provided to existing cardmembers at least once each year.

4. Nothing herein shall preclude American Express from communicating with its cardmembers regarding the compilation or use of cardmember names and/or addresses in a different form or content than as set forth above, provided that any such communication is consistent with paragraph 1 above and does not result in a less frequent notice than as set forth in paragraph 3 above.

5. The Attorney General acknowledges and agrees that this agreement is in full settlement of any issues relating directly or indirectly to the adequacy of American Express' mailing list notification to cardmembers or to American Express' Cardmembers mailing list segmentation practices.

6. The parties agree that the acceptance of this agreement shall not be deemed approval by the Attorney General of American Express' Cardmember mailing list segmentation practices.

7. This agreement shall remain in full force and effect until otherwise agreed to by the parties.

8. In recognition of certain costs incurred by the Attorney General's Office in connection with this agreement, American Express agrees to reimburse the Attorney General its costs in the amount of $10,000.

In Witness Whereof, the parties have executed this agreement as of the date and year first above mentioned.

Robert Abrams	American Express Travel
Attorney General of the	Related Services
State of New York	Company, Inc.
Bureau of Consumer Frauds and Protection	

By: John W. Corwin
By: Phillip J. Riese

Assistant Attorney General	Executive Vice President
in Charge	Consumer Card Group

By: Stephen Mindell	By: Timothy J. Heine
Assistant Attorney General	Assistant General Counsel
Director of Consumer Advocacy	

By: Herbert Israel
Assistant Attorney General

AN IMPORTANT MESSAGE TO OUR CARDMEMBERS CONCERNING PRIVACY

As an American Express Cardmember, you understand and appreciate all that the Card affords you, including the special offers you occasionally receive through the mail.

These offers may come directly from us, from our affiliates, from those establishments that accept the Card, or from American Express in cooperation with an establishment, and each one is carefully considered to ensure that it provides our cardmembers with superior value. Additionally, we try to make sure that these offers reach Cardmembers who would be most likely to take advantage of them.

To do this, we develop mailing lists based on information you provide on your application, information you provide to us in surveys, information derived from how you use the Card which may indicate shopping preferences and lifestyle, as well as information available from public sources.

These lists are used by us and by the establishments with whom we work to develop offers under strict conditions designed to safeguard the privacy of cardmember information. No cardmember information, other than name and address, is ever made available to any party outside American Express.

Cardmembers tell us they appreciate receiving these special offers as well as information of cardmember benefits through the mail.

However, if for any reason you no longer wish to receive these mailings, we offer you the following options:

1. Exclusion from American Express Mailings—including new optional cardmember benefits, travel offers and special offers provided by selected establishments in cooperation with American Express.

2. Exclusion from Establishment Mailings—including special offers provided by selected establishments with approval from American Express.

3. Exclusion from both American Express and Establishment offers and mailings.

If you wish to choose one of these options, either now or in the future, please call us at 1-800————or write to ADDRESS. Six to eight weeks are generally required for your request to become effective. Please remember that if you select any of the options described, you may no longer receive all of our special offerings, many of which are exclusive to American Express Cardmembers, or other information regarding new optional cardmember benefits.

CONTACT: Maureen Bailey of American Express, 212-640-3311.

61. Ibid.
62. "American Express to Disclose Cardmember Info," *Reuters*, 13 May 1992, via NEXIS.
63. Gellene, "Chalk One Up for Privacy," p. D1; see also Ruth Simon, "Stop Them from Selling Your Secrets," *Money Magazine*, March 1992, p. 98.
64. David Bauder, "Credit Card Company Agrees to Tell Customers It Tracks Spending Habits," *Associated Press*, 13 May 1992, Wednesday, AM cycle, via NEXIS.
65. Gellene, "Chalk One Up for Privacy," p. D1.
66. Ibid.
67. "AmEx to Inform Customers When Offering 'Portraits' of Buying Habits," *United Press International*, 13 May 1992, Wednesday, BC cycle, via NEXIS.
68. "AmEx Hit on Data Usage: NY Sets Privacy Hearing," *DM News*, 18 May 1992, p. 1, via NEXIS.
69. Crenshaw, "Credit Card Holders to Be Warned."
70. Maureen Dezell, "Lives On-Line: Privacy in the Age of Data," *Boston Phoenix*, 8 May 1992, sec. 2, p. 5.

71. Public Law 322, Section 300001–3.
72. H.R. 5274, introduced 27 May 1992 into the 102d Cong., 2d Sess., U.S. House of Representatives. The bill was reintroduced into the 103d Congress as H.R. 1344 by Congressman Gary A. Condit, Democrat of California, who succeeded Congressman Wise as chairman of the Subcommittee on Information, Justice, Transportation and Agriculture, of the Government Operations Committee. The statute, if enacted, is to be called the Postal Privacy Act of 1993. *Congressional Record*, H.R. 1261, 16 March 1993.
73. "AmEx Hit on Data Usage."
74. *Virginia Pharmacy Board v. Virginia Citizens Consumer Commission*, 425 U.S. 748 (1976).
75. Title 39 U.S.C. Sec. 4009, P.L. 90–206, Title 3, Sec. 301, 81 Stat. 645, 16 December 1967.
76. *Rowan v. Post Office Dept.*, 397 U.S., pp. 736–37 (1969).
77. "AmEx Hit on Data Usage."
78. Hearing, Testimony of Robert Ellis Smith.

Chapter 2: Who Owns Your Telephone Number?

1. Connie Lauerman, "Now It's Death and Taxes ... and Unsolicited Commercial Phone Calls," *Chicago Tribune*, Sunday Magazine, 24 November 1991, p. 20, zone C.
2. Small Claims Complaint No. 89 SC 1804, filed 7 April 1989.
3. Telephone call to Willis L. Mog, May 1992.
4. Lauerman, "Now It's Death and Taxes." Mog's lawsuit against J. C. Penney was settled out of court under an order of confidentiality, so that neither the amount of the settlement nor its terms are known. He has also filed suit against another telemarketing firm, hoping to establish grounds upon which a court decision can be rendered clarifying the legal issues. However, Mog reports that a number of telemarketers to whom he has sent demands for payment have paid the $100 without protest, indicating they would prefer not to pursue litigation that might offer some insight to policy makers and establish legal precedent. Telephone interview with Willis Mog, 30 April 1993.
5. *Willis L. Mog v. Advanced Telemarketing Corporation and J.C. Penney Financial Services*, No. 89 SC 1804, 20 July 1992.
6. *Willis L. Mog v. The Smith Company*, Small Claims Complaint No. 93 SC 0921, 4 March 1993, Circuit Court of the Twentieth Judicial Circuit, St. Clair County, State of Illinois.
7. Walker Research, Inc., of Indianapolis, reported in Lauerman, "Now It's Death and Taxes."
8. "Correction," *DM News*, 14 December 1991, Final Edition, via NEXIS.
9. Ray Schultz, "Masters of Hypocrisy," *DM News*, 27 January 1992, p. 6.
10. Walter S. Baer, interview, 17 April 1993.

11. Docket No. 78–100, RM 2955, adopted 15 March 1978; Unsolicited Telephone Calls ("Junk Phone Calls"), 67 FCC 2d 1384 (1978).

12. Petition for Issuance of Notice of Inquiry and Notice of Proposed Rulemaking, in the Matter of the Use of Automated Dialing Devices to Present Unsolicited Recorded Messages over the Public Telephone Network, Before the Federal Communications Commission, August 1977.

13. In fact, the Supreme Court has agreed that "[t]he short, though regular journey from mail box to trash can . . . is an acceptable burden, at least so far as the Constitution is concerned," cited in *Lamont v. Commissioner of Motor Vehicles,* 269 F. Supp. 880 (SDNY), aff'd, 386 F. 2d 449 (2d Cir. 1967).

14. Walter S. Baer, "Controlling Unwanted Communications to the Home," *Telecommunications Policy,* September 1978, p. 224.

15. Ibid., p. 225.

16. At the time the companies required that one telephone instrument be permanently wired to the central service, a practice subsequently abandoned.

17. Baer, "Controlling Unwanted Communications," p. 223.

18. *McDaniel v. Pacific Telephone & Telegraph,* 60 Pub. Util. Rep. 3d (PUR), p. 51 (1965).

19. Unsolicited Phone Calls, 77 FCC 2d 1023 (1980).

20. Act of 22 April 1985, Chapter 121, Sec. 1, Washington Legislative Service, p. 315 (St. Paul, Minn.: West Publishing, 1985).

21. Mark S. Nadel, "Rings of Privacy: Unsolicited Telephone Calls and the Right of Privacy," *Yale Journal on Regulation* 4 (1986): 107.

22. Terri Shaw, "Dialing for Your Dollars: Calls from Strangers Could Be Fraud—or Just a Terrible Nuisance," *DM News,* 27 January 1992.

23. For an informative summary of the legislation, see James E. Meadows, "The Telephone Consumer Act of 1991: Consumer Salvation or Unconstitutional Restraint," *The Computer Lawyer* 9, no. 3 (March 1992): 13–18.

24. S. 1462, amending Title II of the Communications Act of 1934, 47 U.S.C. adding a new Sec. 227, "Restrictions on the Use of Telephone Equipment" (P.L. 102–243, enacted by the 102d Congress, 20 December 1991, 105 Stat. 2394). For an excellent analysis of the legislation, see James E. Meadows, "The Telephone Consumer Protection Act of 1991: Consumer Salvation or Unconstitutional Restraint," *The Computer Lawyer* 9, no. 3 (March 1992): 13.

25. 47 U.S.C. Sec. 227(b)(2)(B).

26. 47 U.S.C. Sec. 227(b)(1)(A).

27. For a first and unintended infraction, a fine of $500; if willful, the fine may be extended to three times that amount.

28. Sec. 227(b)(2)(B)(i) and (ii). The regulations to be promulgated by the FCC may exempt calls not made for commercial purposes and calls that will not adversely affect the privacy rights this section was

intended to protect and do not include transmission of any unsolicited advertisement.

29. Seth Mydans, "Names List Leads to Ethics Debate," *New York Times*, 30 July 1991, p. A8.

30. Ibid.

31. Ibid.

32. Sec. 227(c).

33. Sec. 227(e).

34. *Moser and National Association of Telecomputer Operators v. Federal Communications Commission*, 811 F. Supp. 541; 1992 U.S. Dist., LEXIS 20711 (Dist. Ct. Ore. 1992).

35. Ana Puga, "Markey Plans Bill on Privacy Rights," *Boston Globe*, 14 October 1993, pp. 1, 22.

36. New York Telephone, for example, charges an extra twenty dollars annually.

37. Anne W. Branscomb, "Electronic Publishing: A Global View of Videotex," 36 *Federal Communications Law Journal* 38 (September 1976): 135.

38. *United States v. American Telephone & Telegraph Co.*, 552 F. Supp. 131, 180–86, 227, 231 (Dist. Ct. D.C. 1982), affirmed sub nom, *Maryland v. United States*, 460 U.S 1001, 103 S. Ct. 1240 (1983).

39. Judge Greene permitted the RBOC's to provide the transmission of information provided by others, Western Electric Co, Inc., 714 F. Supp. at 2; the Court of Appeals reversed, holding this order, holding the standard too strict, Western Electric Co., Inc., 900 F. 2d, p. 295; upon remand Judge Greene removed the ban but stayed his order pending appeals, *United States v. Western Electric Co., Inc.*, 767 F. Supp. 308, p. 332 (D.C. Cir. 1991) and still opposing the entry of RBOC's into the information market, refused to vacate the stay, *United States v. Western Electric Co., Inc.*, 774 F. Supp. 11, p. 15 (D.D.C. 1991), but the Circuit Court of Appeals removed the stay later, thus freeing the telephone companies to provide information services as well as transmit information services provided by others, *United States v. Western Electric Co., Inc.*, 1991 U.S. APP., LEXIS 33098 (D.C. Cir. 1991).

40. This prohibition was retained in the revision of cable legislation, The Cable Television Consumer Protection and Competition Act of 1992, Sec. 613(b)(1), codified as Title 47 U.S.C. Sec. 533(b)(1).

41. *Chesapeake and Potomac Telephone Co. of Virginia v. U.S.A. et al.*, 1993 U.S. Dist., LEXIS 11822; 1993-2 Trade Cas. (CCH) P70,339 (E.D. VA 1993).

42. *Smith v. Maryland*, 442 U.S. 735 (1979).

43. Ibid., p. 737.

44. Ibid., p. 742.

45. Ibid., pp. 749–52.

46. *U.S. v. Miller*, 425 U.S. 435 (1976).

47. P.L. 95–630, 92 Stat. 3697, enacted 10 November 1978, 12 U.S.C. Sec. 3401.
48. 499 U.S. 340, 111 S. Ct. 1282, 113 L. Ed. 2d 358, 2 CCH Computer Cases 46, 423; 1991 LEXIS 1856 (27 March 1991); for an insightful analysis of what remains capable of copyright protection after *Feist,* see John Rothman, "Copyright of Compilations in the Post Feist Era," (Cambridge, Mass.: Harvard University Program on Information Resources Policy, 1992).
49. 2 CCH Computer Cases, p. 62,958.
50. To quote Justice O'Connor: "Originality is a constitutional requirement. The source of Congress' power to enact copyright laws is Article I, Sec. 8, clause 8, of the Constitution, which authorizes Congress to 'secur[e] for limited Times to Authors . . . the exclusive Right to their respective Writings.' In two decisions from the late 19th Century— The Trade-Mark Cases, 100 U. S. 82 (1879); and *Burrow-Giles Lithographic Co. v. Sarony,* 111 U.S. 53 (1874)—this Court defined the crucial terms 'authors' and 'writings.' In so doing, the Court made it unmistakably clear that these terms presuppose a degree of originality." 2 CCH Computer Cases, p. 62,952.
51. *Rural Telephone Service Co. v. Feist Publications, Inc.,* 737 F. Supp. 610 (1990), reconsideration denied, 1990 U.S. Dist., LEXIS 10011.
52. 1991 U.S. LEXIS 1856, p. °4.
53. *Feist Publications v. Rural Telephone Service,* 1991 U.S., LEXIS 1856°2, 499 U.S., 111 Sup. Ct. 1282 (1991).
54. For more information about the impact of *Feist* on databases, see Baila H. Caledonia, "From Copyright to Copycat," *Publishers Weekly,* 16 August 1991.
55. Sid Moody, "Buying by Mail," *AP Wire Service,* 15 May 1988, BC cycle via NEXIS.
56. Josh Hyatt, "'800' Calls Without AT&T," *Boston Globe,* 28 April 1993, p. 37.
57. Nancy Reider, "Where to Find New Names," *Direct Marketing,* 19 July 1988.
58. These include Home Shopping Channel (HSC) and Quality Value Channel (QVC).
59. Walter Shapiro, "Politics: 1-800-Pound Guerrillas," *Time,* 6 April 1992, p. 17.
60. Tariff FCC. No. 2, Original page 90.4, Specialized Common Carrier Service, 3.23 Assignment and Retention of 800 Service Telephone Numbers, Issued 18 December 1990, effective 1 January 1991.
61. Notice of Rule-Making, 102 FCC 2d 1387 (1986).
62. In the Matter of Provision of Access for 800 Service, FCC 91–249, 38219, 56 Fed. Reg. 51656, 51666, 69 R.R. 2d 1037 (1992).
63. Ibid., p. 1043.
64. Hyatt, "'800' Calls Without AT&T," p. 37.
65. "Comment of the Staff of the Bureaus of Economics and Consumer

Protection of the Federal Trade Commission," In the Matter of Policies and Rules Concerning Interstate 900 Telecommunications Services, CC Docket No. 91–65, 1991 FCC LEXIS 3629, °9; quoting from "900 Numbers: The Struggle for Respect," *Advertising Age,* 18 February 1991, p. S–1.

66. In the Matter of Tele-Compute Corporation Apparent Liability for Forfeiture, Federal Communications Commission, 7 FCC Rcd 6041; 1992 FCC LEXIS 5373; 71 R. R. 2d (Pike and Fischer) 463.

67. Remar Sutton, "Dial '900' for Trouble," *Reader's Digest,* August 1991, p. 40.

68. In the Matter of Policies and Rules Concerning Interstate 900 Telecommunications Services, 6 FCC Rcd 6166; 1991 FCC LEXIS 5525; 69 R. R. 2d (P & F).

69. Ibid.

70. "Comment of Southwestern Bell to the Federal Communications Commission," FCC Docket No. 91–65, 24 April 1991.

71. Ibid., pp. 71–72.

72. In the Matter of Policies and Rules Implementing the Telephone Disclosure and Dispute Resolution Act, FCC Docket No. 93–22, RM-7990, 1993, FCC LEXIS 1562, adopted 11 February 1993, released 10 March 1993.

73. Ibid., °14.

74. FCC Releases on 800 Codes, 900 Codes, and Carrier Identification Codes, Federal Communications Commission, 1993 FCC, LEXIS 792, °13.

75. *Wall Street Journal,* 7 May 1991, p. B1.

76. "Pac Bell Backs Off Selling Lists," *Alameda Times Star,* 16 April 1986, p. 16.

77. "The Phonesmart services are a series of new telephone services based on common Channelling Signalling System (SS7) that permit the transfer of the phone number of the calling party through the phone network. With SS7 the dialing information (the calling party's number) is forwarded from the originating central office to the local switch in the terminating central office. This creates the opportunity to make the phone number of the calling party available to the call recipient. Whether the number is actually forwarded is determined by the phone company." Testimony of Marc Rotenberg, Docket No. 5404, Investigation of New England Telephone and Telegraph Company's PHONESMART Call Management Services, 17 July 1991. State of Vermont Public Service Board.

78. Mary Lu Carnevale and Julie Amparano Lopez, "Party Line: Making a Phone Call Might Mean Telling the World About You: Number Identification Is a Dream for Marketers But a Threat to Privacy," *Wall Street Journal,* 28 November 1989, p. 1.

79. Ric Kahn, "Murdered Woman's Ex-Spouse Queried," *Boston Globe,* 26 August 1992, pp. 31, C1.

80. See, for example, Testimony of Janlori Goldman, Legislative Counsel, on behalf of the American Civil Liberties Union, Washington Office, Before the House Judiciary Subcommittee on Courts, Intellectual Property, and the Administration of Justice, in Support of H.R. 4340, 19 September 1990.

81. *Equifax Report on Consumers in the Information Age*, chap. 8: "The Privacy-Intensive Industries—Telecommunications," p. 78 (Louis Harris, 1990)

82. Ibid.

83. Alan Westin, *Privacy and Freedom* (New York: Atheneum, 1967).

84. Testimony of Marc Rotenberg, Docket No. 5404, Investigation of New England Telephone and Telegraph.

85. See *Seattle Times v. Rhinehart,* 467 U.S. 20 (1984); *Brown v. Socialist Workers Party,* 459 U.S. 87, 95 (1982); *Gibson v. Florida Legislative Investigation Committee,* 372 U.S. 539 (1963); and *Talley v. California,* 362 U.S. 60, 64–65 (1960); *NAACP v. Alabama,* 357 U.S. 449 (1958).

86. *Buckley v. Valeo,* 424 U.S. 1 (1976).

87. *Frisby v. Schultz,* 101 L. Ed. 2d 420 at 431–32 (1988).

88. Statement of Arthur R. Miller, Bruce Bromley Professor of Law, Harvard Law School, on Senate Bill No. 2030, The Telephone Privacy Act of 1990, Before the Technology and the Law Subcommittee, Senate Committee on the Judiciary, 1 August 1990.

89. *David M. Barash et al. v. Pennsylvania Public Utility Commission,* Opinion, 30 May 1990, reversing the Order of the Pennsylvania Utility Commission authorizing the service, No. 2270 C.D. 1989, in the Commonwealth Court of Pennsylvania. *Barash v. Pennsylvania Public Utility Commission,* 133 Pa. Commw. 285, 576 A. 2d 79, PS. Commw. LEXIS 306 (Commonwealth Court of Pennsylvania 1990). The Supreme Court of Pennsylvania confirmed that Caller ID without optional free blocking contravened the Pennsylvania wiretap statute, finding it unnecessary to address the constitutional issue. *Barash v. Pennsylvania Public Utility Commission,* 529 Pa. 523, 605 A. 2d 1198; 1992 Pa. LEXIS 558 (1992).

90. State of New York, Public Service Commission Opinion No. 92-5, Case 91-C-0428, Proceeding on Motion of the Commission to Investigate New York Telephone Company's Proposal to Introduce Caller ID Service, Opinion and Order Authorizing Caller ID Service, 9 April 1992.

91. Ibid, p. 52.

92. State of New York, Public Service Commission, Case 91-C-0428, Proceeding on Motion of the Commission to Investigate New York Telephone Company's Proposal to Introduce Caller ID Service, Opinion No. 92-5 (A) Opinion on and Order Denying Petition for Rehearing, 29 June 1992.

93. Statement of Principles on Privacy in Telecommunications (as modified, September 1991).

94. 103d Cong., 1st sess., H.R. 34323 To Amend the Communications Act of 1934 to prohibit the disclosure of certain information concerning customer's uses of telephone services and for other purposes, introduced 3 November 1993, Title II, Privacy of Calling Party Information, Section 201-204.8.

95. For an excellent pioneering analysis of the impact and policy issues related to TGI, see Thomas E. McManus, *Telephone Transaction Generated Information: Rights and Restrictions* (Cambridge, Mass.: Harvard University Program on Information Resources Policy, Monograph, May 1990), P-90-5.

96. *California Bankers Association v. Schultz*, 416 U.S. 21 (1974).

97. H.R. 3432, Title II, Section 230, (c) (1) and (2).

98. PCS is a digital, low-power mobile telephone technology that could potentially replace much of today's wired and cellular telephone service. A personal service network would have a configuration similar to a cellular network, with several electronic transmit and receive devices installed in neighborhoods and business districts and linked by fiber optics, copper, or microwave to the public switched telecommunications network. However, the outdoor cells and the hand-held consumer receivers are expected to be smaller and less expensive to build than cellular equipment. Very high speed computer systems would be set up in central switching hubs to route the numerous calls to their proper destination. Randall M. Sukow, "PCS—New Set of initials in Cable's Future; Personal Communications Service Cable TV Technology," *Broadcasting* 119, no. 25 (17 December 1990): 73.

99. Thomas A. Monheim, "COMMENT: Personal Communications Services: The Wireless Future of Telecommunications," *Federal Communications Law Journal* 44 (March 1992): 335.

100. Randall M. Sukow, "NTIA Wants $ 1.4 Million for PCS; National Telecommunications and Information Administration; Personal Communications Services," *Broadcasting* 122, no. 14 (30 March 1992): 41.

101. Randy Sukow, "NTIA Asks for More Money for PCS Research; National Telecommunications and Information Administration; Personal Communications Services," *Broadcasting* 122, no. 27 (29 June 1992): 32.

102. FCC Amends Rules to Establish New Narrowband Personal Communications Services (General Docket No. 90–314, ET Docket No. 92–100), 1993 FCC LEXIS 3229, 24 June 1993.

103. Media companies that have been granted experimental licenses for PCS include Time Warner, Continental Cablevision, Tele-Communications Inc., Cox Enterprises, Providence Journal Company, and Viacom International. The telephone companies' roster includes Bell South, Bell Atlantic, Ameritech, NYNEX, AT&T, and a score of others.

See, e.g., Joe Flint, "PCS Ready to Move, But How Far? Issues of Spectrum, Viability and Who Can Participate Remain; Personal Communications Services," *Broadcasting* 122, no. 28 (6 July 1992): 46. See also Edmund L. Andrews, "More Airwaves Are Being Cleared for Communications Without Wires," *New York Times,* 20 September 1993, p. D10.

104. Andrews, "F.C.C. Clearing Airwaves for an Era Without Wires," *New York Times,* 20 September 1993, p. D2.

105. Paul Gilster, "The Bold New World of Wireless Technology," *Triangle Business,* 18 November 1991, p. 11.

106. Angela Gunn, "Future Currents: Where Wireless Technology Is Headed," *PC Magazine,* 4 February 1992, p. 304.

107. Paul Saffo, "Looking Ahead: The Need to Open Radio Bands," *Los Angeles Times,* 5 June 1991, p. D3.

108. Joshua Quittner, "New Wireless Devices Could Put a Phone in Every Pocket, But Will They?" *Newsday,* 10 December 1991, p. 73.

109. Peter Lambert, "PCS Allocations Debated Before FCC; Public Safety and Business Users Doubt Spectrum Sharing; Personal Communications Services," *Broadcasting* 121, no. 24 (9 December 1991): 11.

110. Quittner, "New Wireless Devices," p. 73.

111. Wayne Schelle and Martin Cohen, "Personal Communication Services Will Be Next Major Wave of Advanced Telecommunications," *Broadcasting* 120, no. 17 (29 April 1991): 16.

112. Commissions Requests Comment on Proposed Assignment of the 500 Service Access code for Personal Communications Services, Federal Communications Commission, 5 August 1993, 1993 FCC, LEXIS 4036.

Chapter 3: Who Owns Your Medical History?

1. This item was so newsworthy that every major network and station carried the news and all major newspapers printed the story on 7 November 1991. Next day he was interviewed on the early morning programs and was interviewed subsequently by most of the major talk show hosts.

2. *NBC Evening News,* 7 November 1991.

3. Richard A. Knox, "Magic Johnson Gave AIDS Prevention a Needed Jolt," *Boston Globe,* 10 November 1991, p. 28.

4. Matthew Rees, "Homocons," *New Republic,* 8 June 1992, p. 30: "The old paradigm of the homoconservative is perhaps best represented by Roy Cohn ... Cohn, chief counsel to Joseph McCarthy, was both rabidly anti-gay in public and unabashedly homosexual in private. Even when dying of AIDS in 1986, he refused to be open about his sexuality."

5. Jonathan Alter with Peter McKillop, "AIDS and the Right to Know: A Question of Privacy," *Newsweek,* 18 August 1986, p. 46.

6. Ibid.

7. Martha Smilgis, "The Big Chill: Fear of AIDS," *Time*, 16 February 1987, p. 50.

8. Alessandra Stanley, "AIDS Becomes a Political issue," *Time*, 23 March 1987, p. 24; also Kathleen McAuliffe, "AIDS at the Dawn of Fear," *U.S. News and World Report*, 12 January 1987, p. 62: "Members of the religious right . . . see AIDS as God's rough justice for the sin of homosexuality."

9. 20 U.S.C. Sec. 1400 et seq. (1982).

10. 29 U.S.C. Sec. 794 (1982).

11. 28 U.S.C. Sec. 1983 (1982).

12. *Ryan White v. Western School Corporation*, IP 85–11920 C, 23 August 1985, LEXIS, entry 16 August 1985.

13. *New York Times*, 14 February 1986, p. A12.

14. Ibid., *Doe v. Dolton Elementary School Dist.*, 694, F. Supp., p. 445 (N.D. Ill. 1988) applied the AMA factors to an HIV-infected school-child and found that there was no significant risk of transmission. See also *Chalk v. U.S. Dist. Court Cent. Dist. of Calif.*, 840 F. 2d 701 (9th Cir. 1988), where a child was readmitted to school with the understanding that the identity would be disclosed to teachers but not to students.

15. *Los Angeles Times*, 26 August 1986, p. 18.

16. *Los Angeles Daily Journal*, 15 October 1985, p. C3; *New York Times*, 18 September 1985, p. A20.

17. *Los Angeles Times*, 6 February 1986, p. 32.

18. "Recommendations for Preventing Transmission of Infection with Human T-Lymphotropic Virus Type III/Lymphadenopathy-Associated Virus in the Workplace," Centers for Disease Control, *Morbidity and Mortality Weekly Report* 34 (1985): 682.

19. Erik Eckholm, "Poll Finds Many AIDS Fears That the Experts Say Are Groundless," *New York Times*, 12 September 1985, p. B11; Cristine Russell, "AIDS Stirs Public Concern But Not Panic, Survey Says: Poll Finds Wide Knowledge About Disease," *Washington Post*, 26 September 1985, p. A1.

20. The Public Health Service estimated in 1986 that between one million and one and a half million people had already been infected with the AIDS virus, Centers for Disease Control, *Morbidity and Mortality Weekly Report* 35 (1986): 765.

21. In New Jersey, for example, more than half of the students stayed away in protest of the attendance of a boy whose sister was known to be carrying the AIDS virus. *Minneapolis Star and Tribune*, 26 October 1985, p. 9A.

22. Raymond C. O'Brien, "A Legislative Initiative: The Ryan White Comprehensive AIDS Resources Emergency Act of 1990," *Journal of Contemporary Health Law and Policy* 7 (Spring 1991): 183–205. Act is P.L. No. 101–381, 104 Stat. 576.

23. Those receiving blood transfusions between January 1, 1978, and April 1, 1985 were at risk. See, for discussion, Martin Hirsh, "A Visitation with AIDS, Part VII: Medical Dilemma, Legal and Ethical Quagmire," *Medical Trial Techniques Quarterly* 37 (1990): 1.

24. See "Comment: Protecting Children with AIDS Against Arbitrary Exclusion from School," *California Law Review* 74 (1986): 1373; L. N. Brockman, "Enforcing the Right to a Public Education for Children Afflicted with AIDS," *Emory Law Journal* 36 (Spring 1987): 603; "Note: Discrimination in the Public School: Dick and Jane Have AIDS," *William and Mary Law Review* 29 (1988): 881.

25. "Cruel Twist of Fate Destroys Woman," *The Province,* 21 October 1990, p. 24.

26. CNN News, 8 December 1991.

27. "Fatal Care," *New York Times,* 29 September 1991, p. E7.

28. "Cruel Twist of Fate," p. 24.

29. "Dentist's Role in AIDS Challenged," *Boston Globe,* 25 February 1993, p. 11.

30. Lawrence K. Altman, "An AIDS Puzzle: What Went Wrong in Dentist's Office," *New York Times,* 30 July 1991, p. B6.

31. "Fatal Care," p. E7.

32. "Fear: AIDS Infection Intentional," *USA Today,* 7 June 1993, p. 3A.

33. William Scally, "Senate Wants Jail for Doctors Who Keep AIDS Affliction Secret," *Reuters,* 18 July 1991, via NEXIS.

34. *Morbidity and Mortality Weekly Report* 38 (1989): 9.

35. "Cruel Twist of Fate," p. 24.

36. Mike Williams, "AIDS Victim Infected by Dentist Wants to Protect Others," *Atlanta Constitution,* 19 February 1991, p. D5. See also Charles Seabrook, "DNA Links Dentist to AIDS in 5 Patients, Study Shows," *Atlanta Constitution,* 22 May 1992, p. A2. A pioneering study using DNA fingerprinting techniques provided evidence that linked Dr. Acer with five of his patients who had similar fingerprints to the virus that took Dr. Acer's life.

37. "Kimberly Bergalis Dies; Got AIDS from Dentist," *Washington Post,* 9 December 1991, p. C6.

38. "Myths, Fear Called Widespread in AIDS Litigation," *Boston Globe,* 19 January 1992, p. 2.

39. Ibid.

40. See, for example, Ill. Rev. Stat. ch. 38. Sec. 12–16.2 (1989).

41. Joseph F. Sullivan, "Should a Hospital Tell Patients If a Surgeon Has AIDS?" *New York Times,* 12 December 1989, p. B1.

42. Fifty-seven other health care professionals have admitted to authorities that they are HIV-positive, but of 19,000 of their patients who have been tested, none had contracted the disease from medical treatment. Lawrence K. Altman, "AIDS and a Dentist's Secrets" *New York Times,* 6 June 1993, sec. 4, p. 1.

43. "Doctors and AIDS: New CDC Guidelines," *Newsweek,* 22 July 1991, p. 60.

44. Sullivan, "Should a Hospital," p. B1.

45. Told to the author by Hansell Stedman, M.D., August 1985.

46. Robert Byrd, "U.S. AIDS Cases Top 200,000 Mark; Pace Quickens as Disease Spreads," *Boston Globe,* 17 January 1992, p. 3. The pace with which AIDS was invading the population was indicated by the fact that the first 100,000 cases took eight years to develop, while the second 100,000 appeared in 26 months, and the third was expected to take even less time. Also, the epidemic was spreading throughout the heterosexual population, from 5% to 7% in the second 100,000, while the incidence in homosexual or bisexual men had dropped from 61% to 55% in the second group of cases analyzed.

47. "The State's Hypocrisy on AIDS," *Boston Globe,* 5 May 1992, p. 18.

48. Dawn Webber, "Judge Rules in AIDS Case," from *Los Angeles Daily News,* as reprinted in *Telluride Daily Planet,* 23 June 1993, p. 4.

49. Peter Rhodes Easley, "Comment, the AIDS Crisis in Prison: A Need for Change," *Journal of Contemporary Health Law and Policy* 6, (1990): 221–38.

50. H. Dalton, S. Burris, and the Yale AIDS Law Project, *AIDS and the Law: A Guide for the Public* (New Haven, Conn.: Yale University Press, 1987), p. 238.

51. "AIDS in Prison," National Public Radio Broadcast, 22 November 1988.

52. *National Prison Project Journal* 17 (1988): 5.

53. *Chalk v. U.S. District Court, Central District Court Central District of California,* 840 F. 2d 701 (9th Cir. 1988).

54. Laura D. Estrin, "Comment: Hospitals and AIDS Discrimination: Applicability of Federal Discrimination Laws to HCWS and Staff Physicians," *Journal of Contemporary Health Law and Policy* 6 (1990): 193–220; quotation from p. 201. See also "Note: Between a Rock and Hard Place: AIDS and the Conflicting Physicians' Duty of Preventing Disease Transmission and Safeguarding Confidentiality," *Georgetown Law Journal* 76 (1987): 169. These notes predicted that AIDS victims would be entitled to the protection provided under Sec. 504 of the Vocational Rehabilitation and Other Services Act of 1973, 29 U.S.C. Sec. 794 (1988), and inmates of a prison who were afflicted with AIDS were held to be "handicapped individuals" under the act in *Harris v. Thigpen,* 941 F. 2d 1495 (11th Cir. 1991). Sec. 508 of the Americans with Disabilities Act of 1990, 42 U.S.C. Sec. 12208, precludes those suffering from alcoholism or drug abuse, as well as those with such sometimes perceived disabilities as homosexuality, bisexuality, transvestism, kleptomania, pedophilia, exhibitionism, pyromania, and compulsive gambling.

55. Four of the original cases were reversed. See Estrin, "Comment."

56. Americans with Disabilities Act of 1990, P.L. 101–336, 104 Stat. 327.

57. William Safire, "Candidates' Health," *New York Times,* 23 April 1992, p. A25.

58. Gene Gibbons, "Medical Checkup Shows Bush in Incredible Physical Condition," *Reuters,* 14 September 1991, Saturday PM Cycle, NEXIS.

59. Paul Tsongas, "The Cancer Freed Me. It Freed Me," *New York Times,* 6 May 1992, p. A29.

60. Ibid.

61. Safire, "Candidate's Health," p. A25.

62. Steve Fainaru, "Ashe Has AIDS; Cites Transfusion," *Boston Globe,* 9 April 1992, p. 1.

63. Ibid., p. 14.

64. Faith Daniels reporting on the "Today" show, NBC-TV, 9 April 1992.

65. Richard A. Knox, "For Tennis Star, Infection Came at Time of Great Risk," *New York Times,* 9 April 1992, p. 14.

66. Ibid.

67. Barry Lorge, "Tennis's Conspiracy of Compassion for Arthur Ashe," *New York Times,* 12 April 1992, p. S11.

68. Gene Policinski commenting on NBC's "Today" show, 9 April 1992, in an interview with Katie Couric.

69. Alex S. Jones, "News Media Torn Two Ways in Debate on Privacy," *New York Times,* 30 April 1992, p. B11: "It is not easy for the nation's editors to reconcile the twin American passions for both information—including quantities of gossip—and privacy. On the one hand is an apparent rising tide of advocacy for personal privacy; on the other is a glut of publications and television programs devoted to the most intimate details of people's lives. The public derides the press for revealing the details and yet gives high ratings to the tabloid television shows. Even among journalists and other strong proponents of First Amendment freedoms, there is no agreement on such matters as *USA Today*'s decision to investigate whether Arthur Ashe, the former tennis star, had AIDS. The disclosure of Mr. Ashe's condition touched off the latest round in the debate over privacy."

70. Christine Spolar, "Privacy for Public Figures?" *Washington Journalism Review* (June 1992): 18.

71. Ibid.

72. Ed Smith, professor of journalism at Virginia Commonwealth University, on NBC's "Today" show, 9 April 1992.

73. Spolar, "Privacy," p. 21.

74. See, for example, *Whalen v. Roe,* 429 U.S. 589, p. 605 (1976); also Dalton et al., *AIDS and the Law,* p. 55.

75. Alter and McKillop, "AIDS," p. 46.

76. Susan O. Scheutzow and Anthea R. Daniels, "The Discovery of Medical Records Maintained by Health Care Facilities: Inconsistent Law in Need of Legislative Correction," *Journal of Law and Health* 5 (Winter 1990): 179.

77. *U.S. v. Meagher,* 531 F. 2d 752 (5th Cir. 1975) cert. denied 429 U.S. 1965; J. Wigmore, *Evidence,* Vol. 8, Sec. 2380 (J. McNaughton rev. 1961).

78. D. Shuman, "The Origin of Physician-Patient Privilege and Professional Secrets," *Southwestern Law Journal* 39 (1985): 661.

79. See, for example, *General Motors Corp. v. Director of Ntl. Inst. for Occupational Safety and Health, Department of Health, Education and Welfare,* 636 F. 2d 163 (6th Cir. 1980).

80. For example, Ohio Rev. Code Ann., Sec. 3727.06.

81. American Medical Association, Revised Principles of Medical Ethics (1980).

82. See, for example, for physicians' assistants, for Ohio Rev. Code ANN. Sec. 4730.05(I)(Page's Supp. 1987); for physicians and podiatrists, 4731.22(B) (Page's Supp. 1990); for occupational therapists, 4755.10(G) (Page's Supp. 1990); and for psychologists 4732.17(D) (Page's Supp. 1987).

83. See, for example, *Hammonds v. Aetna,* 237 F. Supp. 96 (N.D. Ohio 1965), motion denied 243 F. Supp. 793 (N.D. Ohio 1965).

84. Scheutzow and Daniels, "Discovery of Medical Records," p. 183.

85. House Conference Report No. 652, 101st Cong., 2d Sess. 58 reprinted in *U.S. Code Congressional and Administrative News,* p. 862 (1990); 42 U.S.C. sections 300 ff (1972), as amended by P.L. No. 101–381, 104 Stat., 602 (1990).

86. U.S. Congress, Office of Technology Assessment, *Protecting Privacy in Computerized Medical Information* (Washington, D.C.: U.S. Government Printing Office, September 1993), p. 15.

87. Ibid., p. 20.

88. William Hafferty, "Whose Files Are They Anyway? Unlocking Your Health Records," *Modern Maturity* (April–May 1991): 68.

89. Family Education Rights and Privacy Act of 1974, 20 U.S.C. Sec. 1232g(b)(1).

90. Hafferty, "Whose Files Are They?" p. 70.

91. Sandra Blakeslee, "Ethicists See Omens of an Era of Genetic Bias," *New York Times,* 27 December 1979, p. B7.

92. Ellen Schultz, "Telling Tales," *Smart Money,* February 1993, p. 84.

93. OAT 1993 Study, p. 31.

94. Lawrence K. Altman, "Researchers Report Much Grimmer AIDS Outlook," *New York Times,* 4 June 1992, p. A1.

95. 42 U.S.C. Sec. 12901f, 102 Stat. 4234, P.L. 100–690, 18 November 1988.

96. *Los Angeles Times,* 20 September 1987, p. 20.

97. Ray M. Anderson, *Infectious Diseases of Humans: Dynamics and Control* (New York: Oxford University Press, 1991).

98. M. Nicole van Dam, "*Note,* The Scarlet Letter 'A': AIDS in a Computer Society," *Computer Law Journal* 10 (Winter 1990): 233–64.

99. Michael D. McDonald and Henrik L. Blum, *Health in the Information Age* (Berkeley, Calif.: Environmental Science and Policy Institute, 1992), pp. 3–4.

100. "President's Health Security Report to the American People"; chapter 5, "Simplicity"; *U.S. Newswire,* 27 October 1993, via NEXIS.

101. Harris-Equifax, "Health Information Privacy Survey 1993," conducted for Equifax by Louis Harris and Associates in association with Dr. Alan Westin, Columbia University (New York: Louis Harris and Associates, 1993), p. 10.

102. Ibid.

103. Ibid., pp. 27, 33.

104. Mitch Betts, "Health Fraud: Computers at War," *Computerworld,* 13 September 1993, p. 1.

105. Ibid., p. 14.

106. S. 1494, 103d Cong., 1st Sess., Sections (5) (B) (i)–(vii).

Chapter 4: Who Owns Your Image?

1. Title 47 U.S.C., Sec. 312.

2. Letter of Janine Ann Petit, 4 January 1992.

3. Ibid.

4. *Channels,* 22 October 1990, p. 19.

5. See comments of Mark Godfrey, director of photography for *U.S. News and World Report,* who described the "first digitized war," in which 35-millimeter negatives were scanned and transmitted over public phone lines or via satellite channels. The equipment manufactured by National Digital Corporation includes a Nikon scanner, a PC-based computer with an image compression card in it, a monitor, a high-speed 19.2-kilobits-per-second modem, and a line that could carry digital data at these speeds. Prints were never made, and a single transmission of a compressed file could take as long as two hours. "Ethics, Copyright, and the Bottom Line," Proceedings of a Symposium on Digital Technologies and Professional Photography (Camden, Me.: Center for Creative Imaging, 1992), p. 40.

6. Arthur C. Clarke, "Beyond the Global Village," *1984 Spring: A Choice of Futures* (New York: Ballantine/Dell, 1984), p. 7.

7. "Ethics, Copyright, and the Bottom Line," p. 30.

8. Ibid.

9. Warren and Brandeis were particularly perturbed by the rise of yellow journalism and the use of cameras to record what had previously been private events. See M. Franklin, *Cases and Materials on Mass Media Law,* 3d ed. (Mineola, N.Y.: Foundation Press, 1987), p. 300.

10. Samuel D. Warren and Louis D. Brandeis, "The Right to Privacy," *Harvard Law Review* 4 (1890): 195.

11. Ibid., p. 209.

12. *Roberson v. Rochester Folding Box Co.*, 171 N.Y. 538 (1902), 64 N.E. 442, 71 N.Y.S. 876.

13. 1903 New York Laws C. 132 Sec. 1, 2; New York Civil Rights Law Sec. 505.51 (McKinney).

14. *Pavesich v. New England Life Insurance Co.*, 122 Ga. 190, 214, 50 S.E. 68, 78 (1905).

15. Cited by Justice Fortas, dissenting in *Time Inc. v. Hill*, 385 U.S., p. 413 (1967).

16. W. Prosser, P. Keeton, D. Dobbs, and R. Owen, *Prosser and Keeton on the Law of Torts,* 5th ed. (St. Paul, Minn.: West, 1984), Sec. 117, p. 851.

17. *Galella v. Onassis,* 487 F. 2d 986; 17 Fed. R. Serv. 2d (Callaghan) 1205; 28 A.L.R. Fed. 879; 1 Media L. Rep. 2425 (2d Cir. 1973).

18. *Galella v. Onassis,* 353 F. Supp. 196 (1972).

19. *Galella v. Onassis,* 487 F. 2d, p. 1001.

20. Ibid., p. 995.

21. Ibid.

22. Ayn Rand, "Man's Rights," *Objectivist Newsletter* (April 1963).

23. ASMP Professional Business Practices in Photography, A Compilation by the American Society of Magazine Photographers (1982).

24. Paul F. Doering, "Protecting Intellectual Property in the Age of Machine-Sensible Art," presentation given at the Conference on Electronic Imaging in the Visual Arts, London, 31 July 1992.

25. Michael D. Remer, "Electronic Rights Contracts: Protecting Your Work in the New World of Electronic Technology," *Northwest Photo Network* (May–June 1992): 28.

26. Doering, "Protecting Intellectual Property," pp. 5–6.

27. David Walker, "ASMP Plans Licensing Agency," *Photo Direct News* (October 1992): 1; idem, "ASMP to Start Licensing Agency," *Photo Direct News* (July 1992): 42.

28. Walker, "ASMP to Start Licensing Agency."

29. David Walker, "Five Stock Agencies Sign with PNI," *Photo Direct News* (November 1992): 1.

30. "Tribune Company Invests in Picture Network International, Electronic Photo Archive and Marketing Company," *PR Newswire,* 1 March 1993, via NEXIS.

31. Nancy Madlin, "Four Stock Agencies Join 3M in CD Venture," *Photo Direct News* (June 1992): 1.

32. It is possible that some trade practices can be established similar to those applied by the book publishing industry. For example, the general practice among book publishers is to require acknowledgment for quotes of over three hundred words and written permission for the use of quotations of over five hundred words. Perhaps with time, ethical practices will evolve that recognize that lifting a certain number of pixels (the minute picture elements) from an image is acceptable but lifting a larger number requires acknowledgment and/or a licensing agreement.

33. Gary Frischling, attorney with the High Technology Group at Irell and Manella in Los Angeles, speaking at the Center for Creative Imaging Conference; "Ethics, Copyright, and the Bottom Line," p. 72.

34. Dow Jones News Service, Doc. no. 120118–0360, 7 January 1984.

35. Ibid., Doc. no. 120706–0544, 6 July 1984.

36. Ibid., Doc. no. 120119–661, 19 January 1984. Until that release, *Flashdance* and *Jane Fonda's Workout* had been the top-selling video-tapes, with 200,000 copies each.

37. Dow Jones News Service, Doc. no. 110512–1159, 5 December 1983.

38. Paul Kagan Associates, Carmel, California.

39. Title 17 U.S.C., Sec. 109(a).

40. Michael Blowen, "Howard's 'Far and Away' Doesn't Come Close: Video Watch," *Boston Globe,* 30 October 1992, "Arts and Film," p. 33.

41. Doug Camilli, "Woman Fends Off Naked Attacker with Umbrella; First to Arrive on Freeway Accident Scene Was No Good Samaritan," *Gazette* (Montreal), 5 November 1992, p. E2.

42. *Sony Corp. v. Universal City Studios,* 64 U.S. 417 (1984).

43. Title 17 U.S.C., Sec. 107.

44. *Williams & Wilkins Co. v. United States,* 420 U.S. 376 (1975).

45. Dow Jones News Service, Doc. no. 110512–1159, 5 May 1983.

46. Paul Page, "Burt Lancaster and James Stewart Reprise Roles Before Congress," *Associated Press,* 16 March 1988.

47. George Lucas, "Lucas and Spielberg: In Defense of Artists' Rights," *Washington Post,* 28 February 1988, p. G1.

48. "Mr. Smith: and Friends: Jimmy Stewart, Movie Colorization," *Broadcasting* 114, no. 12 (21 March 1988): 49.

49. "DeConcini-Hatch Bill Due: NAP, MPAA Battle House Unit Today on National Film Commission Plan," *Communications Daily* 8, no. 116 (16 June 1988): 5.

50. The National Film Preservation Board is authorized P.L. No. 100–446, 102 Stat. 1787, enacted 27 September 1988; codified in Title 2 U.S.C., Sec. 178j (1989).

51. David Goeller, "House Would Discourage But Not Ban Colorized Movies," *Associated Press,* 30 June 1988.

52. Ralph Oman, "Black and White and Red All Over," *New York Times,* 24 June 1987, p. A27. See also 52 Fed. Reg. 2343, 22 June 1987.

53. Michael W. Miller, "Creativity Furor: High-Tech Alteration of Sights and Sounds Divides the Art World," *Wall Street Journal,* 1 September 1987, p. 1.

54. Copyright law experts have decided that the United States could join the Berne Convention without amending the U.S. statute to explicitly include "moral rights" on the assumption that case law adequately protects such rights under the rubric of related legal regimes such as defamation, privacy, and unfair competition. "U.S. to Upgrade Standing in World Copyright Community—Finally," *Channels,* September 1988, p. 22.

55. Miller, "Creativity Furor," p. 1.
56. "Ethics, Copyright, and the Bottom Line," p. 12.
57. Fred Ritchin, "Photography's New Bag of Tricks," *New York Times Magazine,* 4 November 1984, pp. 44–45.
58. "Ethics, Copyright, and the Bottom Line," p. 31.
59. Ibid.
60. Ibid., p. 61.
61. Mark Godfrey, "The Impact of Digital Imaging at *U.S. News and World Report,*" "Ethics, Copyright, and the Bottom Line," pp. 41–42.
62. "Ethics, Copyright, and the Bottom Line," p. 33.
63. Ibid. p. 32
64. Jack Russo and Michael Risch, "Copyright Protection for Virtual Realities," *Computer Law Strategist* 9, no. 6 (October 1992): 1.
65. Ibid., p. 3.
66. "Ethics, Copyright, and the Bottom Line," p. 61.
67. *Stern Electronics v. Kaufman,* 669 F. 2d 852 (2d Cir. 1982).
68. "Photo '92 Update: Looking Back at Photo Midwest," *Photo Direct News* (September 1992): 12.
69. Susan Orenstein, "Digital Multimedia Madness," *Legal Times,* 13 September 1993, p. S29.
70. Remer, "Electronic Rights Contracts," p. 32.
71. "Ethics, Copyright, and the Bottom Line," p. 35.
72. Sandra J. Swanson, "BPA Digital-Imaging Workshop," *Photo Electronic Imaging* (October 1992): 40.
73. Remer, "Electronic Rights Contracts," p. 32.

Chapter 5: Who Owns Your Electronic Messages?

1. IDG Communications, Inc., *Infoworld,* 22 October 1990.
2. Ibid.
3. Glenn Rifkin, "Do Employees Have a Right to Electronic Privacy?" *New York Times,* 8 December 1991, sec. C, p. 8.
4. Bruce Keppel, "Electronic Mail Stirs Debate on the Privacy Issue," *Los Angeles Times,* 23 May 1990, p. D1.
5. Kristi Coale, "Northern Telecom Sees, Hears No Evil," *Infoworld,* 17 February 1992, p. 50.
6. *Alana Shoars v. Epson America, Inc.,* No. SWC112749 (L.A. Super. Ct.).
7. The class action suit by four employees against Epson America, Inc., citing a violation of the California State Penal Code Sec. 631, was filed 31 July 1990, *Flanigan v. Epson America, Inc.,* Case No. BC007036 (L.A. Super. Ct.). The allegations are invasion of privacy by illegally and systematically printing up and reading all E-mail entering and leaving the Torrance site.
8. "Wire Tap?: Class-Action Suit Filed Against Epson America Inc. for Invasion of Privacy. Employee E-Mail Allegedly Tapped," *EDGE: Work-Group Computing Report* 1, no. 11 (13 August 1990).

9. David Bjerklie, "E-Mail; The Boss Is Watching; Electronic Mail Trends," *Technology Review* 96, no. 3 (April 1993): 14.

10. *St. Petersburg Times,* 6 June 1993, p. A1.

11. Title 18, Sec. 1702, Public Law 350, enacted 4 March 1909, 35 Statutes at Large 1941.

12. Michael Stroud, "Rise of Electronic Mail Raises Sticky Privacy Issues," *Investor's Daily,* 22 June 1990, p. 13.

13. Messages entered into the conference during June and July 1993.

14. 103rd Cong., 1st Sess., U.S. Senate, 1993 S. 984, Privacy for Consumers and Workers Act, introduced 19 May 1993. A similar bill had been introduced previously in the House with some 159 sponsors supporting its passage. 1993 H.R. 1900 introduced 28 April 1993.

15. "Employers' Access to Employee E-Mail," *DataLaw Report* 1, no. 1 (July 1993): 1.

16. Ibid., reporting research by the Yankee Group of Boston, Massachusetts, and the Electronic Mail Association of Arlington, Virginia.

17. Rifkin, "Do Employees Have a Right?" p. 8.

18. Wayne Eckerson, "Privacy Suit Forces Users to Examine E-mail Policies: Case Against Epson Raises Troubling Questions," *Network World,* 17 September 1990, p. 1.

19. Ibid.

20. Robert Preer, "E-Mail's Popularity Increases: Computers Foster Connectedness," *Boston Globe,* 11 February 1993, p. 1; see also Stroud, "Rise of Electronic Mail," p. 13.

21. Ibid.

22. Rifkin, "Do Employees Have a Right?" p. 8.

23. 18 U.S.C. A Sec. 2701 et seq.

24. Bart Ziegler, "Lawsuit Raises Question of Whether Electronic Mail Is Private," *Associated Press,* 23 August 1990, Thursday PM cycle, NEXIS.

25. Coale, "Northern Telecom," p. 50.

26. Ibid.

27. W. John Moore, "Taming Cyberspace," *National Journal* 24, no. 13 (28 March 1992): 745

28. John A. Armstrong, "The Silicon Handshake: Doing Business in the Electronic Future," 1992 Regents' Lecture, University of California, Santa Barbara, 18 February 1992.

29. It should be noted that voice mail also achieves many of the same objectives.

30. Armstrong, "Silicon Handshake," p. 19.

31. Some townships, such as Belmont, Massachusetts, limit participation to members elected to speak at the town meeting.

32. John Schwartz, "A Screenful of Venom," *Newsweek,* 4 November 1991, p. 48. See also Jack Rickard, "Prodigy Can't Win as a Censor," *Computerworld,* 11 November 1991, p. 25: "Prodigy's major problem has been that, from the start, it strained to establish its service as a

'publication' under its sole editorial control. It has insisted that what it is running is a 'private' service—just themselves and 1.1 million intimate friends—and further, a 'family' service somehow akin to the Disney Channel."

33. Dean Takahashi, "Prodigy Service Cut Is Censorship, Subscribers Say," *Los Angeles Times,* 7 November 1990, p. D1, via NEXIS.

34. "Computer Bulletin Board Under Fire for Allowing Anti-Semitic Messages," *Agence France Presse,* 23 October 1991, via NEXIS.

35. Telephone conversation with George Perry, General Counsel of Prodigy, 11 June 1992.

36. Charles Leroux, "'Hate Speech' Enters Computer Age," *Chicago Tribune,* 27 October 1991, p. 4.

37. Laurie Petersen, "Between Censorship and Sensitivity," *Adweek Marketing Week,* 28 October 1991, p. 9, via NEXIS.

38. Ted Papes, president of Prodigy, reported in "Prodigy Did Not Publish Offensive Message Cited by Media; Affirms Standards and Free Expression on Bulletin Boards," *PR Newswire,* 23 October 1991, via NEXIS.

39. John Buskin, "Will Free Speech Byte the Dust?" *Newsday,* 30 October 1991, p. 84. However, the message in question was given far more publicity through the mass media coverage than it ever would have received within the Prodigy bulletin board. It was: "Hitler had some valid points, too. Remove the Jews and we will go a long ways towards avoiding much trouble. Pogroms, persecutions, and the mythical holocaust. They only get what they so very richly deserve. Maybe a REAL, and this time, worldwide holocaust is a good idea" (*Agence France Presse,* 23 October 1991).

40. Jerry Walker, "Swift PR Action Chills Anti-Semitism Charges," *Sporting News,* December 1991, p. 36.

41. "Computer Speech—Also Free," *New York Times,* 30 October 1991, sec. A, p. 24.

42. Quoted in Glenn Rifkin, "Mitchell Kapor; There Is an Opportunity for People Who Care About the Social Impact of All This Technology to Take a Stand," *Computerworld* (9 December 1991): 73.

43. Brian Nielson, "Intellectual Freedom in an Electronic Age; PC Monitor," *Online* 15, no. 3 (May 1991): 88.

44. The Feb. 21–22, 1991, meeting in Washington, D.C., was sponsored by the Computer Professionals for Social Responsibility and the Electronic Frontier Foundation; see "Information Policy, Computer Communications Networks Face Identity Crisis over Their Legal Status," *Daily Report for Executives,* 26 February 1991, no. 38, p. A6.

45. Ibid.

46. Jean-Louis Gassee, "Prodigy: Corpocracy at Its Worst; Commentary," *Publishing L.P.* 4, no. 42 (18 December 1990): 17.

47. "Information Policy," p. A6.

48. "Computer as a Forum of Hate Poses Problem," *Los Angeles Times,* 16 November 1991, p. F13.

49. Marianne Taylor, "Users Say Computer Network Is Muzzling Their Give-and-Take," *Chicago Tribune*, 7 January 1991, business sec., p. 1.

50. Singer, who travels frequently for his job, often dials up a computer network from his hotel room to participate in evening political discussions, typing his opinions and observations into a central file available to fellow participants. Ibid., p. 1.

51. *Cubby, Inc. v. CompuServe, Inc,* 776 F. Supp. 135, 1991 U.S. Dist., LEXIS 15545; 19 Media L. Rep. 1525 (1991).

52. This amendment was first proposed by Lawrence Tribe of the Harvard University Law School at a conference sponsored by the Computer Professionals for Social Responsibility, held in Burlingame, California, in March 1991.

53. *NAACP v. Alabama,* 357 U.S. 449 (1958); *Thornburgh v. American College of Obstetricians,* 106 Sup. Ct. 2169 (1986), but see *Buckley v. Valeo,* 424 U.S., pp. 71–72 (1976) requiring disclosure of the names of contributors to campaign committees.

54. Robert B. Charles, "The New World of On-Line Libel," *Manhattan Lawyer* (December 1991): 40.

Chapter 6: Who Owns Video Entertainment?

1. "FCC Thinks It Has Video Intruder," *Chicago Tribune*, 23 July 1986, p. 9.

2. Lawrence Kilman, "HBO Was Victim of Sophisticated Pirate and Its Own Vulnerability," *Associated Press*, 28 April 1986, Monday AM Cycle, via NEXIS.

3. A satellite dish is a parabolic antenna that collects satellite signals. C-band dishes average 7 to 10 feet in diameter. Ku-band dishes range from 3 to 6 feet in diameter. Antenna installed today typically are capable of receiving both signals. Newer versions of direct broadcasting satellites are expected to be capable of delivering signals to much smaller antenna.

4. "Video Pirate Interrupts HBO," *New York Times*, 28 April 1986, sec. 3, p. 24.

5. Kilman, "HBO Was Victim."

6. Quoted in Tom Shales, "On the Air; Look! Up in the Sky; Captain Midnight and HBO's Warning Signal," *Washington Post*, 29 April 1986, p. C1.

7. "Captain Midnight Lashes Out Against HBO," *Associated Press*, 10 May 1986, via NEXIS.

8. Hans Fantel, "Home Video: The Dish Owners vs. the Scramblers," *New York Times*, 15 June 1986, sec. 2, p. 30.

9. Kenneth R. Clark, "Satellite Dish Industry Throws In Towel to Cable Programmers," *Chicago Tribune*, 1 June 1986, p. 10.

10. Gerald Lush, "Perfect Picture for Everyone—Unless Pirates Steal It," reprinted by Burrelle's Service from the *Hardin County Independent,*

Elizabeth, Kentucky, October 1986.

11. "SPACE Helping to Bring the Benefits of Satellite Technology to All Americans," *Satvision* (August 1984): 3.

12. P.L. 98–549, 30 October 1984, 98 Stat. 2779.

13. Sec. 5a amending Sec. 705 of the Communications Act of 1984.

14. Sec. 5(c)(4) "the viewing for private use in an individual's dwelling unit by means of equipment, owned or operated by such individual, capable of receiving satellite cable programming directly from a satellite"; see also *American Television and Communications Corp. v. Floken, Ltd.,* 629 F. Supp, 1462, 1469 (M.D. Fla. 1986), which held that hotel and motel owners' delivery of satellite signals without authorization and for their own commercial advantage falls outside the "private viewing" exception; in agreement, *Entertainment and Sports v. Edinburgh Communication Hotel,* 623 F. Supp. 647, 652 (S.D. Tex. 1985).

15. "[V]ideo programming which is transmitted via satellite and which is primarily intended for the direct receipt by cable operators for their retransmission to cable subscribers."

16. 130 *Congressional Record*—House H10439 (daily ed., 1 October 1984).

17. Peter W. Kaplan, "Sales of TV Dish Antenna Raising Problems," *New York Times,* 9 July 1985, p. C16.

18. "FCC Thinks It Has Video Intruder," p. 9.

19. "Video Pirate."

20. Shales, "On the Air."

21. Ibid.

22. *United Press International,* 23 November 1987, Monday PM Cycle, via NEXIS.

23. Bill McCloskey, "Captain Midnight Arrested, FCC Says," *Associated Press,* 22 July 1986, Tuesday PM Cycle via NEXIS. The videotaped evidence that HBO was able to provide the investigators revealed the sophistication of the equipment necessary to write the message, thus it was essential in identifying the culprit.

24. "Captain Midnight Apologizes," *United Press International,* 24 July 1986, Thursday AM Cycle, via NEXIS.

25. William Trott, "Captain Midnight Strikes Again," *United Press International,* 28 July 1986, Monday BC cycle, via NEXIS.

26. "Captain Midnight Apologizes."

27. Figures supplied by the Satellite Broadcasting and Communications Association of America as of 1 September 1991.

28. Adam Buckman, "FCC Sure Is Mad, Max," *Advertising Age,* 30 November 1987, p. 8; "Pirate," *United Press International,* 23 November 1987, Monday PM cycle, via NEXIS. Adam Buckman, "Nailing 'Headroom' a Cinch, Experts Say," *Advertising Age,* 30 November 1987, p. 70.

29. "CBN Staffer Convicted of Pirating," *Electronic Media,* 1 October 1990, p. 25.

30. Mitchell Miller, "CBN Engineer Convicted on Two Satellite-Piracy Charges," *United Press International,* 25 September 1990, Tuesday BC cycle.

31. "Jury Tries Again on Messages Put in Porn Films," *United Press International,* 24 September 1990, part P, p. 10.

32. "CBN Staffer Convicted of Pirating."

33. P.L. 100–667, enacted 16 November 1988.

34. P.L. 100–667, Sec. 205.

35. *Communications Daily* 10, no. 240 (13 December 1990): 8.

36. *United Press International,* 25 December 1990, BC Cycle, via NEXIS.

37. This story was obtained from law enforcement officials in the Maricopa County, Arizona, sheriff's office.

38. Lush, "Perfect Picture."

39. Calvin Sims, "Cost of Halting TV Signal Thieves," *New York Times,* 16 October 1989, p. D1.

40. "A Tutorial on VideoCipher II Signal Piracy," provided by General Instrument Corporation.

41. "Piracy a Worldwide Problem," *Onsat,* 4–10 December 1988; Calvin Sims, "Business Technology: A New Decoder to Foil Satellite-RV Pirates," *New York Times,* 31 January 1990, p. D6; "2 Million Homes Have Satellite TV Systems," *Advocate* (Newark, N.J.), 30 November 1988.

42. Mary Ellin Arch, "Illegal Descramblers Are Target of 'Cops,'" *Richmond Times-Dispatch,* 21 November 1988, p. B8.

43. "Home Satellite Dishes: Up Against the Wall!" *Channels/Field Guide* (annual publication of *Channels* magazine), 1989, p. 125.

44. "Trade Group Names Piracy Panel," *Satellite TV Week,* 4–10 December 1988.

45. "Amnesty Is Offered Video Pirates," *Richmond Times-Dispatch,* 18 November 1988.

46. Mary Ellin Arch, "Satellite TV Companies Policing Virginia for Illegal Descramblers," *Daily Herald* (Baltimore), 19 November 1988. Matt Whitcomb, a vice president of ACS, Inc., a co-sponsor of the Satellite TV Fair, told reporters that he thought 50% of all Roanoke area descrambler owners were pirates and as many as 75% of the local area dealers had engaged in illegal decoder sales at some time in the past.

47. "Illegal Descramblers 'Fired On' in Roanoke," *Richmond Times-Dispatch* 16 November 1988, p. B2. Terence Luddy, security director for the San Diego–based Videocipher Division of General Instrument, which manufactured the descramblers, said that the company had been able, after extensive investigation, to identify very precise information on the widespread piracy in the area and that they would continue to hit pirate units on a daily basis.

48. "Combating Piracy," *Satellite TV Week,* 11–17 December 1988.

49. "Amnesty Is Offered Video Pirates."

50. "Satellite Dish Users Give Up Outlaw Life, Get New Devices," *Roanoke Times and World News*, 20 November 1988.

51. Mary Ellin Arch, "Amnesty Offered for Illegal Descramblers as FBI Raids Dealer," *United Press International*, 17 November 1988, via NEXIS.

52. "U.S. Customs Raids San Diego Business," *Onsat*, 11–17 December 1988.

53. Marc D. Allen, "FBI Zaps 8 Firms Selling Illegal TV Descrablers," *Indianapolis Star*, 17 December 1988, p. 1; Scott Chase, "Up Against the Wall!" *Channels/Field Guide*, 1989, p. 125.

54. Sims, "Cost of Halting."

55. "Antipiracy Efforts Grow," *Communications Daily* 11, no. 64 (3 April 1991): 3.

56. In the Matter of Regulation of Domestic Receive-Only Satellite Earth Stations, FCC 73–374, adopted 18 October 1979, 74 FCC 2d 205, 216, 44 R.R. 2d 511 (1979).

57. "For Arctic Base, Satellite TV Provides the Outside World," *New York Times*, 9 July 1985, p. C16.

58. SBCA release, 1991.

Chapter 7: Who Owns Religious Information?

1. "Breaking the Scroll Cartel," *New York Times*, 7 September 1991, p. 22.

2. John Noble Wilford, "Computer Breaks Monopoly on Study of Dead Sea Scrolls," *New York Times*, 5 September 1991, p. A1.

3. Robert Leiter, "Dead Sea Scrolls: Out of the Caves, into the Light," *Ethnic Newswatch* 191, no. 13 (27 March 1992): 8x.

4. Hershel Shanks, "Scholars, Scrolls, Secrets and 'Crimes,'" *New York Times*, 7 September 1991, p. 23.

5. "Huntington Library Releases Scroll Photographs," *Biblical Archaeology Review* (November–December 1991): 63. According to Dr. William Moffett, director of the Huntington Library, the decision to open access to the stored images was made in July 1991, prior to the announcement of the computer reconstruction, and intended to be announced in conjunction with the airing of a PBS "Nova" special on the Dead Sea Scrolls scheduled for mid-October. "The Dead Sea Scrolls Are Opened to the Public," *C&RL News* (November 1991): 631.

6. *A Facsimile Edition of the Dead Sea Scrolls*, vols. 1 and 2, prepared with an introduction and index by Robert H. Eisenman and James M. Robinson (Washington, D.C.: Biblical Archaeology Society, 1991).

7. John Noble Wilford, "Monopoly over Dead Sea Scrolls Is Ended," *New York Times*, 22 September 1991, p. A20.

8. Ari L. Goldman, "Lessons Learned from Unscrolling Two Religions' Turbulent Pasts," *New York Times*, 29 September 1991, p. E5.

9. This version of the discovery is the most often recognized by Dead Sea Scroll scholars and referenced by the Library of Congress in its brochure prepared for its exhibition of some fragments (29 April–1 August 1993). Another version of the discovery of the scrolls, described as "fanciful," attributes the discovery to members of a group of nomadic Bedouins of the Ta'amireh tribe who were journeying from Transjordan into Palestine and apparently chose a circuitous route to avoid border checks because they were carrying contraband. See, for example, A. Powell Davies, *The Meaning of the Dead Sea Scrolls* (New York: Mentor Books, 1956), p. 9. Metropolitan Samuel, to whom these first scrolls were taken, in an introduction to one of the first publications several years after the discovery, stated that the truth would never be known except that it was members of the Ta'amireh tribe who discovered the scrolls, implying that there was something clandestine about their discovery. See *The Dead Sea Scrolls of St. Mark's Monastery: The Isaiah Manuscript and the Habakkuk Commentary,* edited for the trustees by Millar Burroughs with the assistance of John C. Trever and William H. Brownlee, foreword by Archbishop Athanasius Yeshue Samuel, Syrian Archbishop–Metropolitan of Jerusalem and Hashemite Jordan (New Haven, Conn.: American Schools of Oriental Research, 1950), p. vii. No doubt some of the fragments were discovered by shepherd boys as well as archaeologists. One account names "a Palestinian Arab shepherd boy, Mohammed el-Dib," as the first; see Joseph Albright, "Rediscovering the Scrolls," *Houston Chronicle,* 29 September 1991, p. A23.

10. "Israelis Relinquish Grip on Dead Sea Scrolls," *Japan Times,* 29 October 1991, p. 19.

11. Davies, *Meaning of the Dead Sea Scrolls,* p. 16.

12. Frank M. Cross, of Harvard University's Department of Near Eastern Languages and Civilizations, was a student of Professor Albright at Johns Hopkins University and was present when Albright identified the Isaiah scroll and its approximate date. (Frank Moore Cross, "Tales of the Early Days in the Discovery and Study of the Dead Sea Scrolls," unpublished manuscript.) For a remarkable feat confirmed years later by carbon-14 dating, see "Carbon-14 Tests Substantiate Scroll Dates," *Biblical Archaeology Review* (November–December 1991): 72. Tests were undertaken at the prodding of Robert H. Eisenman of California State University, Long Beach. Carbon-14 tests were performed on the linen in 1951, but no tests were done on the scrolls themselves. In recent tests done in Zurich, Switzerland, fourteen samples were taken from different texts in the Wadi Qumran and six from five nearby sites—Wadi Daliyeh, Amasada, Wadi Seyal, Wadi Murabba'at, and Khirbet Mird—from the mid-second century B.C. to the mid-first century A.D.

13. Davies, *Meaning of the Dead Sea Scrolls,* p. 12.

14. Avi Katzman, "Chief Dead Sea Scroll Editor Denounces Judaism,

Israel; Claims He's Seen Four More Scrolls Found by Bedouin," *Biblical Archaeology Review* (January–February 1991): 70.

15. The price was reported as $5.60 by "Dead Sea Scrolls Update," *Biblical Archaeology Review* (July–August 1990): 48, but Professor Cross, who purchased many of the fragments, offered the lower figure. However, the price went up as the scrolls became scarcer. The Temple Scroll, which Cross attempted to purchase from Kando on behalf of the ASOR, was purchased by General Yiga'el Yadin for $105,000. See Cross, "Tales of the Early Days."

16. Cross, "Tales of the Early Days."

17. "Israeli Oversight Committee Takes Charge," *Biblical Archaeology Review* (July–August 1990): 46.

18. "Major Players," *Biblical Archaeology Review* (March–April 1991): 53. See also Cross, "Tales of the Early Days."

19. Cross, "Tales of the Early days," p. 9.

20. "Israelis Relinquish Grip on Dead Sea Scrolls," *Japan Times*, 29 October 1991, p. 19.

21. See, for example, Geza Vermes, "Seeing Is Believing," The Higher Education Supplement of the *London Times*, 8 November 1991, p. 19: "Scholars excluded from the circle of the chosen were outraged."

22. Interview with Frank Moore Cross, 9 April 1993.

23. "Why Won't the Scroll Editors Release the Texts? Frank Cross Provides the Answers," *Biblical Archaeology Review* (March–April 1990): 24.

24. "The Story of the Dead Sea Scrolls," National Public Radio, 2 August 1992.

25. Abraham Rabinovich, "New Wind in the Scrollery," *Jerusalem Post*, 11 October 1991, via NEXIS. Under Israel's new antiquities law, archaeological material can be reassigned if not published within five years.

26. "Why Won't Scroll Editors Release Texts?"

27. Davies, *Meaning of the Dead Sea Scrolls,* p. 17.

28. Joseph L. Sax, "Is Anyone Minding Stonehenge? The Origins of Cultural Property Protection in England," *California Law Review* 78 (December 1990): 1554.

29. Ibid.

30. Leiter, "Dead Sea Scrolls," p. 8x.

31. Ibid.

32. The importance placed on the Dead Sea Scrolls by Israelis became apparent when three senior archaeologists, including Dr. Avraham Biran, head of the Israeli Antiquities Department, accompanied paratroop commander Mordechai Gur into Jerusalem to secure the treasures against war damage; see Rabinovich, "New Wind in the Scrollery."

33. Interview with Frank Moore Cross, 9 April 1993; Clyde Haberman, "Israel Protests, But Library Opens Access to Scrolls, *New York Times,* international ed., 23 September 1991, p. A8.

34. United Nations Economic, Scientific, and Cultural Organization Convention on the Means of Prohibiting and Preventing Illicit Import, Export and Transfer of Ownership of Cultural Property (UNESCO Convention), 4 November 1970, 823 U.N.T.S. 231 (1972).

35. John Moustakas, "Group Rights in Cultural Property: Justifying Strict Inalienability," *Cornell Law Review* 74 (September 1989): 1181.

36. The 1983 Convention on Cultural Property Implementation Act, 19 U.S.C.A., Secs. 2601–1613 (West Supp. 1989).

37. Hague Convention for the Protection of Cultural Property in the Event of Armed Conflict, 14 May 1954, 249 U.N.T.S. 240 (1956).

38. See Parliamentary Debate, House of Commons 188 (1984), discussed in Moustakas, "Group Rights in Cultural Property," p. 1198.

39. "Preserve the Dead Sea Scrolls," *Biblical Archaeology Review* (January–February, 1992): 62.

40. Interview with Ben Zion Wacholder, Hebrew Union College, 12 April 1993.

41. Wilford, "Monopoly over Dead Sea Scrolls," p. A20.

42. Interview with ABMC's William Yarchin, who was present when the photographs were taken, 10 April 1993.

43. Interview with William Moffett, 7 April 1993.

44. Wilford, "Monopoly over Dead Sea Scrolls," p. A1; see also "Dead Sea Scrolls Are Opened to the Public."

45. Letter of William A. Moffett to the author, 20 April 1993.

46. Leiter, "Dead Sea Scrolls,"p. 8x.

47. Daniel Williams and Russell Chandler, "Israeli Panel Shifts Stand on Scrolls," *Los Angeles Times,* 26 September 1991, p. A32.

48. "Another View of the 'Dead Sea Scrolls Scandal,'" *Biblical Archaeology Review* (May–June 1992): 64, commends BAR for waging "an extensive propaganda war" against the Scroll Team, beginning in 1985 and continuing up to the present day; see, for example, "Failure to Publish Dead Sea Scrolls Is Leitmotif of the New York University Scroll Conference," *Biblical Archaeology Review* (September–October 1985): 71; "Dead Sea Scrolls Scandal: Israel's Department of Antiquities Joins Conspiracy to Keep Scrolls Secret," *Biblical Archaeology Review* (July–August 1989): 18; "The Dead Sea Scroll Monopoly Must Be Broken," *Biblical Archaeology Review* (July–August 1990): 44.

49. Vermes, "Seeing Is Believing," p. 19; see also John Noble Wilford, "Officials in Israel Ease Stand on Access to Ancient Scrolls," *New York Times,* 27 September 1991.

50. Wilford, "Computer Breaks Monopoly."

51. "Dead Sea Scrolls Update: From the Press," *Biblical Archaeology Review* (November–December 1991): 64–65.

52. "Huntington Library Releases Scroll Photographs," *Biblical Archaeology Review* (November–December 1991): 72.

53. Abraham Rabinovich, "MK's Consider Making Scrolls Available to All

NOTES

Researchers," *Jerusalem Post,* international ed., 26 October 1991.

54. Abraham Rabinovich, "Antiquities Authority Reverses Its Policy on Dead Sea Scrolls Photos," *Jerusalem Post,* 28 October 1991.

55. *A Fascimile Edition of the Dead Sea Scrolls* contains 1,787 plates and was funded by the Irving I. Moskowitz Foundation.

56. Interview with William A. Moffett, director of the Huntington Library, 7 April 1993.

57. John Eckberg, "Dead Sea Scroll Photos to Be Released to Scholars," *Cincinnati Enquirer,* 28 October 1991, via NEXIS.

58. John Noble Wilford, "Open, Dead Sea Scrolls Stir Up New Disputes," *New York Times,* 19 April 1992, p. 22; Emanuel Tov, ed., with the collaboration of Stephen J. Pfann, *The Dead Sea Scrolls on Microfiche* (Leiden, Netherlands: E. J. Brill, 1993).

59. This copy was placed in the Hebrew Union Library in 1989. Interview with Professor Wacholder, 12 April 1993.

60. Brian Hayes, "The Information Age: Reassembly Required," *Sciences* (May–June 1992): 12–15.

61. Ibid.

62. Ibid., 12.

63. Correspondence from Martin G. Abegg, Jr., 31 August 1992.

64. Interview with Ben Zion Wacholder, 12 April 1993.

65. Cross letter.

66. Emanuel Tov, "Expanded Team of Editors Hard at Work on Variety of Texts," *Biblical Archaeology Review* (May–June 1992): 73–74.

67. "Reconstructing the Scrolls Byte by Byte," *Biblical Archaeology Review* (May–June 1992): 71.

68. "Ancient Biblical Manuscript Center Contributes to Photographic Preservation of Dead Sea Photos," *Biblical Archaeology Review* (July–August 1992): 71. In January the Shrine of the Book in Jerusalem invited the center's photographic team to make some 4,000 high-resolution photographs, copies of the original Dead Sea Scroll negatives. The photographers also took new photographs, including some of the Temple Scroll.

69. Ibid.

70. Tov, "Expanded Team."

71. Goldman, "Lessons Learned," p. E5.

72. Davies, *Meaning of the Dead Sea Scrolls,* p. 15.

73. Tov, "Expanded Team."

74. *World Weekly News,* 19 November 1991, pp. 3–5.

75. Michael Baigent and Richard Leigh, *The Dead Sea Scrolls Deception* (London: Jonathan Cape, 1991).

76. Hershel Shanks, "Is the Vatican Suppressing the Dead Sea Scrolls?" *Biblical Archaeology Review* (November–December 1991): 68.

77. "Preserve the Dead Sea Scrolls," *Biblical Archaeology Review* (January–February 1992): 63.

78. Elisha Qimron, a professor at the University of the Negev in Beer-

sheba Israel, was a visiting scholar at the Annenberg Research Institute in Philadelphia during the 1992–93 academic year, where extensive work on the scrolls was in progress.

79. Elisha Qimron, letter to the editors of the *Biblical Archaeology Review* (July–August 1992): 76.

80. "Israeli Court Bans BAR from Selling Book of Dead Sea Scroll Photos," *Biblical Archaeology Review* (March–April 1992): 9. The image in litigation was a picture of the original Hebrew text or a manuscript known as MMT as reconstructed by Qimron and previously published in a Polish journal.

81. Eileen Alt Powell, "Israeli Judge Says Scrolls Book Violated Scholar's Copyright," *Associated Press*, 30 March 1993, AM cycle, via NEXIS.

82. Robert Leiter, "Dead Sea Scrolls Decision Favors Scholar Based Here," *Ethnic Newswatch*, Jewish Exponent 193, no. 14 (April 1993): 19.

83. Tricia Desilets, "Dead Sea Scrolls Prompt Copyright Litigation," *Legal Intelligencer*, 19 April 1993, p. 1; Joel Greenberg, "Court in Israel Supports Editor Who Reconstructed Dead Sea Text," *New York Times*, 31 March 1993, p. A5.

84. John Noble Wilford, "New Accusations Erupt over the Dead Sea Scrolls," *New York Times*, 13 December 1992, p. 28.

85. Ron Grossman, "Scholar Admits 'Indebtedness' on Dead Sea Scrolls," *Chicago Tribune*, 18 December 1992, p. 24.

86. Ron Grossman, "Copyright of Scrolls Text Ignites Court Fight," *Chicago Tribune*, 2 August 1993, zone N, via NEXIS; "Scholars of Dead Sea Scrolls Ask Court to Block Lawsuit," *New York Times*, 1 August 1993, p. 35.

87. "Why Professor Qimron's Lawsuit Is a Threat to Intellectual Freedom," *Biblical Archaeology Review* (March–April 1992): 67.

88. James M. Robinson, "What We Should Do Next Time Great Manuscripts Are Discovered," *Biblical Archaeology Review* (January–February 1992): 66.

89. Ibid.

90. Ibid.

91. *New York Times* editorial, 7 September 1991, p. 22.

92. *Encyclopedia Britannica*, vol. 14 (Chicago: University of Chicago Press, 1972), p. 438.

Chapter 8: Who Owns Computer Software?

1. *Computerworld*, 23 February 1987 p. 16; Letter from D. A. Hult of Chicago.

2. Michael Alexander, "Peace, Love, Not Look-and-Feel; MIT Scientists Lead 150-Strong Anticopyright Protest on Lotus Premises," *Computerworld*, 29 May 1989, p. 93.

3. "Birthing the Visible Calculator," *Byte* 13 (December 1989): 316.

4. Liz Roman Gallese, "Kapor's Crapshoot," *Business Dateline* 3., no. 5 (October 1988): 60.

5. Ibid.

6. The spreadsheet metaphor is essentially an electronic worksheet that remembers the numbers with which you are working and allows you to make small alterations to your calculations to see how they affect the results.

7. "Birthing the Visible Calculator."

8. Ibid.

9. Frank Rose, "The Changing User-MIS Relationship," *Lotus Copyright* 5, no. 12 (December 1989): 110.

10. Ibid.

11. *SAPC, Inc. v. Lotus Development Corporation, et al.,* 921 F. 2d 360, 17 U.S.P.Q. 2d 1146, 2 CCH Computer Cases 46, 391 at 62,790 (1st Cir. 1990).

12. National Research Council Computer Sciences and Telecommunications Board, *Intellectual Property Issues in Software* (Washington, D.C.: National Academy Press, 1991), p. 72.

13. For a more extensive coverage of the history of software protection, see Pamela Samuelson, "A Case Study on Computer Programs," *Global Dimensions of Intellectual Property Rights in Science and Technology* (Washington, D.C.: National Academy Press, 1993), pp. 284–318.

14. 1980 Computer Service Copyright Act, enacted 12 December 1980, P.L. 96–517, Sec. 10; 94 Statutes at large 3028, Title 17 U.S.C. Sec. 101, 117.

15. 450 U.S. 475 (1981).

16. The patent office staff persists in denying that there are "software patents," only software-related inventions.

17. *Vault Corporation v. Quaid Software Ltd.,* 655 F. Supp. 750 (E.D. LA 1987) aff'd. 847 F. 2d 255 (5th Cir. 1988). For a fuller discussion of this issue, see David L. Hayes, "Shrinkwrap License Agreements: New Light on a Vexing Problem," *Computer Lawyer* 9, no. 9 (September 1992): 1.

18. See, for example, John P. Sumner and Steven W. Lundberg, "Software Patents: Are They Here to Stay?" *Computer Lawyer* 8, no. 10 (October 1991): 8.

19. The changes in the copyright law, Title 17, U.S.C. Sec. 407(a) (1988), to conform with entry into the Berne Convention also removed the requirement of deposit of a copy of the protected work, as the Berne countries do not require notice or deposit as a condition of protection. Berne Implementation Act of 1988, P.L. 100–568, 102 Stat. 2853, 2859 (1988).

20. D. E. Sanger, "A Divisive Lotus Clone War," *New York Times,* 5 February 1987, p. D1.

21. *Lotus Development Corp. v. Paperback Software International and*

Stephenson Software, Ltd., 740 F. Supp. 37 (D. Mass. 1990); 15 U.S.P.Q. 2d 1517;2 CCH Computer Cases 46,310.

22. *Whelan v. Jaslow*, 797 F. 2d 1222 (3d Cir. 1986) cert. denied, 479 U.S. 1031 (1987); *Broderbund Software v. Unison World, Inc.*, 648 F. Supp. 1127 (N.D. CA 1986); *Digital Communications v. Softklone*, 659 F. Supp. 449 (N.D. GA 1987).

23. *Lotus v. Paperback*, 740 F. Supp., p. 56.

24. Ibid., p. 67.

25. Ibid., p. 57.

26. One legal writer has called this divergence of philosophies the difference between the "natural law" favoring the deployment of financial incentives to developers to innovate and produce a diversity of products and the "social utilitarian" approach, which favors the interests of society in uniformity and standardization while recognizing that the nature of interface development is of necessity evolutionary. See Bradford P. Lyerla, "Copyrightability of Software User Interfaces: The Natural Law Versus the Social Utilitarian Approach," *Computer Lawyer* 10, no. 1 (January 1993): 21.

27. David Churbuck and Beth Freedman, "Suits Against 1-2-3 Imitators May Have Wide User Impact; Copyright Suit Could Boost Prices of Software and Make Development and Training More Difficult; Computer Software Industry," *PC Week*, 20 January 1987, p. 1, quoting Wayne Maples, an information-center consultant at the Federal Reserve Bank in Dallas, who warned: "Developers will be forced to create products so different that people will be afraid to buy them because they are hard to learn. The real cost of software is not in the package but in the price of training. If the interface is different on all programs, it raises the real cost of the software to the company."

28. *Plains Cotton Coop. Association v. Goodpasture Computer Serv.*, 807 F. 2d 1256, 1262 (5th Cir.), cert. denied, 484 U.S. 821, 98 L. Ed. 2d 42, 108 S. Ct. 80 (1987).

29. *SAS Institute, Inc. v. S&H Computer Systems, Inc.*, 605 F. Supp. 816 (M.D. Tenn. 1985).

30. *Broderbund Software, Inc. v. Unison World, Inc.*, 648 F. Supp. 1127 (N.D. Cal. 1986).

31. Tracy Robnett Licklider, "Cheerios, Snakes, and Squinting Egyptians: Some Thoughts Before Coffee," *PC Report*, December 1992, p. 9.

32. *Brown Bag Software v. Symantec Corp.*, 960 F. 2d 1465 (9th Cir. 1992) cert. denied, 113 S Ct. 198 (1992).

33. *Synercom Technology, Inc. v. University Computing Co.*, 462 F. Supp. 1003, (N.D. Texas 1978); *Lotus v. Paperback*, 740 F. Supp. 37 (Mass. 1990).

34. Brian Kahin, quoted in National Research Council, *Intellectual Property Issues in Software*, p. 66.

35. Decompilation of code is the process whereby a program expressed in machine language is regenerated as source code, that is, it becomes

programming that can be read and understood by a trained programmer. When programs are written in a high-level, English-like language, they must be translated into the binary codes understood by the hardware. Modern compilers are themselves computer programs, designed not only to translate source code into object code but to greatly increase the efficiency with which the program is executed by the machine. Decompilation is a highly complex and difficult process for large and complicated programs; many programmers would rather create a new program than try to decompile one for which they had only the object code.

36. 17 U.S.C. Sec. 102(b); see *Sega Enterprises Ltd. v. Accolade, Inc.*, No. 92-15655 (N.D. Cal. No. C-91-3871 BAC) in the U.S. Court of Appeals for the Ninth Circuit.

37. Ibid., pp. 12–13.

38. Directive 91/250 on the legal protection of computer programs, 14 May 1991, OJ 1991 L122/42, CCH Guide to Computer Law, 44,160, Article 6 (1). For a fuller discussion of the Software Directive, see Thomas C. Vinje, "The Development of Interoperable Products Under the EC Software Directive," *Computer Lawyer* 8, no. 11 (November 1991): 1.

39. EC Software Directive, Article 6 (2)(c).

40. Two extensive reports have been issued on the subject of copyright of software by the OTA, both concluding that there were imperfections in the attempt to thrust computer software into the existing pigeonholes. See, for example, U.S. Congress, Office of Technology Assessment, *Intellectual Property Rights in an Age of Electronics and Information* (1986), and *Finding a Balance: Computer Software, Intellectual Property and the Challenge of Technological Change* (May 1992).

41. See, for example, Pamela Samuelson, "Computer Programs, User Interfaces, and Sec. 102(b) of the Copyright Act of 1976: A Critique of Lotus v. Paperback," *Law and Contemporary Problems* 55, no. 2 (Spring 1992): 311.

42. *Whelan v. Jaslow,* 797 F2d 1222 (3d Cir. 1986).

43. For a discussion of the analytical approach, see David Nimmer, Richard L. Bernacchi, and Gary N. Frischling, "A Structured Approach to Analyzing the Substantial Similarity of Computer Software in Copyright Infringement Cases," *Arizona State Law Journal* (Fall 1988): 625.

44. "Lotus and Paperback Settle Dispute," *Computer Lawyer* 7, no. 11 (November 1990): 31.

45. *Lotus v. Borland,* 799 F. Supp., p. 211, 3 CCH Computer Cases, p. 64,291; also in *Lotus v. Paperback,* 740 F. Supp., p. 61.

46. *Lotus v. Borland,* p. 64,291.

47. 982 F. 2d 693 (2d Cir. 1992) 3 CCH Computer Cases No. 46,744.

48. *Computer Associates International Inc. v. Altai, Inc.,* 982 F. 2d 693 (2d Cir. 1992), 3 CCH Computer Cases 46,744, pp. 64, 192–93.

49. *Sega Enterprises Ltd. v. Accolade, Inc.*, 977 F. 2d, p. 1514 (9th Cir. 1992).

50. Ibid.

51. Notably Pamela Samuelson, of the University of Pittsburgh Law School, in private communication with the author, July 1993.

52. See, for example, *SAS Inst., Inc. v. S & H Computer Sys.*, 605 F. Supp. 816, 832 (M.D. Tenn. 1985).

53. See, for example, the district court case in *Computer Associates, Inc., v. Altai*, 775 S. Supp. 544 (E.D. N.Y. 1991), where the court wrestled with the economics of software production and the intricacies of software architecture and was applauded by the Court of Appeals for its use of outside expertise.

54. See, for example, Arthur R. Miller, "Copyright Protection for Computer Programs, Databases, and Computer-Generated Work: Is Anything New Since CONTU?" *Harvard Law Review* 106, no. 5 (March 1993): 1035; "As the case law involving the idea-expression dichotomy [footnote omitted] attests, the court decisions in this area are, by degree, crystallizing into an understandable and sensible doctrinal matrix, obviating any need for a sui generis approach."

55. Ibid., p. 1009.

56. David L. Hayes, "What's Left of 'Look and Feel': A Current Analysis (Part I)," *Computer Lawyer* 10, no. 5 (May 1993): 2.

57. Anthony L. Clapes, *The "Look and Feel" of the Law* (Westport, Conn.: Quorum Books, 1989).

58. Anthony L. Clapes and Jennifer M. Daniels, "Revenge of the Luddites: A Closer Look at Computer Associates v. Altai," *Computer Lawyer* 9, no. 11 (November 1992): 11.

59. David A. Rice, "Public Goods, Private Contract, and Public Policy: Federal Preemption of Software License Prohibitions Against Reverse Engineering," *University of Pittsburgh Law Review* 53 (Spring 1992): 543.

60. Rachel Parker, "Copyright Cases Reflect Industry's Development; Some Makers Resent Lotus Suit," *Infoworld*, 2 February 1987, p. 29.

61. Sanger, "Divisive Lotus."

62. National Research Council, *Intellectual Property Issues in Software*, p. 64.

63. See testimony of Anne W. Branscomb, *Computers and Intellectual Property*, Hearings Before the Subcommittee on Courts and Administration of Justice of the Committee on the Judiciary, U.S. House of Representatives, 8 November 1989, pp. 33–42.

64. Report of the Advisory Commission on Patent Law Reform (Version 1.1), 27 April 1992. Although this report values the computer software market at only $20 billion, Charles Zraket has found the market to be well over $100 billion; see chap. 9, "Software: Productivity Puzzles, Policy Challenges," *Beyond Spinoff* (Boston: Harvard Business School Press, 1992), p. 283.

65. Ibid., p. 88.

66. Walter B. Wriston, "Technology and Sovereignty," *Foreign Policy* (Winter 1988–89): p. 63; Walter B. Wriston, *The Twilight of Sovereignty: How the Information Revolution Is Transforming Our World* (New York: Scribner, 1992).

67. "Securities, Shearson Lehman Joins Other Brokers, Halts Program Trading," *Daily Report for Executives,* 1 November 1989, p. A18.

68. National Research Council, *Intellectual Property Issues in Software,* p. 67.

69. Ibid., p. 68.

70. *Feist Publications, Inc. v. Rural Telephone Co., Inc.* 499 U.S. 340 (1991), 111 S. Ct., p. 1291; 2 CCH Computer Cases 46,423, reversing 916 F. 2d 718 (10th Cir. 1990).

71. These are a set of principles set forth by the author in an unpublished paper, "Has the Law Adequately Adapted to the Changes in Technology?" presented at a program on "Computer Software–Intellectual Property: Climate for Innovation in the 1990's—A Public Policy Forum," sponsored by the Annenberg Washington Program in Communications Policy Studies of Northwestern University, Washington, D.C., 20–21 May 1991.

Chapter 9: Who Owns Government Information?

1. *Armstrong v. Executive Office of the President,* D.C., No. 89–142 (CRR), decision of 6 January 1993; 61 U.S.L.W. 2427; 93 U.S. Dist., via LEXIS, 95.

2. 44 U.S.C. Sections 2101–2118, 2901–2910, 3101–3107.

3. 5 U.S.C. Sec. 552. Access to information about government deliberations that may affect public policy has normally been obtained through application of the Freedom of Information Act (FOIA). The statute guarantees public access to federal records with a number of exceptions designed to protect national security information, personal privacy, and corporate trade secrets. About a half-million requests a year have enabled citizens to gain access to personal files maintained about them by federal agencies. Furthermore, successful FOIA requests by journalists have played a major role in exposing government scandals such as the Iran-contra affair, harassment of public figures by former FBI Director J. Edgar Hoover, lax enforcement of environment laws, and maltreatment of whistle blowers.

4. 44 U.S.C. Sec. 2201 et seq.

5. 1993 U.S. Dist. LEXIS, pp. 14–15.

6. Even so, there were concerns that some of the material was missing. Some of the tapes ordered to be preserved were lost; some of the dates were missing; and "several sets of tapes had been erased, perhaps inadvertently." John O'Neil, "Some Bush White House Tapes Lost, Archivists Say," *New York Times,* 14 March 1993, p. 25.

7. Joyce E. Beattie, "Information Freedom Bit By Byte," *Government Executive* (December 1992): 32.

8. David L. Margulius, "Your Right to What Uncle Sam Knows: Is Big Business Pulling the Plug?" *PC-Computing Copyright* 2, no. 10 (October 1989): 78.

9. *Dismukes v. Department of Interior,* 603 F. Supp. 760 (D.C. 1984).

10. Ibid., 102d Congress, Senate Bills 1939 and 1940, referred to the Committee on the Judiciary, 7 November 1991; however, the bill has languished in committee since the Department of Justice was lukewarm in support.

11. Government Printing Office Electronic Information Access Enhancement Act of 1993, H.R. 1328 and S. 564, introduced 11 March 1993.

12. "Clinton Administration Aims for Open Information Policy," *U.S. Newswire,* 28 June 1993, via NEXIS.

13. Testimony before the Joint Committee on Printing, 25 April 1991, quoted in Bulletin of the University of Alaska, Anchorage, Center for Information Technology, April 1992, p. 3.

14. Michael Putzel, "White House Notebook—Clinton Lament: Dial O for Obsolete," *Boston Globe,* 4 February 1993.

15. Date: Fri, 29 Jan 93 11:28:50 -0600 ⟩From: lhl@cs.wisc.edu (L. H. Landweber) ⟩To: inet@cs.wisc.edu⟩Subject: White House Network Connection.

16. Anonymous, "A PC President: For Computer Users, Clinton Goes Online," *Boston Globe,* 18 March 1993, p. 21.

17. Stratford Sherman, "Andy Grove: How Intel Makes Spending Pay Off," *Fortune,* 22 February 1993, p. 57.

18. G. P. Hunt, *The Writings of James Madison,* vol. 11 (1910), 103.

19. 1 Statutes at Large 101 (1890), "An Act provided for the enumeration of the Inhabitants of the United States."

20. Barbara Vobeda, "Budget May Crimp Data from Census," *Washington Post,* 18 September 1991, p. A17.

21. Ibid.

22. *SDC Development Corp. v. Mathews,* 542 F.2d 1116 at 1117 (9th Cir. 1976).

23. The Technical Information Act, 15 U.S.C. Sections 1151–57, specifies that "to the fullest extent feasible . . . each of the services and functions provided shall be self-sustaining or self-liquidating and that the general public shall not bear the cost of publications and other services which are for the special use and benefit of private groups and individuals." 15 U.S.C at Sec. 1153.

24. 5 U.S.C. Sec, 552.

25. Ibid., Sec. 552(a)(4)(A).

26. *SDC Development Corp. v. Mathews.*

27. Senate Rep. No. 813, 89th Cong., 1st Sess. 2–5 (1965).

28. This view is enforced by a review of the abuses cited under prior legislation enumerated in House Report 1497, 89th Cong., 2d Sess. 5–6 (1966).

29. Michael E. DeBakey, "The National Library of Medicine: Evolution of a Premier Information Center," *Journal of the American Medical Association* 266, no. 9 (4 September 1991):1252.

30. *National Library of Medicine NEWS* 47, no. 11–12 (November–December 1992):3, 6.

31. Donald A. B. Lindberg, "Message from the Director," *National Library of Medicine NEWS,* in ibid.

32. U.S. Department of Health and Human Services, *MEDLARS: The World of Medicine at Your Fingertips,* Public Health Service, National Institutes of Health, September 1991.

33. 99th Cong., 2d Sess., House Report 99-560, *Electronic Collection and Dissemination of Information by Federal Agencies* (Washington, D.C.: Government Printing Office, 1986).

34. Ibid., p. 53.

35. Ibid., pp. 59–60.

36. Ibid., p. 61.

37. Martha E. Williams, "Online Government Databases—An Analysis," *Online Review* 10, no. 4 (November 1986):227–36.

38. Diane H. Smith and Kent A. Smith, "Online Government Databases: Into the Maelstrom," *Database Copyright* 11, no. 3 (June 1988):56.

39. According to Information USA, which publishes the Federal Database Finder (available for $125 from Information USA, P.O. Box 15700, Chevy Chase, Md. 20815; 301-657-1200).

40. Department of Commerce's Economic Bulletin Board (202377-3870; available 24 hours a day; 8 data bits, 1 stop bit, no parity) is such an example.

41. Ibid.

42. Ibid.

43. "A Copyright Bill Stirs Controversy," *National Law Journal,* 27 July 1992, p. S9.

44. The Reagan administration had also attempted to restrict access to several government databases on the grounds that public access could compromise national security because the Russians could also access publicly available databases.

45. Margulius, "Your Right to What Uncle Sam Knows," p. 78

46. Bill Clinton, "Technology for America's Economic Growth: A New Direction to Build Economic Strength," *Policy Statement,* 22 February 1993, delivered to a group of Silicon Valley executives.

Conclusion: Information as an Asset: From Personal Autonomy to Public Access

1. Patent no. 5,241,671.

2. "Cyberlex," *PC Report* 13 (1994), no. 2, 22.

3. *Council Directive* 93/98, EEC, 29 October 1993.

4. John Perry Barlow, "The Economy of Ideas," *Wired*, March 1984, p.85.

5. Jonathan Rosenoer, "The End of Fair Use," *PC Report* 13, no. 2 (1 February 1994): 19, referring to L. Ray Patterson and Stanley W. Lindberg, *The Nature of Copyright* (Athens: University of Georgia Press, 1991).

6. *Library of Congress News*, PR 930120, 28 August 1993.

7. "Profile of Pacific Bell and Its 1992 Customer Privacy Policy," *Privacy & American Business* 1, no. 1 (September–October 1993): 11–15.

8. William Safire, "Sink the 'Clipper Chip' Notion," *The Times-Picayune*, 15 February 1994, p. B7.

9. S. 1735, "Privacy Protection Act of 1993," 139 *Congressional Record*, no. 162, Senate 16493-5 (daily edition, 19 November 1993).

10. Peter W. Huber, "Assembling the Pieces," pp. 71–78, and Henry Geller, "Competition in Local Telecommunications," pp.37–45, both in *20/20 Vision: The Development of a National Information Infrastructure*, U.S. Department of Commerce, National Telecommunications and Information Administration, NTIA 94-28, March 1994.

11. Anne W. Branscomb, "Beyond Deregulation: Designing the Information Infrastructure," *The Information Society* 1, no. 1 (1982): 167–90 (republished in Japanese); Lewis M. Branscomb, "Balancing the Commercial and Public-Interest Visions of the NII," pp. 1–10, and Charles R. McClure, "Public Libraries, the Public Interest, and the National Information Infrastructure (NII): Expanding the Policy Agenda," pp. 137–153, both in *20/20 Vision*, U.S. Department of Commerce.

12. "Bringing the Information Revolution to Every Classroom, Hospital, and Library in the Nation by the End of the Century," remarks prepared by Vice President Al Gore, Royce Hall, UCLA, 11 January 1994, *CCH Guide to Computer Law* 60,447.

13. Computer Professionals for Social Responsibility (CPSR), *Serving the Community: A Public Interest Vision of the National Information Infrastructure* (1994); Geoff Sears, "Directions of the Highway," *Internet Society NEWS* 2, no. 4 (Winter 1994): 28.

14. *Mayo v. U.S. Government Printing Office*, 4 *CCH Computer Cases* 46,959 (9th Cir. 1993).

15. "Cyberlex,"p. 22.

16. Statute of Anne, c. 19, republished in R. S. Brown, *Copyright* 851 (Mineola, N.Y.: Foundation Press, 1978).

17. Arthur R. Miller, "Personal Privacy in the Computer Age: The Challenge of New Technology in an Information-oriented Society," *Michigan Law Review* 67 (April 1969): 1224–25.

18. Alan Westin, *Privacy and Freedom* (New York: Atheneum, 1967), pp. 324–25.

INDEX